BUILDING CABINETS, BOOKCASES AND SHELVES

FROM THE EDITORS OF POPULAR WOODWORKING

POPULAR WOODWORKING BOOKS
CINCINNATI, OHIO
www.popularwoodworking.com

D1161012

Table of Contents

Introduction

I'm not sure of the date when humans moved from hunter/gatherers to an agrarian society, but I'm pretty sure it was about that same time that we started bringing things into the cave or hut and started storing them. Whether for temporary storage, or because we needed to know where something was the next time we needed it, we've been storing items in our homes for thousands of years. That's not a bad thing, unless hoarding is an issue. Thats' where this book comes in. That may be an over-simplification, but let's say that by building furniture to store our items, we're successfully limiting ourselves to only store what we have space for — unless we build more.

Regardless, this book is about celebrating our human nature for storage. The projects in this book fit into two largers categories of storage: open or enclosed. There are cabinets for storing the items that don't need to be displayed, and there are shelves for those items that we want to share with others, or just need available for easy access. And there are a few projects that don't fit perfectly into either category, but I know we'll find things to store in them.

The projects range in skill level from some very simple furniture pieces requiring very basic skills and only a few tools, to other projects that are best attempted by those with some woodworking experience under their toolbelt. Either way, we've provided step-by-step instructions, cutting lists and diagragms that should make every project approachable to the average builder.

While each of the projects offer instruction to build exactly as shown, we encourage you to step outside your comfort zone and customize the projects as you see fit. Let's face it, we don't all live in the same size house, or have the same size items to store. Feel free to adjust the project to better fit your needs.

Along those same lines, the projects in this book represent a number of different furniture styles. You may find a bookcase that is the right proportion for what you want, but Arts & Crafts isn't your thing. Again, customize as you see fit. Style is usually a function of a couple of design details that can be switched between pieces to best match your furniture style.

Lastly, have fun, and be safe. Plan out your project and the steps involved and things will go much smoother.

— DAVID THIEL, EDITOR

Arts & Crafts Buffet

BY ROBERT W. LANG

I designed this buffet cabinet a couple years ago for a weekend seminar on Arts & Crafts joinery. After the class I added a 3-D model to the *Popular Woodworking Magazine* online SketchUp collection. It was an easy way to provide detailed plans for those in attendance. As time passed, the model rose to the top of the collection, based on popularity.

My goal in designing it was to combine several classic elements from the early 20th century, without building a reproduction of any one piece in particular. I was looking to design a piece with a contemporary feel, but that was grounded in traditional Arts & Crafts period elements. Apparently I swiped the right details from the right sources to make a successful piece.

The wide overhanging top with breadboard ends, the finger-jointed drawer and the sculpted handles were all borrowed from the designs of Charles and Henry Greene. The proportions of the door stiles and rails were lifted right from the Gustav Stickley stylebook, and the double-tapered legs are a Harvey Ellis element turned upside down.

Equally important are the overall proportions and the rounded edges that ease the transitions where there is a change of direction or a change in plane. The light color of the soft maple keeps the cabinet from looking too formal or too masculine. Absent are the elements often seen in new pieces based on old designs. Corbels and spindles were banished to the land of overused and misapplied design features.

Skinny Legs & All

The legs are important visually; the upward taper leads the eye to the top, and the wide portion near the bottom makes the base appear substantial. Combined with the wide rails on the bottom of the doors, the case sits on a firm visual foundation, and it looks larger and heavier than it really is.

The legs are also key elements in the structure. Each leg is a corner for two different frames. There is a lot of joinery in each, and to help keep track of the leg locations, I laid out the tapers after resawing the legs from 8/4 stock. My local supplier didn't have material available simply to mill the legs to the 1¼" finished dimension, so I bought thicker than I needed, resawed the boards to 1⅜" and saved the thin offcuts for the bottom of the drawer.

My method is to work out all the joinery first, then cut pieces to shape and round the edges just before final assembly. I cut the ⅜"-wide stopped grooves for the side and back panels first, using a plunge router. I then lowered the depth setting and cut the mortises in the wide faces of the legs with the same router.

There isn't enough of a flat area on the narrow sides of the legs to support the router, so I moved to the hollow-chisel mortiser to add the mortises for the front and back rails. Then I cut the tenons on the ends of the top and bottom side rails. I used a backsaw for the shoulder cuts, then cut the cheeks on the band saw.

I dry-fit the side rails to the legs, forming side sub-assemblies without panels. Then I made the joints for the front and back rails. In the back, the mortises fall within the grooves for the back panel. In the front of the case, the mortises are the only joinery.

To keep the backs of the front and back rails flush with the back of the legs, I set my marking gauge directly to the edge of a mortise. Then I used that setting to mark out the tenons. I cut the tenon shoulders with my backsaw and the cheeks on the band saw. After fitting these joints, I did another dry run, connecting the two side assemblies with the front and back rails.

Come Together

With a complex piece such as this, the best way to ensure that everything fits together is to make careful dry runs, then pull the actual dimensions for the next piece to be fabricated from the subassembly. With the legs connected side to side and front to back, I made sure the carcase was square before making the bottom.

The bottom fits between the front and back rails, and at the ends there is a pair of through-tenons. The critical distance is from shoulder to shoulder on these tenons. After ripping the bottom to width, I held the bottom in place below the rails on the carcase and marked the shoulder locations directly.

Then it all came back apart to cut

CLASSIC COMBINATION. This buffet has a contemporary feel, but it is a combination of classic design elements of the American Arts & Crafts period of the early 20th century.

the through-mortises in the bottom side rails. These pieces are too short to clamp to the bench and have room for the plunge router, and too wide to fit easily in the mortiser. I drilled out the bulk of the waste with a Forstner bit at the drill press, then cleaned up the mortises with chisels and a float.

The first step in making the tenons was to cut a wide rabbet on both the top and bottom of the shelf. I clamped a straight-edge on the shoulder line and used a router with a straight bit and a top-mounted flush guide bearing.

I made a cut on both ends on the top side, then I clamped the straightedge on the bottom. I carefully made a cut, then measured the thickness of the tenon, comparing it to the height of the mortise. When I could force a corner of the bottom into the mortise, I knew I was as close as I wanted to come with the router.

I held the backside of the rail against the end of the cabinet bottom and marked the ends of the tenons from the mortises. I cut the ends of the tenons with my backsaw, then turned the bottom 90° and used the same tool to make the two end cuts. I used a jigsaw to remove the material between the tenons and stayed about ⅛" away from the shoulder's edge.

There is just enough material from the first router cut that defines the shoulder to guide the bearing of a flush-trim router bit. That took care of making a straight edge between the tenons, except for a small quarter circle in the corners. A little chisel work removed that extra material, and I was ready to test the fit.

With a chisel, I cut a small chamfer around the back edges of the mortises, and I used my block plane to chamfer the ends of the tenons. A few taps with a mallet revealed the tight spots on the tenons. Some work with a shoulder plane and float brought the tenons down to size, and after achieving a good fit with both rails on the ends of the bottom, I was ready to dry-fit the rest of the case.

Shapes of Things

After another test-fit and a bit of tweaking, I was ready for a break from joinery,

BETTER THAN NUMBERS. Setting the marking gauge directly to the edge of the mortise ensures exact alignment of the rail and leg.

KNOWLEDGE IS POWER. Measuring with calipers reveals the exact thickness of the tenon and how far to set the depth of the router bit.

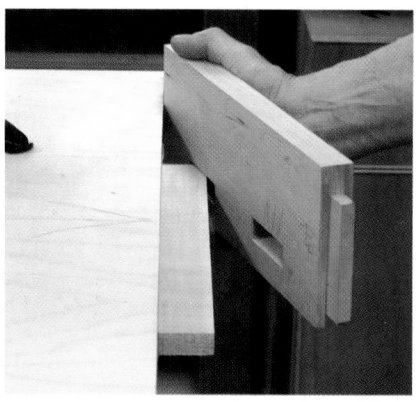

WHEN TO STOP. When a corner can be forced into the mortise, the thickness is close. Then it's time to cut the edges of the tenons.

WHERE IT BELONGS. Marking the tenons directly from the mortises is faster and far more accurate than measuring.

so I cut the tapers on the legs at the band saw. I cleaned up the saw marks with a light pass across the jointer, then began smoothing surfaces and rounding edges. I began smoothing all the flat surfaces with a plane to remove mill marks and evidence of beatings from my test assemblies.

I took my cue for the edge treatment from Greene & Greene. Instead of running a roundover bit in a router around the edges, I used my block plane to hand-form a radius on all the exposed edges. This doesn't take as long as you might think, and this method allows for variation of the edge radius.

The radius on the legs is larger at the bottom than at the top. This follows the taper of the legs and adds a subtlety to the edges that a router couldn't provide. My method for doing this efficiently is to open wide the mouth of my block plane and skew the blade as far as I can.

EASIER BY HAND. These cuts could be made at the table saw, but that would be an awkward operation. Cutting the tenons by hand allows me to see what is going on.

With the blade cocked, the plane takes a big bite on one side and a fine cut on the other. By shifting the position of the plane as I tilt it on the edge of the board, I can remove a large chamfered edge to begin the cut, then make fine finishing cuts to remove the arrises and form a nice curve. Shifting the position of the plane laterally allows it to do coarse, medium and fine work without fiddling with the tool.

I also cut the arches at the bottom edge of the front and side rails at the band saw, and used a series of rasps to refine the curves and round the edges. I made 5/8"-thick panels for the sides, making a rabbet around the perimeter to form a tongue on the panel that fits in the grooves of the legs.

Then I made 3/8"-thick shiplapped panels for the back before turning to the last bit of joinery for the case. A simple web frame supports the drawer, and two rails (one at the front and one at the back behind the visible rails) support the top.

The web frame is mortise-and-tenon construction; I assembled and fit this frame with the cabinet dry-assembled. I put the cabinet together and took it apart several times to fit parts as the joinery progressed to ensure that the complex assembly would all fit together. And it served as good practice for the final glue-up.

I cut the two top rails to the outside width of the case and marked the inside edges to the top side rails. I made a 1/4"-wide rabbet on the bottom of the ends, then cut a dovetail on both ends of each

DRY-FIT NOW, PANELS LATER. The only way to know if things will really fit is to put the carcase together. The panels will be added the next time around.

rail. With the rails in position, I marked the top side rails to cut the sockets.

I used a wheel marking gauge to mark the bottom of the dovetail sockets in the rails and a knife to mark the vertical cuts. After sawing the outside edges with my

dovetail saw, I used a chisel to remove the waste (vertical saw cuts into the waste may make waste removal easier). On a small joint such as this, the marking gauge can be used as a small router, providing a flat bottom for the socket.

WHY THIS SLIDES. Opening the mouth of the block plane provides room to skew the iron.

BIG MOUTH, QUICK WORK. This side of the plane will take a coarse cut, removing a lot of material in a hurry.

FINE ON THIS SIDE. The other side of the plane takes a small finishing cut. The amount of material removed and the quality of cut is controlled by moving the plane laterally.

Arts & Crafts Buffet

	NO.	ITEM	DIMENSIONS (INCHES)			DIMENSIONS (MILLIMETERS)			MATERIAL	COMMENTS
			T	W	L	T	W	L		
❏	4	Legs	1¼	3¾	30¾	32	95	781	Maple	
❏	2	Upper side rails	⅞	3	13⅜	22	76	340	Maple	¾" TBE*
❏	2	Lower side rails	⅞	4¼	13⅜	22	108	340	Maple	¾" TBE
❏	2	Side panels	⅝	12⅝	23½	16	321	572	Maple	
❏	1	Cabinet bottom	⅞	11⅞	30¼	22	301	768	Maple	1¼" TBE
❏	6	Back panels	⅜	4⅞	23½	10	124	572	Maple	Shiplap edges
❏	1	Upper back rail	⅞	3	27	22	76	686	Maple	1¼" TBE
❏	2	Lower front/back rails	⅞	4¼	27	22	108	686	Maple	1¼" TBE
❏	1	Top front rail	⅞	⅞	27	22	22	686	Maple	1¼" TBE
❏	1	Front drawer rail	⅞	1¼	27	22	32	686	Maple	1¼" TBE
❏	2	Inner top rails	¾	3	29½	19	76	750	Maple	DTBE**
❏	2	Web frame rails	¾	2¼	23¾	19	57	603	Poplar	1¼" TBE
❏	2	Web frame stiles	¾	3¼	11⅞	19	82	301	Poplar	
❏	2	Hinge strips	½	1	18⅞	13	25	479	Maple	
❏	2	Door hinge stiles	⅞	3⅝	18⅞	22	92	479	Maple	
❏	2	Door lock stiles	⅞	2⅞	18⅞	22	73	479	Maple	
❏	2	Door top rails	⅞	3⅜	7¾	22	86	197	Maple	1¼" TBE
❏	2	Door bottom rails	⅞	4⅝	7¾	22	118	197	Maple	1¼" TBE
❏	2	Door panels	⅝	6	11⅝	16	152	295	Maple	
❏	1	Top	¾	15⅞	46½	19	403	1181	Maple	1¼" TBE
❏	2	Breadboard ends	⅞	2¼	16⅛	22	57	409	Maple	
❏	2	Drawer sides	¾	4¾	13	19	121	330	Maple	
❏	1	Drawer front	¾	4¾	24½	19	121	623	Maple	
❏	1	Drawer back	¾	4¼	24½	19	108	623	Maple	
❏	1	Drawer bottom	¼	12	23½	6	305	572	Maple	
❏	1	Drawer handle	1¼	1½	16	32	38	406	Maple	
❏	2	Door handles	1¼	1¾	5	32	45	127	Maple	

*TBE = Tenon both ends; **DTBE = Dovetail both ends

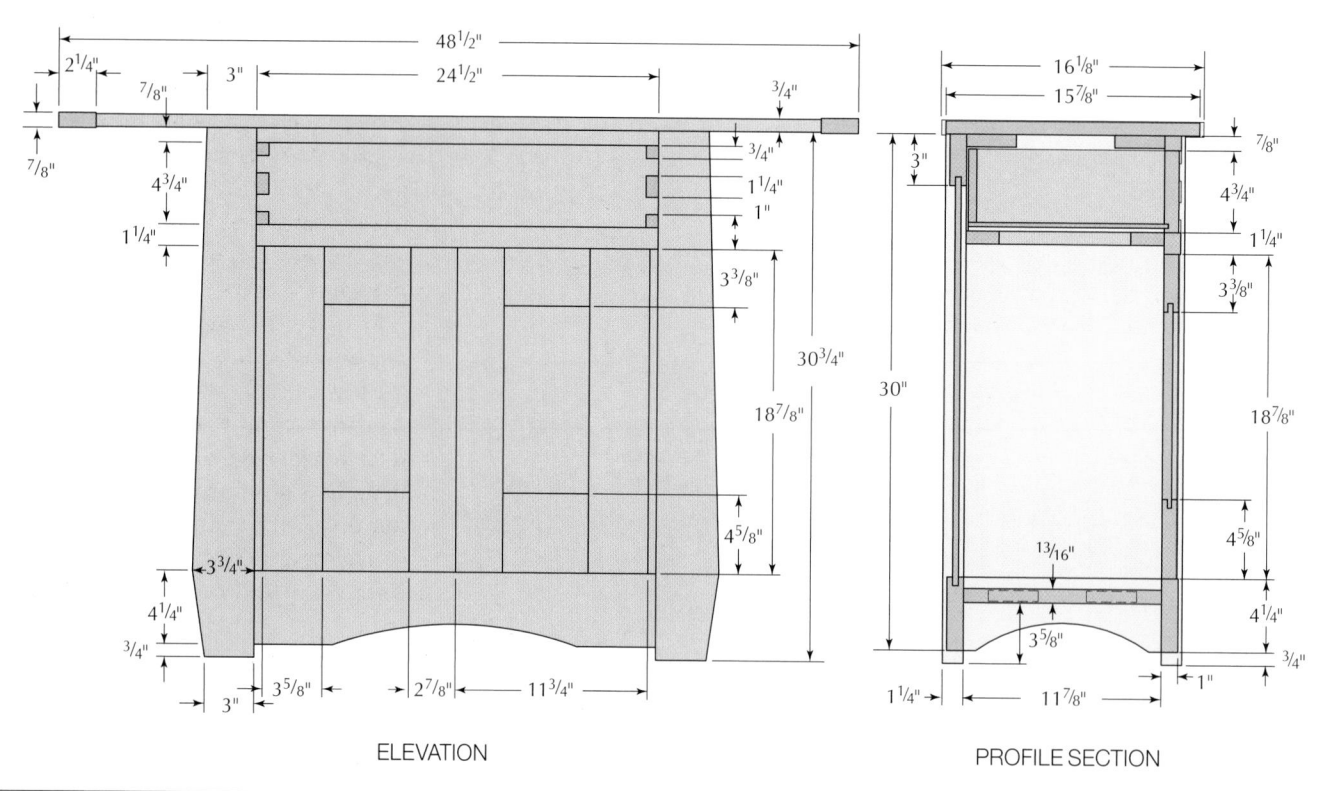

ELEVATION   PROFILE SECTION

NO-SPREAD ZONE. A single through-dovetail on each of the top rails locks the sides of the case together and adds an attractive detail.

E PLURIBUS UNUM. Subassemblies minimize the number of pieces to contend with during the final assembly. After clamping, check to see that they are square.

WHERE BOTTOM AND SIDE COLLIDE. This isn't as hard as it looks; the side will be one piece, and trial runs ensure that everything fits.

TAPE FOR THE TAPERS. Offcuts from tapering the legs are taped in place to provide a flat surface for the clamps.

Tighten Up

Fighting off the urge to glue the entire box together, I went over all the parts with a card scraper then fine sandpaper. Then I put the side panels in place and glued the rails between the legs, then let these subassemblies dry overnight. This simplified the final assembly by reducing the number of parts.

The obvious tricky part of putting things together for real is down low. The through-tenons for the cabinet bottoms need to slide through the mortises in the rail at the same time the tenons in the front and back rails go into the legs. I put the entire cabinet together without any glue to practice my technique and to avoid any trauma during the real thing.

The other tricky part is that, with the legs tapered, there isn't a good surface to place any clamps. Fortunately one of my bad habits was ready to provide a solution. I rarely throw anything away,

so I found the tapered offcuts from the legs over by the band saw. Good old blue painter's tape held these to the legs, providing a flat place to put the clamps.

I put one of the side assemblies on my bench with the inside of the case facing up, applied glue to the mortises and put the rails in place. I started the tenons on the end of the bottom into the side rail mortises, then brushed glue on the inner portion of the tenons. This kept the glue off the exposed ends of the tenons. That was the easy end.

I slid the shiplapped back panels into position, then brushed glue on the tenons in the rails before I started the through-tenons into the mortises in the lower side rail. At the same time, I lined up the other tenons with their matching mortises. I tapped down on the rail until all but about ½" of the through-tenon was visible between the tenon shoulder and the rail.

I reached in to brush more glue on the tenons, then tapped on the outside of the side subassembly to close the joints. I tried to tap directly over each tenon on the legs as the second side of the cabinet moved into place. When the side was about ⅛" away from closing, I put down the mallet and picked up my cabinet clamps.

I tightened the clamps and went on a hunt for glue squeeze-out near the joints. I try to control squeeze-out by applying just enough glue to the joint. The goal is to apply the glue so that it almost squeezes out. The last step in the carcase assembly was to jockey the web frame into position and glue the long edge to the rail below the drawer opening. At the back, a couple pocket screws from below attach the back of the frame to the back legs.

I had a little glue bead appear here and there, and those were scraped off with the back of a sharp, wide chisel before the glue had time to dry. I keep a wet rag handy to keep the chisel clean and don't wipe the wood unless I have to.

Feeling Groovy

The doors are standard frame-and-panel construction; ¼"-wide grooves run along the inside edges, and haunched

SLIDING HOME. Start all the mortises and get the parts close with a rubber mallet. A few clamps close the joints side to side.

SIMPLE FIX. A pocket screw at each end attaches the drawer frame to the inside of the back legs.

tenons in the rails fit mortises in the stiles. The elements of the doors are all wider than they need to be. This enhances the overall appearance of the doors in the opening; there is a better balance in the middle, and the wide lower rails reinforce the sense of visual weight toward the bottom of the cabinet.

The combined width of the doors is 1" less than the width of the opening; thin strips are glued inside the legs to carry the hinges. This detail allows the doors to be set back from the front edges of the rails while still able to swing freely past the inside edges of the legs. These features are common in Gustav Stickley designs. The variation of planes adds visual interest to the unadorned surfaces.

The drawer is joined at the front with Greene & Greene-style finger joints. The fingers are graduated in width, and they extend about ⅛" past the drawer front. I made a simple L-shaped fixture and attached it to the table saw's miter gauge to assist in cutting the joints. After attaching the fixture, I ran it through the saw blade to cut a slot in the lower portion.

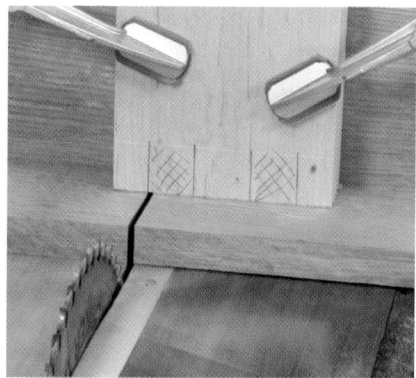

L OF A SOLUTION. A simple jig attached to the table saw's miter gauge supports the work and indicates the exact line of the cut.

I laid out the fingers on one of the drawer sides, making sure to clearly mark the waste area. Then I adjusted the height of the blade to match the marked depth of the cut between the fingers. I placed the two drawer sides together and aligned the pencil marks on the wood with the saw cut in the fixture.

When the sides were in position, I clamped the stacked sides to the back of the fixture. I cut the ends of each finger

BALANCING ACT. After cutting the first set of fingers, place the end of a side on the drawer front to mark the matching parts of the joint.

before removing the waste material in between. When the sides were finished, I placed them on each end of the drawer front to transfer the cutlines.

After marking the waste area in the drawer front joints, I lowered the height of the saw blade to leave the ends of the drawer front barely proud of the drawer sides. I then cut the fingers in the drawer front in the same way that I cut the mating ends of the drawer sides.

HOLD THE LINE. Place the pencil line next to the kerf in the guide to cut just inside the line.

EASY NOW. The two parts should slide together easily — but without any slop. If it's too tight, file the fat fingers.

When I was happy with the joints at the front of the drawer, I cut grooves with a small plunge router in the sides and front for the drawer bottom. The grooves in the sides stop at the front to match the depth of the groove in the drawer front. The groove falls within the first finger, so it can run from end to end through the drawer front.

The back of the drawer is narrower than the sides. It comes down from the top of the drawer and ends at the top of the groove, allowing the drawer bottom to be slid into place after the drawer is assembled. The drawer bottom is one solid panel, glued up from the leg leftovers and planed to ¼" thickness. The back and sides of the drawer are joined with through-dovetails.

Roundabout

Like the cabinet it lives in, the drawer was put together and taken back apart several times. With the sides in place, I marked the front edge of the drawer front on the fingers of the drawer sides. This provided a target for rounding the edges of the fingers. I clamped the sides in my vise and went to work with a small rasp.

As with the other radiused edges, I began by cutting a 45° chamfer, working in the direction of the grain. When the edge of the chamfer reached about two-thirds of the distance from the end to the pencil line, I removed the sharp edges and began to transform the faceted edges to a gentle curve. When I got close to the

lines, I switched to a piece of #180-grit Abranet to remove the rasp marks.

I didn't want any glue to squeeze out when I assembled the drawer, so I carefully applied glue to the recesses between the fingers with an acid brush. I began with the end-grain surfaces, let the glue soak in for a few minutes, then applied glue to all the mating surfaces. I clamped the drawer box together at the front, placing small blocks of scrap between the fingers to provide a bearing surface for the clamps.

I planed the bottom edge of the drawer front before assembly to keep the edge of the front ¹⁄₁₆" above the bottom edge of the sides. When I fit the drawer in the opening, I was able to plane the sides to get a good fit and keep a slight gap between the drawer front and the case rails. Drawer guides are glued on to the web frame to keep the drawer sliding

straight. A rabbet on the bottom edge of the guide allowed me to reach in with a block plane to tweak the fit.

Speaking in Tongues

The breadboard ends have a ¼"-wide, ½"-deep groove along each inside edge. I made each groove with a straight bit in a small plunge router, stopping the groove about 1" in from the ends. I located the matching tongue on the top by clamping a plywood straightedge to the line, and made the cut with a flush-trim bit in the router.

The tongue is 1¼" long; the extra ¾" was used to make three tenons to hold the breadboard in place. The tenons are about 2" wide; the outer tenons end about ⅛" in from the end of the groove. After cutting the tenons, I marked their locations on the breadboard and cut the mortises with the hollow chisel mortiser.

The middle mortise fits the tenon tightly in width, but the end two were cut wider to give the top some room to move. These joints are pinned with square walnut plugs that go completely through the breadboard and the tenons. The square holes for the ¼" and ⁵⁄₁₆" plugs we made with punches developed by Darrell Peart. These punches work in conjunction with a drill bit, so it was simple to start from the show side, punch the square and drill the holes through the assembled joint.

After drilling, I took the joint apart and placed the drill bit in each hole, then used the punch to square the sides. I elongated the holes in the two outer tenons so they could move in the mortises

CUTTING CORNERS. Mark where the end of the drawer side intersects the fingers on the drawer front. Round over the edges to the pencil line.

ROOM TO MOVE. Elongate the sides of the holes that pass through the tenons. This will allow the top to expand and contract against the breadboard ends.

ADJUSTABLE GUIDE. The drawer guides are glued to the web frame. The short length and rabbeted bottom edge provide room to adjust the width with a block plane.

as the seasons change. On final assembly of the top, I applied glue to the center tenon only. The outer joints are held in place with pegs.

Maxwell's Silver Hammer

I also added decorative pegs (3/16", 1/4" and 5/16") to the joint locations on the front legs, the door stiles and the drawer front. Recesses of about 1/4" deep for the plugs were made with the square punches. The plugs were ripped from some quartersawn walnut. I cut square strips on the table saw, about 1/32" larger than the recesses.

I smoothed the long edges of these strips with my block plane, and I measured the width and thickness with calipers until they were close in size, but still a bit larger than the holes. I dropped the end extension of the calipers into the holes to find the correct length for the pegs, then used the jaws of the calipers to transfer this measurement to the strips.

I rounded one end of each strip with a coarse file, followed by sandpaper, before cutting the pegs to length. After cutting, I used a chisel to chamfer the back edges of the pegs to make it easier to start them in the holes. After the pegs were sanded, I treated them with a solution of vinegar in which I'd soaked iron, then cut them to length. This solution reacts with the tannic acid in the walnut and turns the wood black. (Brian Boggs explains an alternative ebonizing process in the June 2009 issue of *Popular Woodworking* (#176).)

I used an artist's brush to coat the inside of each hole with glue, inserted a peg and tapped it in place with a brass hammer. The smooth hard surface of the hammer burnished the faces of the pegs.

Because the doors hang on strips glued to the inside of the door opening, mortising the hinges was simple. I trimmed the doors to 3/32" less than the height of the opening and cut the strips to an exact fit. I put a door (hinge stile up) in my vise and placed a strip along the edge, using a dime to space the top of the strip with the top of the door.

Then I marked the locations of the hinges. I cut the hinge mortises in

Supplies

Lee Valley
leevalley.com or 800-871-8158

1 set • square hole punches
#50K59.20, $24.50-$26.50
each, $129 for set of six

2 • ball catches
#00W12.00, $1.50 each

Prices correct at time of publication.

the doors with a small plunge router equipped with a fence. I put a block of wood behind the door and adjusted the position of the door in the vise so that the edge of the door was flush with the top of the block. This kept the base of the router flat on the thin edge without any danger of tipping.

The mortises in the hinge strips were cut with the strips clamped flat to the benchtop. After routing, I squared the corners of the mortises then screwed the hinges in position on the doors and on the strips. Then I removed the hinges, and glued the strips to the inside of the legs, with the back of the strips flush with the back of the legs.

I glued a small block of wood behind the rail of the face frame above the doors to provide a place to mount brass ball catches to keep the doors shut. The handles were shaped at the band saw, then the edges were rounded with a block plane and rasps. I made relief cuts on the back of the handles with a carving gouge to provide a finger grip. Those cuts were refined with a gooseneck scraper.

The first coat of finish is clear shellac. I used the canned stuff from the hardware store and thinned it about 30 percent. This left the color a bit cold to my eye, so I added about 25 percent amber shellac to the mix for the second, third and fourth coats. After letting the shellac dry, I buffed the surface with a nylon abrasive pad, then applied a coat of paste wax.

ONE-TWO PUNCH. Locate the punch and smack it a couple times with a hammer. This cuts sharp corners and straight sides for the plug hole.

WASTE REMOVAL: Follow with a drill through the hole in the punch body. This removes the waste within the square recess.

Chimney Cupboard

BY MEGAN FITZPATRICK & GLEN D. HUEY

There's a backstory to this chimney-cupboard project. Last March, I planned a week off to renovate the 6½' x 8' bathroom in my 110-year-old house (I was sure it wouldn't take long – after all, I only had to gut it to the studs and joists, hang new drywall, reroute plumbing …). Three months later, I finally had the tile in and grouted, and a working shower. A month after that, I installed a medicine cabinet and put up the wainscoting and the trim. So close on a year later, I'm almost done. But the small space allowed no room for built-in storage, and I was unwilling to tear out adjoining plaster walls to enlarge the space.

So I needed a tall, free-standing cabinet that fit with my amalgamation of Victorian and Arts & Crafts design elements, and it had to fit into the narrow area between the shower door and commode, making the most use of available space. This three-drawer chimney cupboard was designed to accommodate a variety of storage needs, and fit a specific location. At 10½" the depth, due to space limitations, is fairly shallow. And, I wanted the piece to match the exact height of the shower wall, 78½" (I've been told I can be a tad persnickety). The point (yes, I do have one) is that it's easy to start with a design idea in mind, and adjust the dimensions and design elements such as inset versus lipped drawers, or hardware and mouldings, to meet your specific needs.

First Steps

Before heading to the shop, we first designed the project in Google SketchUp (sketchup.com), a powerful (and free) design program that allows you to build in virtual space and get all the elements and measurements just as you want them (the files for this project are available at popularwoodworking.com under the *Sketchup* menu tab).

Then, based on the measurements established in the drawings, we headed to the shop and pulled rough maple planks from our rack, selecting straight-grained boards for the face frame and side panels, and laid out the various elements. We rough cut the pieces to length for the face frame pieces and sides, adding 1" to the final lengths, then milled the stock to ¾" on the jointer and through the planer.

Face First: Mortise-and-Tenon

This is a face-frame cabinet, so building that frame is the initial step in the process. By completing it first, you can then use the finished frame to make any necessary size adjustments to the other pieces.

At the table saw, we ripped the rails, stiles and drawer dividers from the same S4S board, and crosscut them to final length. Then it was on to laying out the mortises on the rails.

Determine the face of each frame member, then clamp the stiles together with the working edge facing up. Use the drawing to locate each rail and divider along the length of the stiles and mark the top and bottom edge of each rail with a line completely across each stile. Next, move in a ½" from the top end of the stiles and draw a line setting the location of the mortise for the top rail. Move toward the center of each layout area ¼" and place a partial line for each of the remaining rails. Mortise only between these partial lines.

Using ¾" stock makes this a simple process. Set up a marking gauge to find the center of the workpiece. Using the marking gauge you've already set up, strike the centerline of one of your mortises (you'll use that mark to line up the bit at the mortiser).

You're now ready to make the cuts. Chuck a ¼" hollow-chisel mortising bit in the mortiser, set the depth for 1¼" (setting the depth of cut on the strong side), then line up the bit point with the centerline you marked in the top mortise. Bore a series of holes across the mortise, leaving a little less than ¼" in between each hole (this helps to keep the chisel from deflecting). Go back and clean out the remaining waste, then make another series of passes from end to end in the mortise to clean out any remaining waste, and to break up any large chips (this will make it easier to knock out the sawdust). Then move on to the next mortise. Because each mortise is centered on your ¾" stock, you can flip the workpiece end-to-end and the setup will remain consistent.

With all your mortises cut, it's time to move on to the tenons on the rails. Again, ¾" stock makes it easy to center the tenons in your workpieces, and not have to change setups or spend much time measuring. Glen suggests using ¾" stock for all face frames when possible; that way the layout becomes second nature (after so much time in the shop, he can eyeball it to within a millimeter, so he spent a lot of time rolling his eyes every time I reached for my 6" rule and/ or sliding square).

Each tenon is $1\frac{1}{4}$" in length and $\frac{1}{4}$" in thickness. Raise the blade in your table saw to just a hair under $\frac{1}{4}$". Set your fence at $1\frac{1}{4}$" to the outside edge of the blade, and make the cuts on all four shoulders of each end of each rail. Raise the blade to $\frac{1}{2}$" when cutting the edge shoulder cut on the top rail. We used a tenon jig (the one Senior Editor Robert W. Lang built for the August 2007 issue, #163) to cut the shoulders. Your fence setting will vary depending on your jig, but the idea is to leave a matching $\frac{1}{4}$" tenon when finished, with the blade raised to $1\frac{1}{4}$".

Cut the shoulder off the outside of the rail to keep from trapping waste material between the blade and the rail. It's a good idea to check the fit of that tenon in your mortises to see if you need to make any slight adjustments in your saw settings before you finish the rest of the cheek cuts. The goal is a snug fit. You should be able to insert the tenon into the mortise using hand pressure and maybe a little

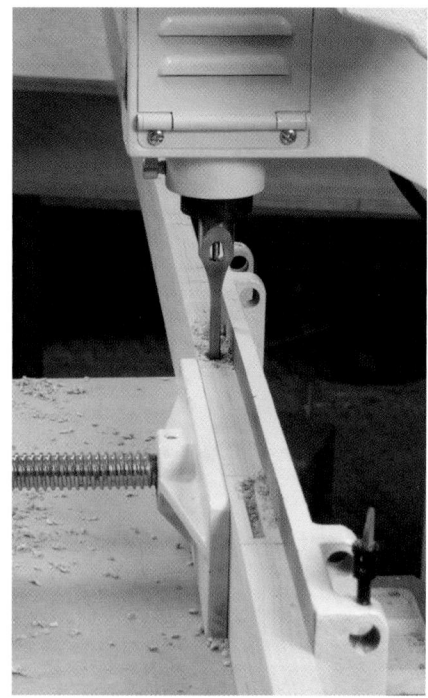

SQUARE CUTS. To ensure you get a nice, squared mortise, first make a series of cuts spaced a little less than $\frac{1}{4}$" apart; this will help keep the chisel from deflecting.

VERSATILE STORAGE. This tall chimney cabinet is perfect for any narrow space, whether in the kitchen, bath or elsewhere in your home.

ROLLING SHOULDER CUTS. Make all four cuts on one end of each rail at the table saw, using a sled or sliding table.

TENON JIG. This tenon jig keeps the workpiece secure as you cut off the cheeks of your tenons.

mallet tap – if too much force (or too little) is necessary, you'll want to adjust your fence accordingly.

Once you have that right, make the rest of your cheek cuts then head to the band saw to remove the remaining waste.

Set up your fence a heavy ¼" from the outside edge of the blade so you're cutting away waste on the inside of each tenon (that way you can just flip the piece to make the second cut, without having to adjust the fence). This will

make each tenon just a little loose from top to bottom in the mortise, allowing room for minor adjustments. Exercise caution to get the depth of your cut just right – if you cut past the proper depth, the kerf will show on your finished frame

Chimney Cupboard

	NO.	ITEM	DIMENSIONS (INCHES)			DIMENSIONS (MILLIMETERS)			MATERIAL	COMMENTS
			T	W	L	T	W	L		
❏	2	Face frame stiles	¾	2¾	78	19	70	1981	Maple	
❏	1	Top face frame rail	¾	5½	18	19	140	457	Maple	1¼ TBE*
❏	1	Bottom face frame rail	¾	3	18	19	76	457	Maple	1¼ TBE
❏	3	Face frame drawer dividers	¾	1¼	18	19	32	457	Maple	1¼ TBE
❏	2	Sides	¾	9¾	78	19	248	1981	Maple	
❏	1	Top	¾	9	20	19	229	508	Maple	
❏	1	Fixed shelf	¾	9	20	19	229	508	Maple	
❏	3	Drawer extensions	¾	1¼	19½	19	32	496	Maple	
❏	6	Drawer runners	¾	2¾	7¾	19	70	197	Maple	½ TOE*
❏	6	Drawer guides	¾	¾	8	19	19	203	Maple	
❏	1	Nailing strip for backboards	¾	2¾	19½	19	70	496	Maple	
❏	2	Door stiles	¾	2	44	19	51	1118	Maple	
❏	1	Top door rail	¾	2¼	14	19	57	356	Maple	1¼ TBE
❏	1	Bottom door rail	¾	2¾	14	19	70	356	Maple	1¼ TBE
❏		Back	⅝	20½	78	16	521	1981	Maple	
❏	1	Top drawer front	⅞	4	15⅜	22	102	391	Maple	
❏	1	Middle drawer front	⅞	5	15⅜	22	127	391	Maple	
❏	1	Bottom drawer front	⅞	6	15⅜	22	152	391	Maple	
❏	1	Top frame front	½	2⅛	23¾	13	54	603	Maple	45° ABE*
❏	2	Top frame sides	½	2⅛	11⅞	13	54	301	Maple	45° AOE*
❏	1	Top frame back	½	2⅞	19½	13	73	496	Maple	
❏	1	Front crown	13/16	2	22⅝	21	51	575	Maple	
❏	2	Side crowns	13/16	2	11 5/16	21	51	287	Maple	
❏	2	Long retainer strips	5/16	5/16	39¾	8	8	1010	Maple	
❏	2	Short retainer strips	5/16	5/16	11⅜	8	8	289	Maple	

* TBE, Tenon both ends; TOE, Tenon one end; AOE, Angle both ends; AOE, Angle one end

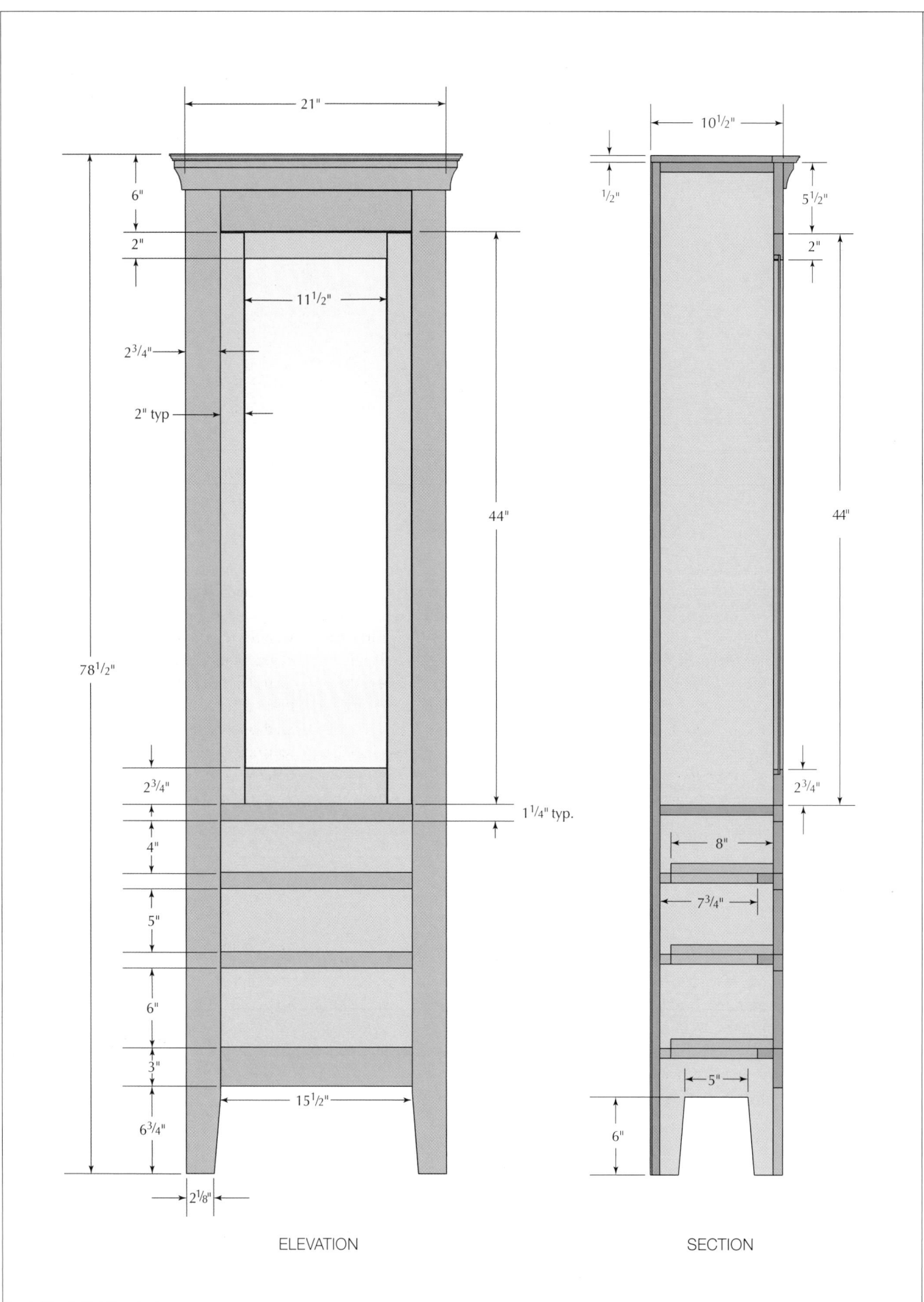

ELEVATION

SECTION

DRY FIT, THEN GLUE. With everything squared up and fitting, add glue and clamp your face frame together and set it aside to dry.

(see the door-construction photo at the bottom of page 21).

Dry-fit, Then Glue

Now dry-fit the frame together, and when everything looks good, take it back apart and squeeze glue into the mortises of all stiles, using an acid brush to coat all the surfaces. Then spread a thin layer of glue on the face of each tenon and mate the two. Remember: you left a little wiggle room on the mortise from top to bottom, so you can knock it one way or the other as necessary so that all your openings are square. Now do the same on the other side, check all the openings for square, and clamp it together to dry.

How much glue? Glen suggests that you look for a little bit of squeeze-out, so you know you've got enough. You can clean it up after it dries with a chisel or card scraper, or wipe it off while wet with a rag and warm water (though there is some argument that this could give you finishing problems later).

Side Panels

Because the side panels have to be glued up from two pieces (unless you're lucky enough to find wide stock), it's important to take a close look at the pieces you're using, and work with any grain patterns and color variation to get the best-looking panels possible. I wanted the panel seam to be dead center, so I ripped from both edges of my surfaced boards to get the best look, and took the final passes for the glue line at the jointer. We then glued the panels and set them aside to dry.

With the panels dry, we lined up the top edges and marked the dado location at the top drawer divider (behind which is a ¾" solid shelf) then routed a ¾"-wide x ¼"-deep dado in each side panel using a shopmade straightedge guide for the router. We also routed a rabbet of the same size at the top end of the side panels to accept the top. We then moved to the table saw to cut a ¾" x ⁷⁄₁₆" two-step rabbet at the back edge of each side panel, to later receive shiplapped backboards. The ¾" flat cut is made first. I used a featherboard to help support and secure the second cut; for me, it's hard to hold a 9¾" piece of stock steady though a 78" long cut without it moving.

Before gluing the sides to the face frame, we used a plywood jig we made at the drill press to drill ½" deep x ¼" holes for shelf pins to hold the three glass adjustable shelves (you could instead buy a plastic shelf-pin jig, or use peg board as a template.)

Then, we stuck a ¾" offcut into the dado, both to check the fit and to use it as a guide to line up the dado location with the top drawer divider, ran a bead of glue along the edge of the side panel, then clamped the panel and face frame flush. After it was dry, we did the same on the opposite side. We then made a template for the side cutouts, clamped it to the bottom edge of the side panel, and used a ¼" top-bearing router bit to cut

SHELF GROOVE. Set up a straightedge jig to guide your router through your shelf-groove cut.

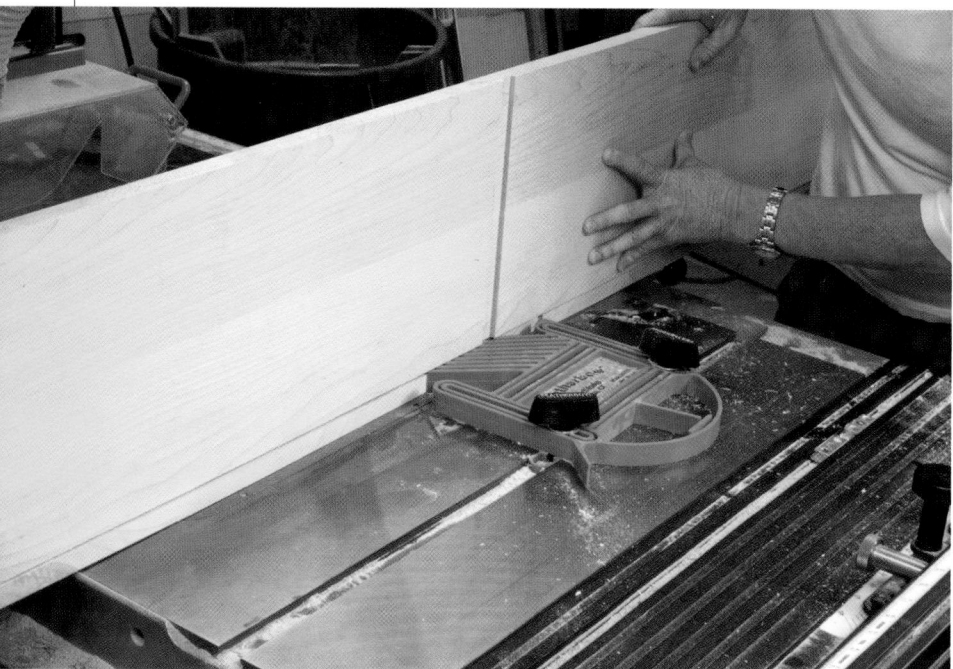

TWO-STEP. This two-step rabbet cut is made more secure and safe by using a featherboard to help hold the workpiece.

out the shape on both sides after trimming it with a jigsaw.

Next, we cut and fit the shelf and case top into the side/face frame assembly. The shelf is held with 1¼" brads installed from below the shelf, into the side panels; the top is attached with brads coming in from the top.

Next up were the drawer extensions, the runners and the drawer guides. Cut the extensions according to the cut sheet and fit each to the case directly behind the top edge of the dividers. Before they are glued in place you'll need to create

the ¼" x 2¼" x ½" mortises to accept the runners. These mortises begin a ¼" from the end of the extension.

The runners are milled to size and a tenon is created on one end of each runner. I elected to notch the back edge of each runner so I could use a 1½" cut nail

to hold the rear portion of the runner in place. The notch is ⅞" x 1¾". Add glue to the mortise and tenon, then add the nail to complete the installation of the runners.

Each runner needs a drawer guide. The guides are set square to the case front and flush with the face-frame edge.

Door Construction

The door is also constructed of ¾" stock, and it's the same mortise-and-tenon process and setup as was used on the face frame.

Once the door was glued, clamped square and the glue was dry, we fit it to the door opening in the frame using a nickel to gauge the offset on all four sides, and took passes at the jointer (one for one on each side) until the fit was perfect.

And here's Glen's hint to avoid tear-out along the top or bottom of the door frame: Because you'll be taking jointer passes off the end grain of the stiles, there's a very good chance that you'll splinter the outer edge of the stile. To avoid that, make a short cut from what will be the trailing end of the cut, then reverse the work and make the full cut.

CHEAP AND EASY. Chucking an offcut into the shelf dado makes it easy to line up the face frame with the sides.

OFFCUT

TAKING SIDES. Make sure everything is lined up flush before tightening down the clamps. Secure the ends first, then adjust as necessary through the middle to compensate for any slight bowing.

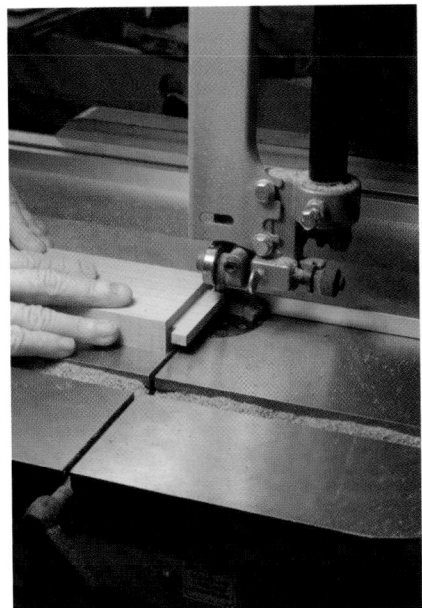

CAREFUL NOW. Cut the remaining waste on the tenon at the band saw, being careful not to overshoot your mark. If you do, the resulting kerf will show on the front of the door.

Because the material at the end is already gone, you won't have any tear-out.

Drawer Construction

I wanted inset drawers, which I was told (after the fact) are a little trickier to make than lipped drawers, because the fit has to be perfect or they won't look right. Because the fronts involved half-blind dovetails, we milled maple to ⅞" thick (you can go as thin as ¾", but the extra thickness provides a more antique look).

The drawers are graduated in size, from 4" - 6" in height, all are 15⅜" wide. (I just hope that bottom one will be deep enough to hold my hair dryer). First, we carefully examined the surfaced stock to select the best faces for the drawers, then crosscut each front to length before ripping each front to width, making the fit very snug. We then pared each front to finished width, taking thin passes at the jointer on each edge until we had a penny-thickness offset on all four sides of each.

We milled the ½" drawer sides and backs out of poplar and cut them to size; I then hand cut half-blind dovetails for the front, and through dovetails at the back.

After dry-fitting each drawer then knocking them apart, it was back to the table saw to cut a ¼"-wide x ¼"-deep groove ½" up from the bottom edge of each of the six side pieces, and on the three drawer fronts, for the drawer bottom. Add glue to your tails and pins, knock the drawers together and check for square, then set them aside to let them dry.

Next, mill poplar (or whatever secondary wood you choose) to ⅝" for the drawer bottoms, and cut them to size. What you're about to make is basically a country-style raised panel. At the table saw, set the fence to ³⁄₁₆", angle your blade to 12° and raise it so the blade exits cleanly through your workpiece.

Check the fit of the panels in your drawer grooves, mark a line where the inside edge of the drawer backs and the bottom panels meet. Pull the bottoms out and measure to find the center of each bottom (if, like me, you're anal-retentive … Glen prefers to eyeball it) and cut a saw slot set to the height of the line. Insert the bottoms into each drawer (you'll have an overhang at the back of ¼"), drill a pilot hole into the drawer back, then drive a cut nail through the slot in the drawer bottom, into the drawer back. This provides support for the bottom while allowing for seasonal movement. (In wider drawers that require more support, space two slots across the back.) Glen admits that you could simply eschew the slot and nail straight through the drawer bottom, but the slot more easily accommodates seasonal movement in the drawer bottoms.

STACKED. Here, the finished drawers are stacked and waiting for drawer bottoms and the finish.

CLIMB CUTTING

FINISH CUT

ROUT A RABBET. To rout the rabbet for the glass, you'll be making some climb cuts, To avoid tear-out, first make a shallow climb cut with the router, then go back and cut to full depth.

SQUARE YOUR CORNERS. Use a 6" rule to extend the line of the rabbet, then clean the corner square with a chisel.

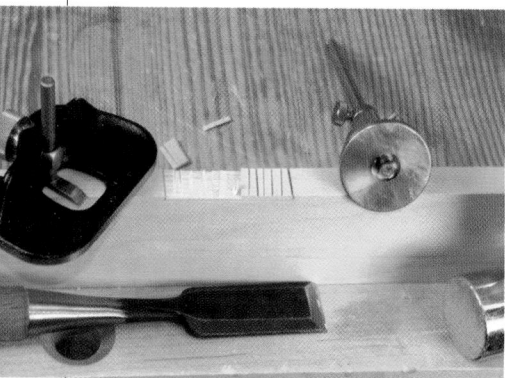

HINGE MORTISE. I cut the hinge mortises by hand using two marking gauges, a wide chisel and a router plane. If you don't have a router plane, use a chisel to pare the flat bottom.

Back to the Door

Now we need to rout a ³⁄₈" x ¹⁄₂" rabbet for the glass (or mirror, if you prefer) for the door. Set up your router with a rabbeting bit, set the depth to ¹⁄₂", then clamp your door face-down on your bench (you'll have to change the workpiece setup several times while routing the rabbet so you don't cut into your bench). Cutting the rabbet involves some climb cutting, so make sure you have a good grip on the router, and are holding it tightly and flat against your workpiece (a D-handle router makes this a little easier). To avoid ugly tear-out on the finish cut, first climb cut a shallow pass to waste out just some of the material. Then reverse directions (regular routing operation) and remove the rest, working your way around the interior of the door.

With the rabbet routed, you need to square the corners with a chisel. Press a rule against the inside of the rabbet, and extend the lines at each corner with a pencil to mark the area to be chiseled. First, make sure your chisel is sharp, then pare your way down ¹⁄₂" to the bottom of the existing rabbet.

Measure from side to side and top to bottom, and give your glass purveyor a call for both the panel glass and adjustable glass shelves. We ordered ¹⁄₁₆"-thick glass for the door, and ³⁄₈"-thick glass for the shelves.

Now it's time to cut mortises for the hinges. While you could set up a router for this operation, with only two hinges to install, I opted for hand tools: two marking gauges, a chisel and mallet,

A RAISED PANEL. To angle the drawer bottoms so they'll fit in the ⁵⁄₈" groove, you're basically making a raised panel on the table saw. Angle your blade to 12° and raise it so the angled blade exits cleanly through your workpiece.

and a small router plane to clean up the finished depth (which could be accomplished with a wide chisel, and a little more care).

Drill pilot holes for the hinge screws, and seat two screws in each hinge to make sure the fit is correct then transfer the hinge locations to the face frame, and remove the hinges from the door (you'll need them to mark around on the face frame). Cut your hinge mortises on the face frame, drill pilot holes for the screws, then install the hinges on the door. Hint: Put a smidge of paste wax on the screw, and it will seat more easily.

Now grab a buddy and have him or her hold the hinges in place on the frame as you install the door to ensure it fits. You'll then have to take it off and remove the hardware before finishing.

Building a Top Hat

The top frame and cove moulding completes the construction for the case. Mill the material to thickness and size according to the cut sheet.

The top frame houses another of our joints, the biscuit. The biscuit joint is used to join the two front mitered corners as well as the rear frame piece to the sides of the frame.

Cut the 45° miters at the miter saw, locate the center of the angled cut and use the plate joiner to create the slot for the biscuits. The wider rear frame has the slot centered on the ends with matching slots on the inside edge of the frame sides.

Assemble the rear frame to the sides with glue and biscuits, then clamp. Next, add glue into the remaining slots and assemble the frame. The trick to getting a square glue-up is to add another clamp across the front with one clamp along each side. Then, tighten the clamps so the mitered joints align.

Once the glue has dried, sand the frame to #180 grit and profile the edges at the router table. We used the new Freud Quadra-Cut beading bit to profile the top frame.

Attach the frame to the case using #8 x 1¹⁄₄" wood screws ensuring the frame is centered on the case and flush with the back.

The cove moulding is created with a raised panel bit at the router table. Use the full profile taking shallow passes until the top of the cove just touches the panel; there's no reveal.

Next, cut the mitered corners of the moulding, sand the profile smooth using

Supplies

Horton Brasses
800-754-9127 or
horton-brasses.com

2 • Hinges
#PB-407B; satin nickel

3 • Bin pulls
#BN-2; satin nickel

1 • Door latch
#SL-4; satin nickel

1 • Clout nails
#N-7; 1/4 pound (53 nails)

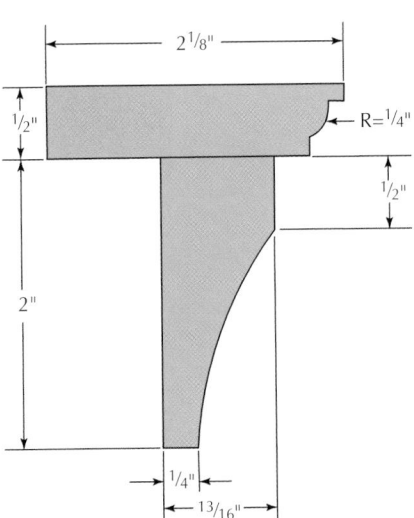

COVE MOULDING PROFILE

#180-grit sandpaper and add the pieces to the case with 1" brads applied both to the case and into the top frame.

Backboards

I built a shiplapped back with three evenly spaced boards (a plywood panel would work, too). We ran two-step rabbets at the table saw, and I used a block plane to chamfer the edges that would show on the inside. Before installing the backboards, I painted the interior display area for some contrast with the clear finish on the outside, and to tie it in with the rest of the bathroom woodwork. Using the same template as for the side cutouts, we marked the back and made the cuts with a jigsaw.

Next, install a nailing strip at the bottom to which to attach the backboards. The piece is screwed to the bottom of the bottom drawer runners with two #8 x 1¼" wood screws.

To install the backboards so that they'll accommodate seasonal movement, the idea is to use as few nails as possible. Two of the boards have only three nails: one at the top, one at the fixed shelf and one into a nailing strip at the bottom edge. The third board, because it has no lap to secure it flat, has two nails at either edge, in the same locations.

Finishing Touches

For the finish, we simply used a coat of sanding sealer and a coat of lacquer (sanding between coats) then wax.

Finally, you're ready to install the glass. It's held in the door with simple retaining strips pulled from the scrap bin and tacked in place with ½" headless pins (make sure you shoot the pins at an angle, wood to wood, so you don't hit and break your glass). Now install the catch for the door; we simply put it where we thought it looked good. For the final step, center the drawer pulls in each drawer, drill pilot holes then screw the pulls in place.

Arts & Crafts Bookcase

BY KARA GEBHART

My mom has a bookcase in every room of my parents' house. Most of them are stuffed two-rows deep with paperbacks, hardbacks, picture books and travel books. And still, whenever I visit, I find even more novels piled on top of end tables, underneath coffee tables, near the sides of chairs and on the backs of toilets. But I'm like her – I love collecting books.

Tired of moving my own piles of books every time I needed a place to set a drink down, I decided to build a bookcase of my own. This project serves as a nice challenge for the beginning woodworker and as a great weekend project for those more skilled. Its Arts & Crafts style is emphasized by mortise-and-tenon joinery, wedges and Stickley-style (sans ammonia) finish. While the ends remain forever assembled, a few good whacks to the wedges and the whole project comes apart, stacks together and can be transported easily in the trunk of a car.

Getting Started

In keeping with the Arts & Crafts tradition, I bought rough quartersawn white oak for this project, which I jointed and planed. Don't have a jointer or planer? No problem. Head out to your local home center and purchase dimensional lumber. The shelves can be cut from 1 x 8s, as can the rails and stiles, with some waste.

When purchasing your lumber, be picky. Choose knot-free heartwood (you don't want pieces with a lot of sap) that has lots of figure. Determine which pieces are the most attractive and mark those for the most visible parts of the project.

Cut all your pieces to size according to the cut list.

Test Mortise

The first step to building this bookcase is tackling the joinery and assembling the sides. It's important that the project's tenons fit snugly into the mortises, which means first making a test mortise. This will allow you to check the size of your tenons throughout the tenon-cutting process, ensuring accuracy. There are 24 mortises in this project. Do yourself a favor and, if you don't already have one, buy a hollow chisel mortising machine (about $250). A mortising attachment for your drill press or a $3/8"$ Forstner bit also are acceptable options.

To make your test mortise, first select a piece of scrap from this project. Some sappy waste will do just fine. As a rule of thumb, mortises should be half the thickness of your tenon's stock. Because this project's tenon stock is $3/4"$ thick, the mortises need to be $3/8"$ thick. It's also a good idea to make your mortises about $1/16"$ deeper than the tenons are long. This will keep the tenons from bottoming out in the mortises. The depth isn't as important as the width in a test mortise, so simply make your test mortise as deep as your longest tenon is long. Because the rails have $3/4"$-long tenons and the stiles have 1"-long tenons, your test mortise for this project needs to be $1^{1}/_{16}"$ deep.

If you've never used a hollow chisel mortiser before, check out "A New Manual for Mortisers" (August 2001 issue #123). Cut your test mortise.

Table-saw Tenons

Now it's time to cut the 24 tenons. Sure this sounds like a lot, but with a dado stack and a miter gauge, you'll breeze through this step in no time.

First, install a $5/8"$ dado stack in your table saw. Set the fence for the finished length of your tenon and set the height of the dado stack to about $3/16"$, which is the depth of your shoulders on your tenon. I cut the rails' tenons first, so the finished length was $3/4"$. Hold the piece about $1/16"$ from the fence and push it through the blade, using your miter gauge. Now hold the piece directly against the fence and, using your miter gauge, push it through the blade again. Repeat this same procedure for the edges of the tenon.

After you've cut your first tenon, make sure that it fits snugly into your test mortise. If satisfied, keep cutting. Remember to set the fence for 1" once you're ready to cut the tenons on the end of the stiles.

Back to the Mortiser

To cut the mortises, first use the diagrams to measure where the rails start and stop along the stiles. Now use your rails to lay out the locations of your mortises. Cut each mortise a little over each measured line so that you're able to maneuver the rails for perfect positioning during glue-up. Cut all the stiles' mortises. You'll cut the mortises in the feet after the sides of the bookcase are assembled.

Before assembling the sides, use your table saw, plane or chisel to cut a $3/16"$ x

A few quick passes are all it takes to cut one side of the rails' tenons, using a dado stack and a miter gauge.

$\frac{3}{16}$" chamfer on the stiles' top four edges, which is a traditional Arts & Crafts look.

Assembling the Sides

Now that the rails and stiles are complete, it's time to assemble the sides. First, dry-fit everything together. Choose the face sides of your pieces carefully. Remember: Your most visible pieces should be your most attractive. Clamp the assembly together.

Check for gaps, squareness, mistakes or anything else that might cause panic during gluing. Use the extra space you cut (when you mortised slightly over the measured lines) to maneuver the rails until they're in their appropriate places. If it's tight, try hitting them with a mallet. Once you're positive that everything is perfectly positioned, use a ruler to draw lines across the joints. These lines will be your guides during glue up. Now take everything apart, put glue in the mortises, clamp and let dry.

Band-sawn Feet

Once the glue has cured, it's time to cut the feet. Each foot has two mortises and a detail cut using the band saw. Use the diagram to lay out the shape of the feet on each piece. Lay out and cut your mortises, again going a little over each line for maneuverability during assembly.

Now head over to your band saw. Cut the feet to shape as close to your lines as you possibly can. The closer you get, the less cleanup you'll have to do. Remove the saw marks with a chisel or a plane. Dry-fit the sides and feet, draw your guide lines, take the sides and

Use a test mortise to check the fit of your tenons throughout the tenon-cutting process. This ensures accuracy.

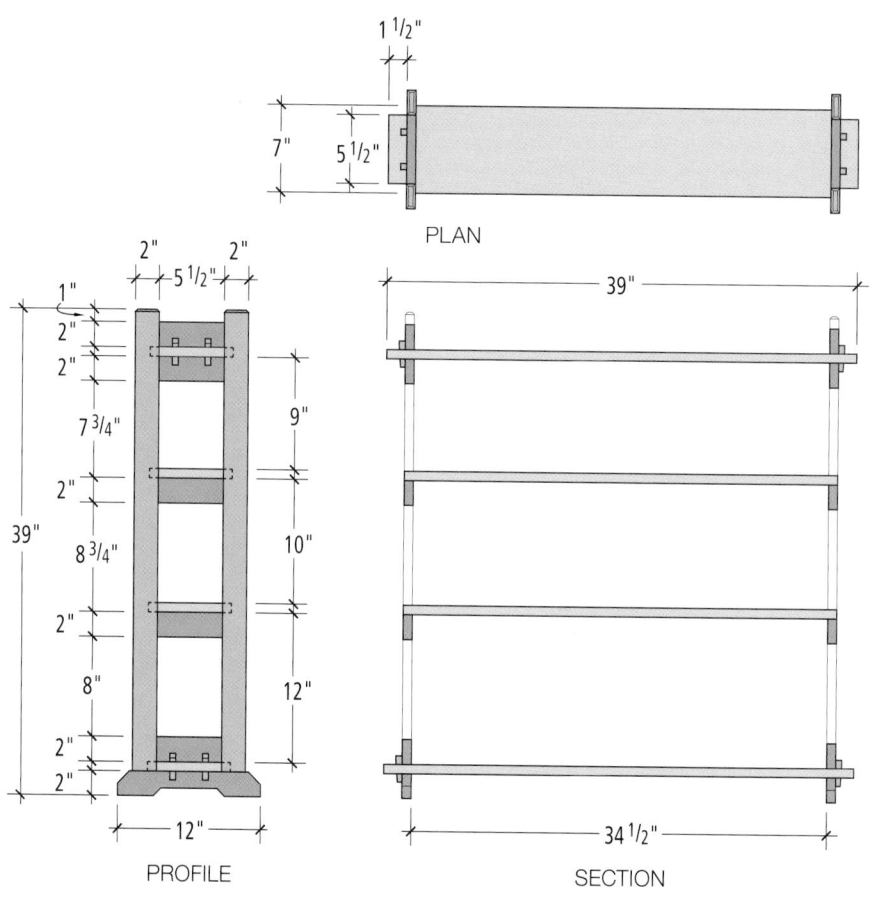

PLAN

PROFILE

SECTION

Use the edges of the rails' tenons like rulers to mark the beginning and end of each mortise in the stiles.

feet apart and then glue the assembly together.

Sturdy Shelves

With the sides now assembled, it's time to cut the shelves. First you need to cut notches in the shelves' corners. The top and bottom shelves' notches are 2¼" long by ¾" wide, allowing enough overhang for the wedges. The notches in the two middles shelves are ¾" long by ¾" wide.

Once you've measured and drawn where the notches start and stop, head to the table saw to cut the notches on the top and bottom shelves. Because the table saw's blade is curved and because you won't be running the entire length

Slide an extra rail (which is ¾" thick) into the space between the top two rails to ensure a perfect slot for the top shelf.

Use the diagrams to measure where the stiles start and stop on the feet. Like the rails, use the edge of the stiles' tenons like rulers to mark the beginning and end of each mortise.

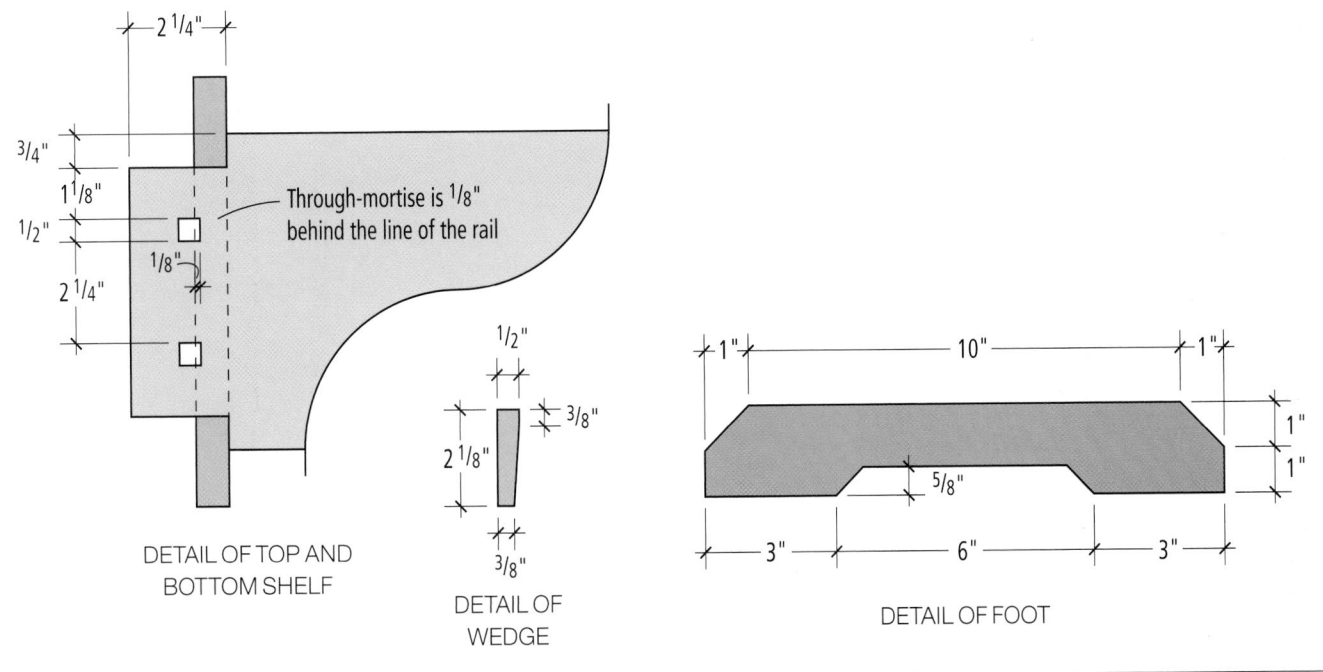

Through-mortise is ⅛" behind the line of the rail

DETAIL OF TOP AND BOTTOM SHELF

DETAIL OF WEDGE

DETAIL OF FOOT

of the board through the blade, you must be a little creative in your cutting. First, correctly position your fence and raise your blade to its appropriate height. Then, with a grease pencil, draw a line on the fence where the blade enters the table. Now, draw a line on your work where the cut should stop. Run the piece through until the two lines meet, stop and pull the piece back. Carry the line on the piece over to the other side, flip the shelf over and again run it through until the two lines meet, as shown in the top photo.

LINE ON FENCE

When cutting the shelves' notches, draw a line on your table saw's fence to determine when to stop cutting. Because of the table saw's curved blade, more material will be cut away on the underside of the piece than on the top.

Wedges slide through mortised holes in both the top and bottom shelves. Use the diagrams to lay out the locations of the $1/2$" x $1/2$" mortises. Note on the diagram how the mortises are located $1/8$" behind the line of the rails.

Head to your band saw and cut the remaining part of the top and bottom shelves' notches away. Now cut the notches on the middle shelves, using the band saw.

The whole bookcase is held together tightly by tapered wedges that snug into through-mortises in the top and bottom shelves. Cut the mortises in the top and bottom shelves, as shown at far right.

Tapered Wedges

If you haven't done so already, plane the stock for your wedges down to $1/2$" thick.

Most of the tapered part of the wedges should slide through each mortise. As the wedge gets wider, you will need a mallet and a block of wood to finish pounding them down to a uniform height.

Measure and make a mark $3/8''$ from the top of each wedge, and another mark $3/8''$ wide from the bottom of each wedge. Draw a line, connecting your marks. Cut the taper, using either your band saw or a sander. Clean up the wedges with your chisel. Test fit the wedges, as shown in the photo at the bottom of page 28.

Finishing Touches

After all your hard work, the last thing you want to do is slack off when it comes to sanding. First, clean up all your edges with a sanding block and a chisel. Next, sand everything, starting with 100 grit and moving on to 150. Hold each piece up to a light, making sure you have all the scratch marks removed. Don't forget to break the edges.

Because this is an Arts & Crafts piece, I decided on a Stickley-style finish, without ammonia's danger. First apply J.E. Moser's Golden Amber Maple water-based aniline dye. Let it dry overnight. Next, apply Valspar's Professional

warm-brown glaze. Let it, too, dry overnight. Finally, apply your favorite topcoat. Check out the Supplies box at right for ordering information. For complete instructions on how to create this ammonia-fumed-looking hue, check out "Arts & Crafts Finish" (June 2002 issue #127, available for sale online at shopwoodworking.com).

Supplies

Woodworker's Supply
800-645-9292 or woodworker.com

J.E. Moser's Golden Amber Maple water-based aniline dye

1 oz. • #844-743, $5.29

4 oz. • #844-750, $12.99

8 oz. • #844-757 • $22.59

Woodfinishingsupplies.com
507-280-6515

Valspar Professional Glaze, choose the color "warm brown/mahogany"

1 quart • #WL6100-25, $10.99

1 gallon • #WL6100-1, $34.99

$3/4''$-long tenons on rails

EXPLODED VIEW

$1''$-long tenons on stiles

Arts & Crafts Bookcase

	NO.	ITEM	DIMENSIONS (INCHES)			DIMENSIONS (MILLIMETERS)			MATERIAL	COMMENTS
			T	W	L	T	W	L		
❑	4	Stiles	$3/4$	2	38	19	51	965	White oak	1" TOE
❑	10	Rails	$3/4$	2	7	19	51	178	White oak	$3/4$" TBE
❑	2	Feet	$3/4$	2	12	19	51	305	White oak	
❑	2	Top & bottom shelves	$3/4$	7	39	19	178	991	White oak	
❑	2	Middle shelves	$3/4$	7	36	19	178	914	White oak	
❑	8	Wedges	$1/2$	$1/2$	$2 1/8$	13	13	54	White oak	

TBE = tenon, both ends; TOE = tenon, one end

Knockdown Bookcase

BY DAVID THIEL

The Arts & Crafts movement was part of an interesting social change in America — the advent of mail-order purchases. Catalogs from Sears, Roebuck and Co. and Montgomery Ward were all the rage, and many companies took their cue and offered their wares for sale through catalogs rather than set up expensive retail establishments throughout the country. While it was a great idea, it raised a difficult problem with furniture. The majority of space in any piece of furniture is air. While air is very light, it's also bulky and expensive to ship. So furniture makers perfected a style of furniture that continues today — knockdown furniture. Finished disassembled, the furniture could be shipped flat, then assembled by the owner. Through-tenons with tusks were the turn-of-the-20th-century answer, while hidden cam-locking hardware is the answer today.

Slanted Construction

This project is actually a very simple bookcase made challenging by slanting the sides. Many of the knockdown bookcases had straight sides, but why do things the easy way?

Start construction by preparing the panels for the sides and four shelves. If you aren't fortunate enough to have oak that's wide enough to make your sides using a single board, glue up the shelves or sides using two boards, but make sure the joint falls in the center of the finished panel. This is less important on the shelves; but since the sides come to a peak at the center, the joint becomes obvious if you're off the mark. Also, you

can cut the top and bottom shelves to length, but leave the two center shelves long at this time. When the through-tenons are cut and fit, you can measure for the exact length of the center shelves.

Critical Pencil Lines

With the sides prepared, lay out the shelf locations, mortise locations and the overall shape in pencil on one of them. To allow you to do a minimum of angled or beveled cutting on the pieces, the shelves all fit into $\frac{3}{4}$"-wide by $\frac{3}{8}$"-deep dados cut at a 5° angle in the sides using the table saw. Because of this, the location of the shelves actually falls at an angle on the sides. A $\frac{1}{16}$" difference in shelf height one way or the other won't dramatically affect the use of the bookcase, but you must make sure that the dados are cut at the same locations on each side.

If you happen to have a sliding table on your table saw, you're in great shape. Most people don't, so the next best option to cut the angled dados is to use your miter gauge. If you don't have a substantial wooden fence attached to your gauge, now is a good time. A fence that is 18" to 24" long and about 3" high will work fine. You'll need to determine which way to orient the sides on your saw depending on the way the arbor of your saw tilts. With some of the cuts, the majority of the side will be supported by the miter gauge, and you can use your rip fence to guide your cut. When the larger section of the side will be between the blade and rip fence, this is an unsafe cut. The board can twist and bind against the blade and cause a kick-

back. Move the rip fence out of the way, mark the sides and make the next cuts with only the miter gauge fence. With the dados complete, swap the dado with a crosscut blade, and bevel the bottom edge of each side at that angle.

Angled Mortising

The next step is the through-mortises. For these to work correctly, they also need to be cut at a 5° angle, and they must fall directly in the dados you just cut on the saw. You could cut them by hand, but the 5° angle is tricky to maintain. You could also set up a mortiser to do the job, but I got a little smarter and came up with a router template.

By using a piece of $\frac{1}{2}$" Baltic birch with a strip added beneath one end, I made a router template that would make cuts at a 5° angle. It takes some rearranging of the guide for the different cuts, but the results work rather well.

Careful layout lines are critical here. To make the 5° ramp, I used a scrap piece of $\frac{1}{2}$" material for the back strip, nailed to the template 14" from the end. Check this dimension carefully on your materials to get as close to 5° as possible.

The rest is fairly simple. Check the offset on your router template guide from the bit, and add this to the $\frac{3}{4}$" x 2" dimension for the mortise. Mark that size on the template and use a drill and jigsaw to make a square hole.

Clamp the template in place over the mortise locations and cut your through-mortises using two or three depth settings. Depending on the router bit you're using, you may want to use a backing board

After carefully laying out the shelf locations, use a dado stack (set at a 5° angle) and the saw's miter gauge to cut the angled dados.

This simple scrap-wood jig made angled mortises a fairly simple task.

With the sides clamped together and mounted in my vise, shaping the sides simply took some sanding and planing.

behind the side to reduce tear-out. I used a jigsaw and chisel to square up the corners.

Shaping up the Sides

The next step is to cut the sides to their "spade" shape. I used my band saw for most of this work, but used a jigsaw to cut the radii under the top shelf and the arch at the bottom. Cut a little wide of your layout lines, then clamp the sides together, aligning the sides by the shelf grooves on the inside surface. Plane and sand the sides to matching shapes.

Fitting the Through-Tenons

Now it's time to fit things together. Start by checking the fit of your shelves in the dados in the sides. Mine were a hair

thick, so I was able to run them down on the planer to make an almost-perfect fit. Check the width of the bottom shelf against the width of the sides at the shelf location, now that the sides are shaped. Rip the shelf to size. Next, fit the shelf into the dado and, from the outside, mark the tenon location through the mortise on the end of the shelf. Remove the shelf and mark off the 2" length of each mortise, then head for the band saw again. The width of the tenons is the critical cut. The shoulder of the tenons should be neat, but that edge is buried in the side's dados, so it doesn't have to be perfect.

With the tenons cut for the bottom shelf, fit the shelf and sides together. You want a snug fit, but not too loose and

Detail of shelf joinery

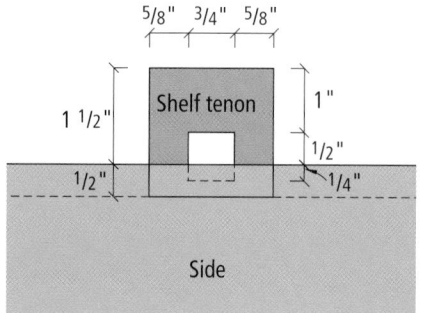

not too tight. A chisel, file or rasp and some sanding should do the job. Take your time and get it right.

With the bottom shelf fit, check the dimensions on the top shelf, mark the tenons and repeat the fitting process. When that task is complete, fit the two center shelves and slide them into position. These shelves are designed to be left loose, but if they slide a little more than you like, a nail through the side into the center of the shelf will make a permanent solution, or you can drive a short wedge into the joint under the shelf for a temporary fix.

A close look at the wedged through-tenons shows the recess behind the side that allows the wedge to pull the sides tight.

Tusks and the Home Stretch

To hold the top and bottom shelves in place — and the whole case together — disassemble the case and mark the $\frac{3}{4}$" x $\frac{3}{4}$" through-mortises on the shelf tenons as shown in the diagrams. I used my mortising machine to cut these holes. Another option is to use a drill press to cut the mortises and then square up the corners using a chisel.

Reassemble the case, then cut the eight tusks. Appropriately, the tusks should seat with their center at the shelf tenon. Fit the tusks as necessary, and tap them into place to make the whole case rigid. Now take it all apart one last time and sand everything to 150 grit.

For a finish, I used a simple dark-colored gel stain, wiping off the excess until I was happy with the depth of the color. I then top-coated the case with a couple of coats of lacquer.

The nicest thing about moving this bookcase is that after you knock out the eight tusks, everything fits in the trunk of a compact car.

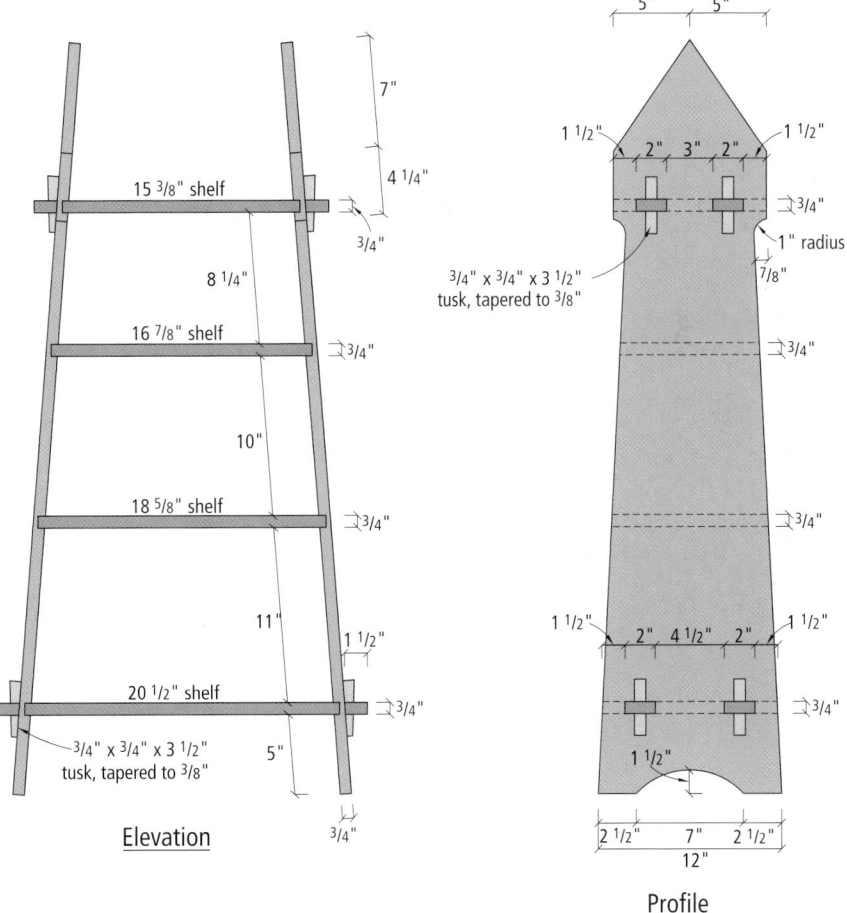

Elevation

Profile

Knockdown Bookcase

	NO.	ITEM	DIMENSIONS (INCHES)			DIMENSIONS (MILLIMETERS)			MATERIAL	COMMENTS
			T	W	L	T	W	L		
❏	2	Sides	$\frac{3}{4}$	12	48*	19	305	1219		
❏	1	Bottom shelf	$\frac{3}{4}$	11$\frac{1}{8}$	24$\frac{1}{2}$	19	282	623		2"TBE
❏	1	Top shelf	$\frac{3}{4}$	10	19$\frac{3}{8}$*	19	254	493		2" TBE
❏	1	Third shelf	$\frac{3}{4}$	9$\frac{7}{8}$	19*	19	251	483		
❏	1	Second shelf	$\frac{3}{4}$	8$\frac{11}{16}$	17*	19	220	432		
❏	8	Tusks	$\frac{3}{4}$	$\frac{3}{4}$	3$\frac{1}{2}$	19	19	89		

* Oversized for fitting; TBE = tenon, both ends

Craftsman Bookcase

BY ROBERT W. LANG

There are many bookcases in my house, but they're a motley collection – poor cousins to the rest of the furniture. The really nice bookcases I've made have gone to live with clients, while I have kept the prototypes and the also-rans. They are nicer than concrete blocks and pine planks, but not my best work. The cherry bookcase in my living room was a test case – both of a dovetail jig and the wood's moisture content.

It was time for something nicer. This design is an adaptation of early 20th-century Gustav Stickley bookcases. I wanted to use nice wood, and show off a bit with the joinery.

I didn't have a specific species of wood in mind when I went to the lumberyard, but I knew I wanted something attractive and wide enough to avoid gluing up individual boards. I found a nice batch of sapele, also known as African mahogany, and brought home 50 board feet of wide planks.

Off to a Good Start

My lumber had been surfaced to $15/16$", but it wasn't quite flat. After cutting the parts to rough sizes, I ran the material over the jointer and through the planer to remedy that, ending up with stock slightly thicker than $13/16$". I planed off the mill marks with a smoothing plane, and dressed all of the stock with a scraper before working on the joinery.

This exercise served two purposes: I now knew the material was straight and true, and having the faces at a nearly finished state would save work later on. It's a lot easier to work on a plank on a bench than it is to work inside an assembled cabinet.

When the faces were smooth, I cut the sides and fixed shelves to their final sizes. I determined which side should be right and which should be left, situating the most attractive faces on the outside. I put a 1"-diameter straight bit in my plunge router, and set the fence to cut a $7/8$"-wide, $1/2$"-deep rabbet on the back edge of each side, stopping at the bottom edge of the lowest shelf.

Doing this step first established the sides as right and left, and it kept me from confusing the inside and outside faces as I worked on the remaining joints. Each of the three shelves connects to the cabinet sides with a pair of wedged through-tenons. On the inside of the case, each shelf sits in a $1/8$"-deep dado.

The dados aren't really needed structurally, but they ensure that the inner surfaces of the joints always look good, and they help to locate the through-mortises with the jigs that I used. With a dozen through-mortises to fit, I needed a method to make the process efficient and idiot-resistant, if not idiot-proof.

Jigs and Joints Work Together

Because I didn't have a router bit the exact size to match the thickness of the shelves, I decided to use a $5/8$"-diameter, $1/2$"-long bit with a guide bearing mounted above the cutters. I made a jig to match the thickness of the shelves by clamping an offcut from one of the shelves between the two fences.

I then screwed a straight piece of scrap to one end of the fences, making

certain that the inner edge was square to the working edges of the fences. I screwed another piece of scrap to the opposite end of the fences, and I was ready to make a test cut. The resulting dado was just a bit narrow, and a few swipes with the smoothing plane on the bottom of the shelves made for a snug fit.

After routing the three dados in each of the case sides, I began to make the second jig, which is used to cut the mortises. The mortises are $5/8$" wide and $2\frac{3}{4}$" long, and they are equal distances from the front and back of the case sides with a 3" space in between. Rather than cut the mortises in the jig, I made them by assembling pieces of $1/2$"-thick plywood in two layers.

I laid out the locations of the mortises on the larger, bottom part of the jig, then I glued and nailed smaller pieces along the layout lines. I drilled holes in the waste area, and with a flush-trim bit in my router, I trimmed the bottom of the

DEDICATED JIG. This dado jig is made to fit the thickness of the shelves, and utilizes a flush-cutting bit with the bearing on top.

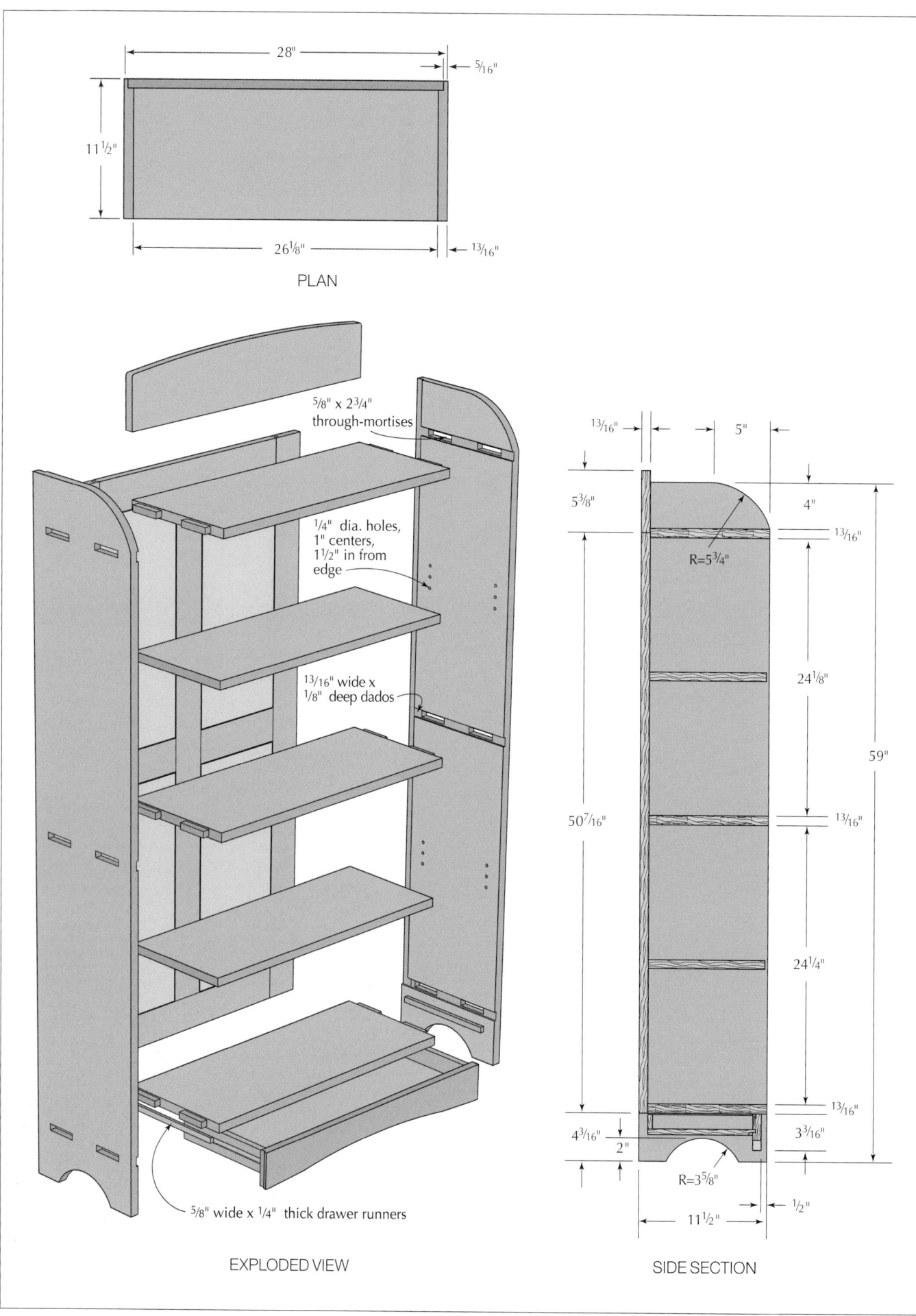

PLAN

$^5/_8$" x $2^3/_4$"
through-mortises

$^1/_4$" dia. holes,
1" centers,
$1^1/_2$" in from
edge

$^{13}/_{16}$" wide x
$^1/_8$" deep dados

$^5/_8$" wide x $^1/_4$" thick drawer runners

EXPLODED VIEW

SIDE SECTION

28"

$^5/_{16}$"

$11^1/_2$"

$26^1/_8$"

$^{13}/_{16}$"

$^{13}/_{16}$"

5"

$5^3/_8$"

4"

$^{13}/_{16}$"

R=$5^3/_4$"

$24^1/_8$"

$^{13}/_{16}$"

59"

$50^7/_{16}$"

$24^1/_4$"

$^{13}/_{16}$"

$4^3/_{16}$"

2"

$3^3/_{16}$"

R=$3^5/_8$"

$11^1/_2$"

$^1/_2$"

Craftsman Bookcase

NO.	ITEM	DIMENSIONS (INCHES) T	W	L	DIMENSIONS (MILLIMETERS) T	W	L	MATERIAL	COMMENTS
☐ 2	Sides	13/16	11 1/2	59	21	292	1499	Sapele	
☐ 3	Fixed shelves	13/16	10 11/16	28 1/8	21	271	714	Sapele	
☐ 2	Adjustable shelves	13/16	10 7/16	26 1/4	21	265	666	Sapele	
☐ 2	Back panel outer stiles	13/16	3 5/16	50 7/16	21	84	1281	Sapele	
☐ 1	Back panel inner stile	13/16	3	46 5/16	21	76	1176	Sapele	1 1/4" TBE *
☐ 1	Back panel top rail	13/16	3	23 1/4	21	76	590	Sapele	1 1/4" TBE *
☐ 1	Back panel bottom rail	13/16	3 5/8	23 1/4	21	92	590	Sapele	1 1/4" TBE *
☐ 2	Back panel middle rails	13/16	3	11 3/8	21	76	289	Sapele	1 1/4" TBE *
☐ 4	Back panels	3/4	9 5/8	21 1/8	19	245	536	Sapele	
☐ 1	Back splash	13/16	5 3/8	27 1/2	21	137	699	Sapele	
☐ 1	Lower apron/drawer front	13/16	3 3/16	26 3/8	21	81	670	Sapele	
☐ 2	Drawer sides	5/8	1 3/4	10 1/16	16	45	256	Maple	
☐ 1	Drawer back	1/2	1 1/4	26 1/8	13	32	663	Maple	
☐ 1	Drawer bottom	1/2	9 3/4	25 3/8	13	248	645	Poplar	
☐ 2	Drawer runners	3/8	3/4	9 1/16	10	19	231	Maple	

* TBE=Tenon both ends

jig to match the top. A few cuts with a chisel to clean out the corners and I was ready to make mortises – almost.

The mortises need to be exactly centered in the dados, and I needed a way for the jig to be clamped to the case sides. I made an edge piece the thickness of the case side, plus the thickness of the jig, and used the same jig that I used to cut the dados in the sides to cut a notch across this piece. This notch aligns the jig to the shelf dados.

After carefully centering this piece on the mortises, I screwed it in place and made a test cut. I used an offcut from one of the shelves to align the jig

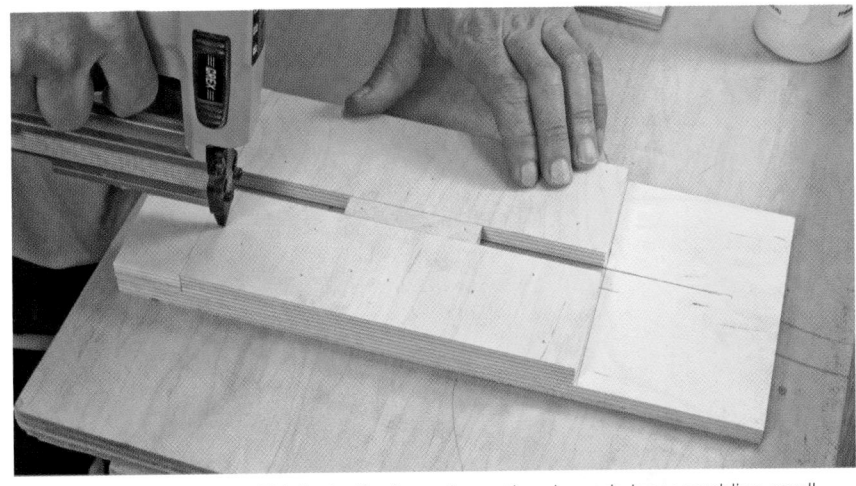

BUILT AROUND THE HOLES. This jig for the through-mortises is made by assembling small pieces to a backer. The openings are then cut with a router and a locating fence is added.

DOUBLE DUTY. After routing, the mortising jig also serves as a guide for the chisel to square the corners of the through-mortises.

GETTING IN SHAPE. After cutting the lower arch with a jigsaw, the curve is smoothed with a rasp.

ONE SIDE MAKES ANOTHER. After the curves on one side are completed, the first side is used as a template to make the second side.

for routing. I jammed the offcut in the dado in the case side, leaving an inch or so protruding from the edge of the side. This allowed me to knock the notch in the jig over the scrap. With the jig properly aligned to the case side, I clamped it in place. After drilling a hole to get the bit started, I cut the mortises with a flush-trim bit in my router.

After routing each pair of mortises, I left the jig clamped in place, flipped the side over and used the jig as a guide to cut the corners of the mortises square with a chisel.

At this point, I walked away from mortise-and-tenon territory and went to work on the curved profiles at the top front corner of each side, and the arched cutouts at the bottom. After laying out the curves on one side, I cut close to the line with a jigsaw and cleaned up the edges with a rasp.

The first side was put into service as a template for the second. I put the finished side on top of the other and traced the curves. After cutting the curves in the second side, I clamped the two

MARKED IN PLACE. The tenons are marked directly from the mortises, ensuring that the locations match.

SHOULDERS FIRST. A shallow rabbet is cut on each side of the shelves to start the making of the tenons.

ENDS SECOND. The ends of the tenons are cut by hand, then the waste in between is removed.

TEST, DON'T GUESS. Penciled hatch marks on the tenons will smear reveal tight spots within the joints during test fitting.

A LITTLE OFF THE TOP. The pencil lines smear where material needs to be removed. A planemaker's float gives good control and leaves a smooth surface.

HOW IT OUGHT TO BE. The ends can be a bit loose because the wedges will expand the tenons.

together, and used a flush-cutting bit in the router to make the second side an exact match of the first.

A Trip to Through-Tenon Territory

The next step is where the dados in the case sides saved a tremendous amount of time and prevented the formation of even more grey hair. The layout for the tenons needs to match the mortise locations exactly.

At this point I looked at the three shelves, marked the best face and edge of each, and decided which one would be the top, middle and bottom. I clamped the entire cabinet together and with a lumber crayon, marked the locations of the shelves in relation to cabinet sides.

Some hand fitting would be needed, and putting a carefully fit bottom shelf upside down in the top shelf location wouldn't be a good thing. With the case together, I ran the point of my knife around the perimeter of each mortise, marking the location of the tenons in the ends of the shelves.

I set up a small plunge router with a fence set to leave the tenons slightly proud of the outside of the cabinet sides. I set the depth to the top of the knife marks, checking both sides of each end to be sure that the tenons were centered. I wanted to make the cheek cuts quickly, but I didn't want to go too far.

I cut the edge cheeks of the tenons with a dovetail saw, and used a jigsaw to

ONE SIZE FITS ALL. In theory, the tapered wedges will fit anywhere. In reality, I fit each one and kept them in order.

remove the waste between the two tenons. With the end of each shelf housed in the dado these cuts didn't need to be pretty; I only needed to get material out of the way.

Before starting the fitting process, I took a chisel and chamfered the inside edge of each mortise, and with a piece of sandpaper I broke the sharp edge of each tenon to prevent damge to the outside of the mortises during fitting.

With a soft pencil, I made a series of hatch marks on the tenon cheeks and eased them into place. When I met resistance, I removed the shelf and examined the marks. The tight spots showed as smears in the pencil lines and I used a float to reduce the thickness until I had a good fit.

THE EASY PART. Each wedge is pared flush with the surrounding tenon. Then they are removed and stuck to a piece of blue painter's tape.

A Further Complication

Clearly in the grips of an obsessive-compulsive exposed-joinery episode, I laid out each tenon end for a pair of wedges. Unable to leave well enough alone, I decided it would look nice to set the wedges on a slight angle, making dovetail-like shapes in the end of each tenon.

I marked the distance to the edge of each cut on the ends of the tenons with a combination square, then marked the angles with a bevel gauge and knife. The slots for the wedges are at a compound angle, but I only fussed about the start of each cut. Using a dovetail saw, I cut the vertical angles by eye.

This meant that the wedges also had to be a complex shape. I began by cutting simple wedges from a piece of purple-

tongue on three edges of the drawer bottom. The back of the drawer is ½" narrower than the sides to allow the bottom to slide in after the drawer is assembled. A couple screws in elongated holes secure the thick back edge of the bottom to the drawer back and allow for seasonal wood movement.

With the drawer completely assembled, I measured in from the front of the case 2⁵⁄₁₆" (the ¹³⁄₁₆" thickness of the drawer front, plus the 1" distance from the back of the front to the end of the groove in the side, plus the ½" set-back of the drawer front from the front of the case).

I measured down from the bottom of the lowest shelf and drew a line parallel to the shelf to locate the runner. With the drawer front ½" behind the edge of the shelf, the top of the drawer front can't be seen when it is closed, so I left a ¹⁄₁₆" gap so the drawer wouldn't scrape the shelf on its way in and out. When I had the positions of the runners located, I screwed them to the inside of the case with #6 x ⁵⁄₈" flathead screws.

Easy Elbow Grease Finish

Because I had planed and scraped all the large flat surfaces before assembly, there wasn't much to be done to get ready for finishing the bookcase. I planed the front edges of the fixed shelves flush to the cabinet sides, chamfered all of the edges slightly with a block plane, and gave everything a light sanding with #240 grit.

The first coat of finish was Watco Light Walnut Danish Oil. I saturated the surface, wet-sanded it with a nylon abrasive pad, kept the surface wet for about 45 minutes, then wiped off the excess. This was followed by two coats a day of Waterlox for three days. After allowing the finish to cure for a couple days, I wet-sanded it with Watco Satin Wax and #400 grit wet/dry paper, leaving a nice sheen and a surface that is pleasant to the touch.

The joinery, details and finish on this bookcase are more than what is needed to store some books, but that really wasn't the purpose in making it. The idea was to leave something behind that demonstrates what a bit of extra effort looks like. It makes me look like a competent craftsman. Now to fill it with some books that might make me look intelligent, as well.

SLIDING HOME. The drawer bottom slides past the drawer back and into grooves in the sides and front. Screws in elongated holes will hold the bottom to the back and allow the bottom to shrink or swell.

SIMPLE ENOUGH. Maple runners below the bottom shelf support and guide the hidden drawer.

Harvey Ellis Bookcase

BY ROBERT W. LANG

Gustav Stickley once wrote that the best way to learn furniture design was to build a proven design. He wrote that the student "learns from the start the fundamental principles of design and proportion and so comes naturally to understand what is meant by thorough workmanship." This bookcase is one of the finest examples of proportion and detail that make the Craftsman style more than just a simple piece of furniture.

In 1903 Harvey Ellis designed this glass-door bookcase while working as a designer for Stickley. The first time I saw an original example of this piece of furniture I was struck by how perfectly proportioned it was and how well all of the details combine.

These details also present some challenges in building. While this is a relatively simple piece, the joinery must be precisely executed. Before I began, I spent some time tuning up our table saw and jointer, made sure my squares and measuring tools were in order, and sharpened my chisels and planes.

True to the Original

Original Craftsman furniture was occasionally made in mahogany or figured maple, but the vast majority was made from quartersawn white oak. This method of sawing yields more stable material than plain sawn oak, and the distinctive rays can be absolutely stunning. White oak is much more of a furniture wood than red oak, giving a smoother and more refined appearance.

In addition to using this wood, I also decided to use the same method of fin-

ishing that was originally used, fuming the finished piece with ammonia, and using shellac followed by wax.

Tannic acid in the wood reacts with the fumes from the ammonia, yielding a distinctive coloration in the rays and flecks, as well as in the rest of the wood. Staining, glazing and dyeing can come close to the color of an original Stickley piece, but fuming can match it exactly.

I had to glue stock together to obtain the widths required. Because the final color was dependant on a chemical reaction, and the tannic acid content of white oak will vary from tree to tree and board to board, I was careful to match boards for color as well as for figure. I also cut most of the parts for the door from the same piece of wood so that the color would be as close as possible.

Mortising With a Template

I began the joinery work with the through mortise-and-tenon joints at the bottom of the case sides. I made a template from ½"-thick plywood, which helped me locate the mortises and the arched cut-outs. I cut the mortises in the template with a ½"-diameter bit in my plunge router, guided by the router's fence, and squared the ends with a chisel and a rasp.

I could have used this same method on the actual cabinet sides, but by using the template I only had to do the layout work once, and if I slipped with the plunge router, the damage would be to a piece of plywood, not my finished end panel.

With the template clamped to the bottom of the end panel, I drilled most

The template locates the through mortises precisely, as well as the arched cut-out and the location of the dado for the bottom of the case.

of the mortise with a ⅜" Forstner bit, and then used a router with a flush trim bit to trim the sides of the mortises flush to the template. I used the smallest diameter flush trim bit I had to minimize the amount of material left in the corners. With the template still clamped to the panel, I used the edges of the mortise in the template to guide the chisel in the corners. A riffler and a flat rasp completed the work on the mortises.

Dados and Rabbets

On the inside of the end panels there is a dado to hold the bottom and a rabbet from the top down to the dado to house the back. I made both of these cuts with a router and a ¾"-diameter straight bit. I used a shop-made T-square jig for the dado, and used the router's edge guide to make the rabbet, stopping at the dado for the bottom. I also ran a ¾"-wide by ¼"-deep rabbet along the back edge of the cabinet bottom.

With the work on the side panels complete, I turned to the tenons on the ends of the two arched rails that sit below the bottom and penetrate the sides.

I always like to "sneak up" on the fit of tenons, especially when they are exposed. The tricky part with through tenons is that the final cut that yields a good fit must also be smooth enough to give a good finish. I made the initial cuts on the table saw, using a jig that rides on the fence as shown.

With the bottom in place in its dado, I held the rails in place, and marked the locations of the top and bottom of the tenons directly from the mortises in the end panels. I made these cuts on the band saw, then I cleaned up all the saw marks with a shoulder plane. As I got close to a good fit, I switched to a

After the tenons are trimmed to fit with a shoulder plane and scraper, the exposed ends are rounded with a block plane.

card scraper. Once I had the tenons fitting nicely, I took a piece of ³⁄₃₂"-thick scrap, and placed it on the outside of the cabinet with its edge against the tenon. I then marked a pencil line around the tenons. This established a starting point for the rounded ends of the exposed tenons. I used my block plane and a rasp to bevel and round over the ends of the tenons, shown above.

After the tenons were complete, I marked the midpoint of the arch, and drove a finishing nail ⅛" below that point. I also made a mark ⅜" in from each end at the bottom edge of the rail. I then bent a ⅛"-thick strip of wood across these three points, and marked the curve with a pencil. The curves in the end panels had been marked from

the template, and all of these cuts were made with my jigsaw.

The next task was to join the two stiles and top rail that make up the face frame of the carcase. I cut tenons on the end of the rail with a stack dado set in the table saw, and made the mortises at the top of the two stiles with a hollow chisel mortiser. I glued the rail between the stiles, and set this subassembly aside while I worked on the back panel.

Panelled Back

Backs in original Craftsman pieces varied depending on when they were made, and could be V-grooved or shiplapped planks, or frame-and-panel assemblies. I chose to make a back panel, as this would help keep the cabinet from racking.

The long mortises on the ends of the rails are cut with this tenoning jig that rides along the table saw fence.

With the rails already glued to one stile, the shiplapped boards for the back panel are slipped into the groove in the rail. When they were all in place, I glued on the remaining stile.

The stiles and rails for the back are all ¾"-thick material, with a ¼"-wide by ⅜"-deep groove centered in one edge. Mortise-and-tenon joints hold the panel together, and the ¼"-thick shiplapped panels float in the grooves in the stiles and rails. You also could use ¼"-thick plywood for the back panels, or make the entire back from one piece of ¾"-thick plywood.

To assemble the back, I first glued one end of each of the three rails into one of the stiles. After letting the glue dry overnight, I slipped the shiplapped panels into place, then applied glue to the tenons on the rails, and clamped on the remaining stile.

Assembling the Case

With one of the end panels flat on the end of my assembly table, I inserted the tenons for the bottom rails part way in their mortises, and then applied glue to the tenons. This keeps the glue from

To control glue squeeze-out on the exposed tenons, I get the tenon started in the mortise, then apply glue directly to the tenon.

Harvey Ellis Bookcase

	NO.	ITEM	DIMENSIONS (INCHES)			DIMENSIONS (MILLIMETERS)			MATERIAL	COMMENTS
			T	W	L	T	W	L		
CARCASE										
❑	1	Top	¾	14	36	19	356	914	Oak	
❑	2	Sides	¾	13	57¼	19	330	1454	Oak	
❑	1	Bottom	¾	13	31½	19	330	800	Oak	
❑	1	Bottom edge trim	½	¾	32	13	19	813	Oak	
❑	2	Arched rails	¾	5	33¼	19	127	844	Oak	31" between tenons- tenons extend ⅜" past sides
❑	2	Face frame stiles	⅞	1½	50½	22	38	1283	Oak	
❑	1	Face frame rail	⅞	1⅛	29	22	29	737	Oak	28" between tenons
❑	2	Applied pilasters	¼	1	50½	6	25	1283	Oak	
❑	2	Capitals	⅞	2⅛	1⅛	22	54	29	Oak	
❑	2	Shelves	¾	11⅛	30⅞	19	282	784	Oak	
DOORS										
❑	2	Stiles	¾	2½	49⅜	19	64	1255	Oak	Door opening is 28" x 49⅜"
❑	1	Top rail	¾	2½	24½	19	64	623	Oak	23" between tenons
❑	1	Bottom rail	¾	3½	24½	19	89	623	Oak	23" between tenons
❑	2	Intermediate stiles	¾	1¼	44⅜	19	32	1128	Oak	43⅜" between tenons
❑	1	Intermediate rail	¾	1¼	24	19	32	610	Oak	23" between tenons
❑	3	Top lights	⅛	7 5/16	7 5/16	3	186	186	Glass	
❑	3	Lower lights	⅛	7 5/16	35 13/16	3	186	910	Glass	
❑	18	Glass stops	¼	¼	7 5/16	6	6	186	Oak	
❑	6	Glass stops	¼	¼	35 13/16	6	6	910	Oak	
BACK										
❑	2	Stiles	¾	1½	50⅞	19	38	1292	Oak	
❑	2	Rails	¾	1½	29½	19	38	750	Oak	28½" between tenons
❑	1	Mid rail	¾	2	29½	19	51	750	Oak	28½" between tenons
❑	12	Back panel slats	¼	4⅞	23 7/16	13	124	595	Oak	Shiplapped

squeezing out on the outside of the joint. I tapped the rails home with a dead-blow mallet, and then eased the bottom in to its dado, as shown at right. With these parts together, I put glue on the tenons of the rails, and edge of the bottom before clamping down the remaining side panel.

I then laid the cabinet on its back, and glued and clamped the face frame in place. After letting the glue dry for an hour, I glued the trim piece on the front edge of the bottom. The seam between the face frame and the end panel is covered by a 1/4"-thick strip that runs from the top edge of the bottom to the bottom of the top face-frame rail.

These small additional pieces add interest to the design by creating steps in an otherwise flat surface. They also hide the joints and display quartersawn figure on the front of the cabinet.

I made a template out of 1/2"-thick baltic birch plywood that located the holes for the pegs that support the two adjustable shelves. After drilling the holes, the carcase was complete, except for the two blocks that cap the trim on the top front of the cabinet. I laid out the blocks on each end of a piece of wood about a foot long to give me room to hold them while cutting them on the band saw.

This extra material also provided a way to hold the blocks in my bench vise while cleaning them up with a rasp.

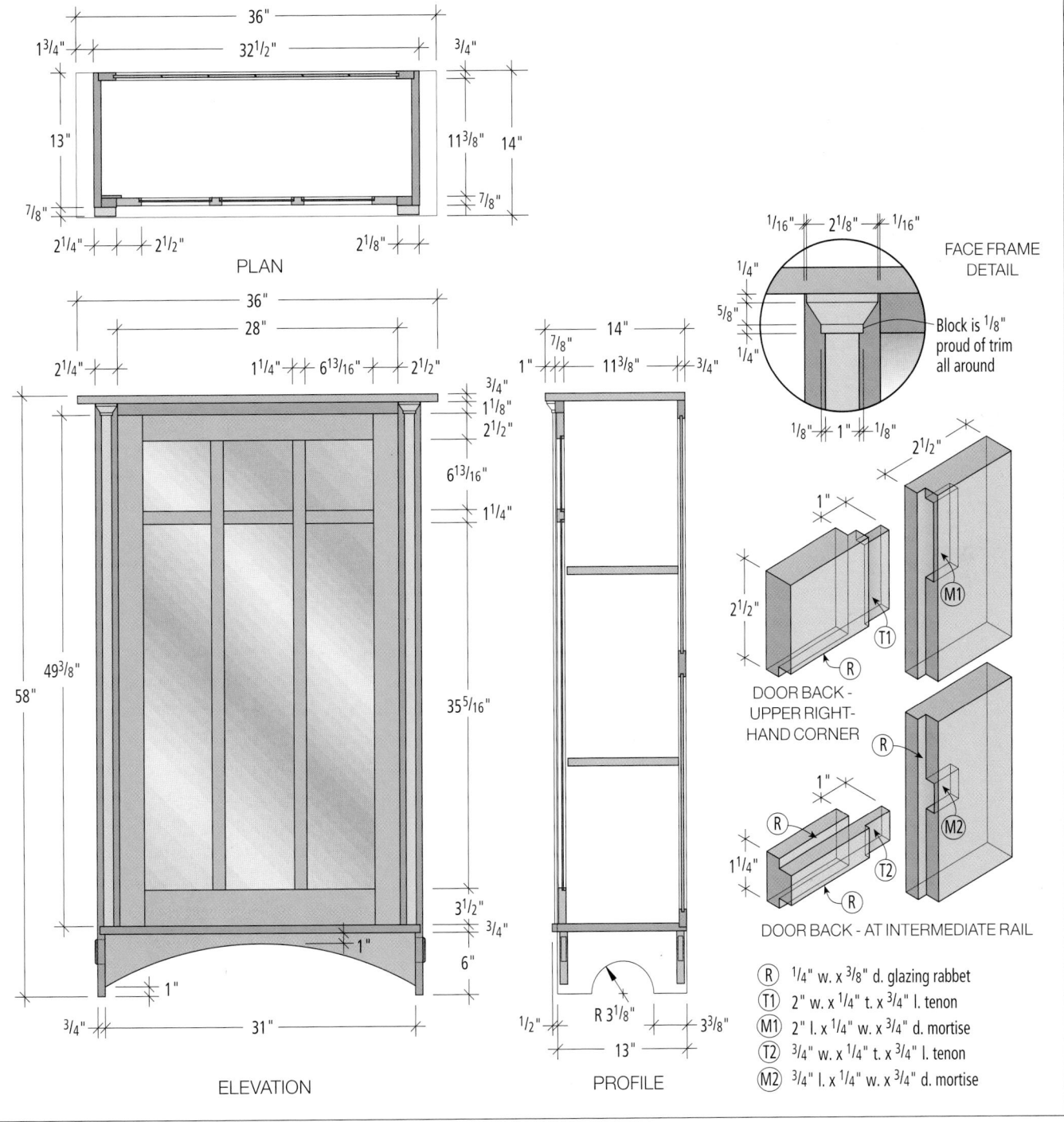

PLAN

ELEVATION

PROFILE

FACE FRAME DETAIL

Block is 1/8" proud of trim all around

DOOR BACK - UPPER RIGHT-HAND CORNER

DOOR BACK - AT INTERMEDIATE RAIL

R 1/4" w. x 3/8" d. glazing rabbet
T1 2" w. x 1/4" t. x 3/4" l. tenon
M1 2" l. x 1/4" w. x 3/4" d. mortise
T2 3/4" w. x 1/4" t. x 3/4" l. tenon
M2 3/4" l. x 1/4" w. x 3/4" d. mortise

With the two bottom rails in place, I spread glue on the top edges of the rails and in the dado before tipping the bottom in to place.

After spreading glue on the end of the bottom, and the cheeks of the tenons, the remaining cabinet side is carefully put in place.

After all the surfaces were smooth, I glued them in place.

Door

With the back panel completed, and the case parts assembled, It was time to work on the door. The glass sits in a ¼"-wide by ⅜"-deep rabbet and is held in place with ¼"-square strips of wood. This glass stop is nailed in place after the cabinet is finished. The outer stiles and rails are held together with mortise-and-tenon joints. The intermediate stiles and rail also have tenons on their ends. The door tenons all have a step in them to accommodate the rabbet for the door's glass. The ¼"-wide mortises are in line with the inside of the rabbet.

At the upper portion of the bookcase door, the intermediate rail joins the two narrow stiles with a half-lap joint as shown top, near right. I made the joints for the outer stiles and rails, and then clamped the door together to lay out the joints for the intermediate stiles and rails. I cut these joints, as well as the all tenons for all the door parts, with a stack dado set in the table saw.

I assembled the door in stages, to avoid putting together a lot of parts at once. I assembled the half-lap joints first. The top and bottom rails were then put on the ends of the smaller stiles and clamped. While this assembly was drying, I cut the mortise for the lock, and carved the recess to inlay the brass escutcheon for the keyhole.

I secured one of the long stiles in my bench vise (as shown bottom right),

The trapezoid shaped block is laid out on each end of a long piece of wood to make cutting and handling easier.

Because of the mechanical fit of the rails and bottom, it only take a couple clamps to secure the bottom of the case assembly.

All of the cuts to form the capital block were made on the band saw, as shown here. The final cut will be made after the block is smooth.

Leaving the block attached gives me plenty of material to clamp in the vise while I smooth out the saw marks with a rasp, followed by a file, and then #150-grit sandpaper.

The half-lap joints, as well as all of the tenons for the door were cut with the dado head on the table saw as you can see here. The block clamped to the saw's fence locates the cuts without trapping the parts between the dado cutter and the fence.

Half-lap joints hold the intermediate stiles and rails of the doors together.

and put glue in the mortises before placing the tenons of the rail assembly. Next I put some glue on the top edges of the tenons on the rails. Then I tapped the second rail in place before I began clamping.

Fumed Finish

Fuming white oak with ammonia is an exercise in faith; the color doesn't look right until the piece is finished with shellac and dark wax. There is also a distinct

Supplies

Lee Valley Tools
800-871-8158 or leevalley.com

1 • 1³⁄₈" mortise cabinet lock
#00N25.35, $10.80

1 • ½" extruded brass
escutcheon
#00A03.01, $2.30

Rockler
800-279-4441 or rockler.com

2 • Antique brass ball tip hinges 3" long
x 2" wide
#56962, $27.99 pair

8 • Desktop fasteners
#21650, $4.49/package of 10

Craftsman Plans
craftsmanplans.com

1 • Large format shop drawings,
includes full size details and cut list,
#GST700, $16.95

Prices as of publication date.

I assemble the door in stages. Here I'm placing a subassembly of the intermediate stiles and rail to one of the door stiles. The remaining stile will be placed on top and clamped.

After sanding all of the parts, I placed them in an airtight fuming tent, located by the back door of the shop.

After "fuming" for 24 hours the tent was aired out and the plastic removed. Here you can see the construction of the tent frame, and the change in color.

risk that some parts won't come out the same color as others, or, perhaps worse, that there will be some sapwood present that won't take on any color at all.

Twenty-six percent ammonia is used in blue print machines, and is a much stronger solution than household ammonia, which is about five percent. Such a strong chemical requires great care in handling, as the fumes can quickly damage eyes, skin and lungs. Make sure to where gloves, goggles and a respirator when handling it. I also took steps to minimize the time that the ammonia was exposed to the environment in our shop.

Before fuming the entire piece, I did some tests on scraps. As I worked on this project, I saved the cutoff pieces from the end panels and top. I put these, along with other scraps in a plastic container with an airtight lid. I put some ammonia in a small plastic bowl in the larger container, sealed the lid, and let this sit for 24 hours. Satisfied that the final result would be close to matching, I built a frame from inexpensive 1 by 3 pine and covered it with 4-mil-thick plastic sheet, as shown above left.

I tucked the plastic under the wood frame at the floor, and secured it to the frame with spring clamps to get an airtight seal. I left one end open so that I could place the assembled cabinet and all of the parts inside. Once everything to be fumed was inside, I clamped most of the opening closed, leaving just enough room at the bottom to reach in and pour the ammonia in to a plastic container. After this, I sealed the rest of the end and waited a day.

When it came time to remove the cabinet from the tent, I put on my goggles, gloves and respirator, opened the bottom of the end, and put a lid on the plastic container inside. I then put a fan in the opening, and exhausted the fumes outside. After letting the fan run for an hour, I opened the tent completely.

Most of the pieces came out close in color, but there were a few parts that were a bit lighter, and a couple edges that didn't take at all. Overall though, I was happy with the results, and prepared to deal with the inconsistencies.

The first step after fuming was to smooth all of the surfaces with a nylon abrasive (Scotchbrite) pad, and give everything two coats of garnet shellac, in a two-pound cut. I then mixed some aniline dye (Liberon Fumed Oak light) with some alcohol. With a 1"-wide sash brush, I applied the dye to the lighter areas, brushing on slight amounts until the color was close. I followed this with two more coats of shellac.

The shellac changes the dirty-looking brownish gray of the fumed oak to warm brown. The photos at right show the progression of the color from raw wood, fuming and shellac. The color from the shellac, however, is just a bit too orange,

The quartersawn white oak in its natural color.

After exposure to ammonia fumes for 24 hours, the oak has turned a grayish brown color.

and needs to be waxed to achieve the desired rich brown I was looking for. I smoothed all the surfaces with #320 -grit sandpaper, followed by a Scotchbrite pad.

The final step in finishing was to apply dark paste wax, which fills the open pores of the oak, and tones down the color from the garnet shellac, leaving the piece a rich warm brown.

With the finish complete, I installed the glass in the door, holding it in place with ¼" x ¼" glass stop. I mitered the corners, and attached the stop to the inside of the openings with 23 gauge pins.

All that remained was to install the lock and escutcheon in the door, hang the door and attach the top with figure-8 fasteners. I placed three fasteners in the front and back rails, and one in the center of each of the end panels.

Harvey Ellis's association with Gustav Stickley lasted only a few months before Ellis died in January 1904. Ellis's influence on Arts and Crafts design however was tremendous. The details he produced for Stickley have served as hallmarks of the period.

Ellis related the arrangement of spaces in good design to the notes in a musical chord. This bookcase combines the practical and architectural elements that he is known for in perfect harmony, and serves as a fitting tribute to his genius.

Garnet shellac adds some color, and highlights the distinctive grain. Dark wax will complete the finish.

Knockdown Media Center

BY JIM STACK

If you've every had a chance to inspect an antique armoire, you might have noticed something unusual. Many of these old pieces were designed to be knocked down easily to travel – even the really expensive fancy ones.

In that tradition, this project also knocks down easily, but it uses some high-tech hardware installed with a biscuit joiner.

These plans show you how to build the project as an entertainment center with a shelf large enough to hold two or three video components. The drawers can be fitted with CD, DVD or VCR-tape organizers. The back has a removable panel for easy access to all the electronic components.

However, if you'd prefer a go-anywhere armoire, it's simple work to remove the top shelf and add a hanging rail. It has as much space as a small closet.

For this project I picked ash boards with lots of colors and figured grain patterns for the panels and used the straighter-grained pieces for the rails, stiles and legs. The finish is a clear topcoat.

One more thing: The project is built entirely with biscuits. Even the knockdown hardware and hinges are installed using a biscuit joiner. If this project doesn't convince you of the utility of this tool, nothing will.

Frame First

Create a template of the curve at the base, and use it to trace the pattern onto the legs. The curve begins 6" up each of the six legs and the bottom of each leg ends up 2" wide. Rough-cut the waste material away using a jigsaw. Use your template as a guide to rout the curves smooth.

Now is a good time to cut a ½" x ½" rabbet on the back legs to hold the back (I waited until after assembly and made the rabbet using my jointer's rabbeting ledge). Miter one long edge of each of the four front legs. Tape the outside of the joint and apply glue in the miter. Fold the leg assembly together. I made some clamping cauls (as shown in the photo below) to hold the assembly square while the glue sets.

Now set up your router in a router table to cut all the grooves for the panels in this project. I used a ¼" straight bit that was set to make a ½"-deep cut. Cut this stopped groove on the legs, and cut the groove on the long edges of all the rails for the side assemblies. This is the same groove that will be used to assemble the doors, so leave the router set up for now.

Cut the #20 biscuit slots to join the legs and rails. Glue up and finish sand the ¼"-thick panels before assembling the sides. As always, get all the clamps, glue, biscuits and an assistant (if you need one)

Make the curve at the feet by first creating a template. Rough-cut the shape using a jigsaw and use a router to make the edges smooth.

together before you start assembling the sides. Be sure to use glue only in the biscuit slots and not in the grooves. You want the panel to float in the grooves so it can expand and contract.

Once the panels are complete, drill the shelf pin holes for the adjustable top shelf.

Knockdown Hardware

With the sides assembled, you now need to prepare the shelves, top and bottom that join them. All of these parts are made from ¾" plywood with a ¼"-thick strip of ash on the front edge. The front edge of the sub top is held flush with the front of the face frame, so you'll need to notch the front corners around the front legs.

Now cut the slots for the knockdown hardware. I used Lamello Simplex plates – which consist of two interlocking metal bits that you glue into #20 biscuit slots. You can purchase a box of 100 for

$42 from Lamello's U.S. representative, Colonial Saw (csaw.com or 781-585-4364).

These #20 slots go in the bottom and middle shelves and the sub top. Use a carpenter's square as a guide for cutting the #20 slots for the knockdown hardware in the sides. The bottom edge of the middle shelf should be located 29¾" up from the bottom of the legs. Then cut matching slots in the ends of the bottom, the middle and the sub top.

You need to use a two-part epoxy to glue the aluminum hardware into the slots. I mixed a batch of epoxy about the size of a 50-cent piece (remember

those?), which was enough to glue five or six pieces of hardware into the slots. I used toothpicks to put the epoxy into the bottom and halfway up the sides of the slots. Don't use too much epoxy or it will get in the inside of the hook on the knockdown hardware and on the top sides of the slot. This makes it impossible to put the two parts together after the epoxy has cured. I recommend practicing putting the epoxy into the slots in scrap material before starting.

Once the epoxy has cured, you can knock the case together to see how everything fits.

Here is one method that works well for holding the leg assembly square during gluing.

Cove moulding on the table saw is safe if done correctly. It works best if you use a sharp, carbide-tooth blade.

Cut biscuit slots in the ends of the bottom, middle and top shelves for the matching knockdown hardware.

Here you can see the ¹⁄₁₆" lip created by the straight moulding when attached to the inner top panel.

Use spacers to hold the hardware parallel to the cabinet bottom. The spacers also ensure the hardware will be located at the same height on both sides of the cabinet.

This is what the door stiles look like before assembly. It's a quick and simple way to make frames (with or without panels).

Top Cap

The top is made up of a few layers. Begin by cutting the inner top panel to size from plywood. You also could make it from ¾" scrap pieces biscuited together if you're short on plywood.

Miter and nail the straight moulding to the underside of the inner top panel. Let the moulding hang over the panel about ¹⁄₁₆". This lip will make it easier to align the cove moulding (see the photo below, near left, for details).

I made the cove moulding on the table saw. Before you set up for the cove cut, cut a flat face on the moulding material. Set up a fence behind the blade at about a 45° angle to the blade. Clamp it in place and raise the saw blade about ⅛". Test the cut until it is centered in the moulding material and the cove is the proper radius. To center the cut, move the fence toward or away from the blade, keeping the angle the same. To change the radius, change the angle of the fence.

Make your first cut in all the moulding pieces. Raise the blade another ⅛" (or a little less if your saw sounds like it's working too hard). Continue until the cove depth is to your liking. You'll probably need to move the fence slightly toward or away from the blade to keep the cut centered, but try not to change the angle of the fence when you move it.

Miter and nail the cove moulding to the inner top panel by holding it against the lip you created with the straight moulding. Then glue the outer top panel onto the top of the assembled cove moulding.

Insides and Doors

The drawers are made of soft maple with ash fronts. The sides are biscuited to the drawer fronts, and the back of the drawer is captured between the sides. The bottom slides into a ¼"-wide by ¼"-deep groove in the sides and front.

First make the cutout on the drawer front using a jigsaw and then sand the edge smooth.

These drawers use full-extension hardware, so the drawer fronts need to have a ⁷⁄₁₆" lip extending past both sides. This lip conceals the hardware when the drawer is closed. Mark the location of the sides on the back of the drawer front and biscuit them in place. Biscuit the sides to the back. Glue and clamp the drawer assemblies.

The drawer slides need to be able to clear the legs, so you have to install spacers at the front and back that you will screw the slides to. First, lay out on the spacers where the hardware will be mounted on the drawers and transfer this to the cabinet sides. Screw the spacers in place. Attach the slides to your drawer boxes and the spacers, and turn your attention to the doors.

The frame-and-panel doors are built using the same setup as the side panels. Cut the necessary stopped grooves in the stiles and the through-grooves in the rails. Cut biscuit slots to join the rails and stiles. Glue the doors together at the biscuit joints only (allow the panel to float) and clamp.

Finishing Touches

The hinges for this cabinet are installed with the biscuit joiner. They're called Duplex Hinges and can be purchased from Colonial Saw ($36 for a box of 10 nickel-plated hinges). Fit the doors in the case with the spacings you want and set your biscuit joiner to cut a #20 slot. Center the cutter on that space between the door and leg. Then cut the slot. You'll have a mortise cut into both the door and the cabinet side at the same time. (If you prefer, you also can set the cutter to make the entire mortise in the door instead of both pieces.)

The adjustable shelf needs clearance at the back edge for cables and wires. An easy way to create that space is to rip 2" off the back side of the adjustable shelf, then glue two wings to the back of the shelf at both ends. (Use biscuits to hold these wings in place, of course!)

Cut out an opening in the upper part of the back panel for cable and wire access. Then mount the back panel by first adding a frame around the inside edges of the opening to create a ½" lip.

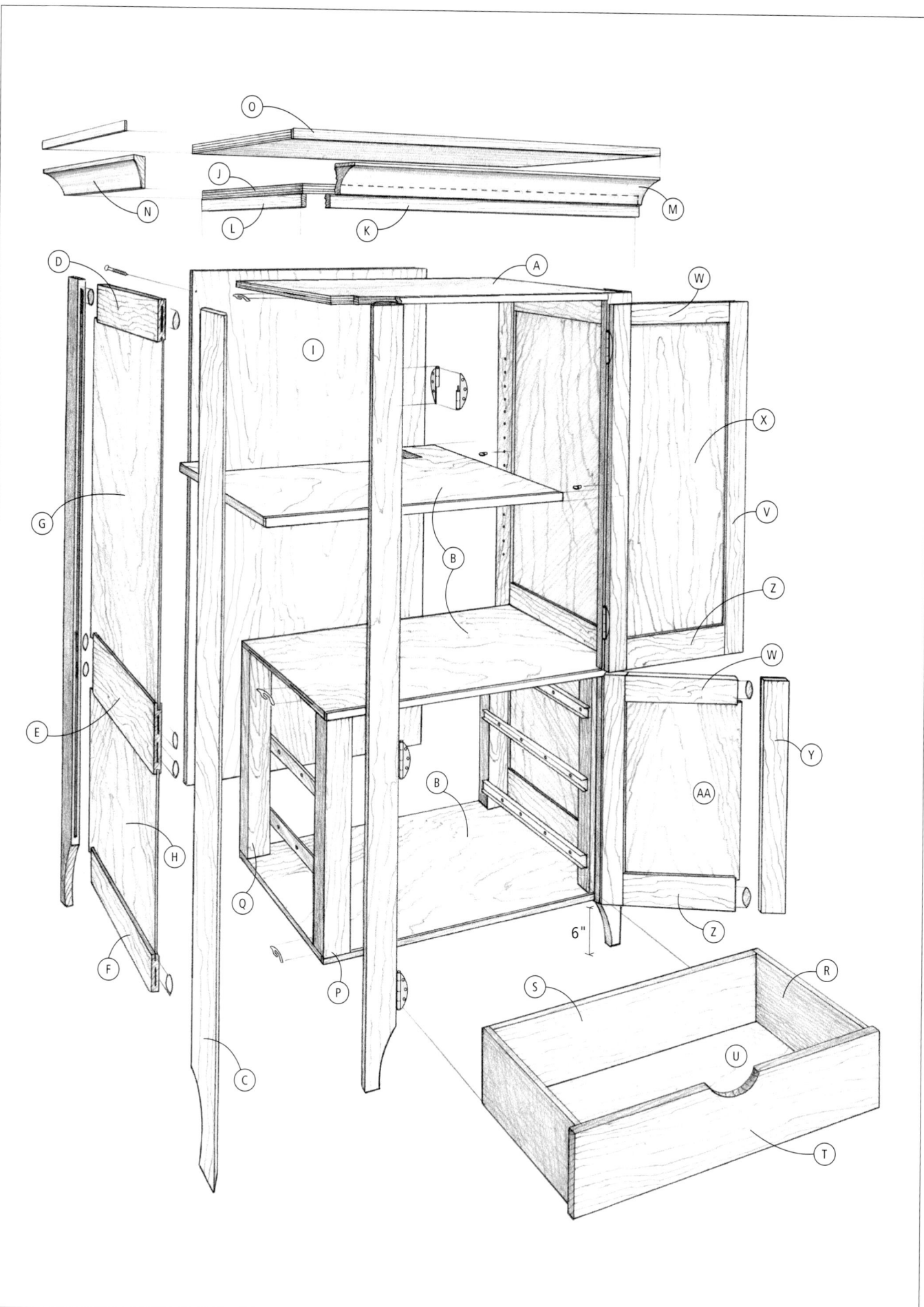

6"

This essentially creates a shop-made wire grommet.

Cut a panel to fit in the cutout from the back of the cabinet and attach it with screws. Now screw the back in place on the case.

Use small magnetic catches to hold the doors closed. These are mounted so that both the top and bottom doors use the same magnet; the top door overlays the top half of each magnet, while the bottom door overlays the bottom half of each magnet.

These catches are one of the few things you can't install in this project using your biscuit joiner. But just give the biscuit people some time and I bet they'll come up with a way.

When mortising the Duplex hinges for the cabinet, add an auxiliary fence to the biscuit joiner because the cabinet face is 3" wide and the fence on your tool probably won't extend that far.

AUXILIARY FENCE

Knockdown Media Center

	NO.	LET.	ITEM	DIMENSIONS (INCHES) T	W	L	DIMENSIONS (MILLIMETERS) T	W	L	MATERIAL	COMMENTS
CASE											
❏	1	A	Sub top	$3/4$	$23^1/2$	$34^1/2$	19	572	877	Birch ply	Includes $1/4$" x $3/4$"ash strip on front
❏	3	B	Shelves	$3/4$	$22^3/4$	$34^1/2$	19	578	877	Birch ply	Includes $1/4$" x $3/4$" ash strip on shelf fronts
❏	6	C	Legs	$13/16$	3	71	21	76	1803	Ash	$1/4$" x $1/2$" groove for panels
❏	2	D	Top rails	$13/16$	$3^3/4$	18	21	95	457	Ash	$1/4$" x $1/2$" groove for panels
❏	2	E	Center rails	$13/16$	$5^3/4$	18	21	146	457	Ash	$1/4$" x $1/2$" groove for panels
❏	2	F	Bottom rails	$13/16$	$3^1/2$	18	21	89	457	Ash	$1/4$" x $1/2$" groove for panels
❏	2	G	Top panels	$1/4$	$18^3/4$	$34^1/4$	6	476	870	Ash	
❏	2	H	Bottom panels	$1/4$	$18^3/4$	$19^5/8$	6	476	499	Ash	
❏	1	I	Back	$1/2$	$35^1/2$	65	13	902	1651	Birch ply	Screwed into $1/2$" x $1/2$" rabbet in legs
TOP MOULDING ASSEMBLY											
❏	1	J	Inner top panel	$3/4$	$24^{11}/16$	$37^3/8$	19	627	950	Birch ply	
❏	1	K	Front straight trim	$3/4$	$1^1/2$	$37^1/2$	19	38	953	Ash	Nailed to underside of inner top panel
❏	2	L	Side straight tim	$3/4$	$1^1/2$	$24^3/4$	19	38	629	Ash	Nailed to underside of inner top panel
❏	1	M	Front cove trim	$1^1/2$	$1^1/2$	$40^1/2$	38	38	1029	Ash	Nailed to front edge of inner top panel
❏	2	N	Side cove trim	$1^1/2$	$1^1/2$	$26^1/4$	38	38	666	Ash	Nailed to sides of inner top panel
❏	1	O	Outer top panel	$3/4$	$26^1/2$	41	19	673	1041	Birch ply	Includes $3/8$"-thick ash strips on front and sides
DRAWERS											
❏	2	P	Front drawer spacers	2	$3^1/2$	23	51	89	584	Ash	Allow drawer slides to clear legs
❏	2	Q	Rear drawer spacers	$1^1/2$	$3^1/2$	23	38	89	584	Soft maple	Allow drawer slides to clear legs
❏	6	R	Sides	$1/2$	$7^1/2$	20	13	191	508	Soft maple	$1/4$" x $1/4$" groove for drawer bottom
❏	3	S	Backs	$1/2$	$6^1/4$	$25^1/2$	13	158	648	Soft maple	
❏	3	T	Fronts	$3/4$	$7^1/2$	$27^3/8$	19	191	696	Ash	$1/4$" x $1/4$" groove for drawer bottom
❏	3	U	Bottoms	$1/4$	$20^1/4$	26	6	511	660	Luan ply	Nail bottom to underside of back
DOORS											
❏	4	V	Top door stiles	$13/16$	$2^1/4$	$39^1/4$	21	57	997	Ash	$1/4$" x $1/2$" groove for panels
❏	4	W	Top rails	$13/16$	$2^1/4$	$10^3/8$	21	57	264	Ash	$1/4$" x $1/2$" groove for panels
❏	2	X	Top door panels	$1/4$	$11^1/8$	$34^1/4$	6	282	870	Ash	
❏	4	Y	Bottom door stiles	$13/16$	$2^1/4$	$24^1/8$	21	57	613	Ash	$1/4$" x $1/2$" groove for panels
❏	4	Z	Bottom rails	$13/16$	$3^1/2$	$10^3/8$	21	89	264	Ash	
❏	2	AA	Bottom door panels	$1/4$	$11^1/8$	$19^3/8$	6	282	493	Ash	$1/4$" x $1/2$" groove for panels

Bibliophile's Bookcase

BY MEGAN FITZPATRICK

This large case-on-case shelving unit is adapted from similar pieces I've seen in private libraries and in stately homes. I also dug up a few pictures from the Sotheby's and Christie's auction sites, where the form is referred to as a "bibliotheque" (also the French word for library).

Those examples, however, all feature intricate mouldings and fancy corbels and are more adorned than would look right in my less-than-stately 1895 home. I do, however, have 10' ceilings and an embarrassment of books, so while I didn't want fancy, I did want big. So I reconceived the form in a Shaker-on-steroids style – the piece is just shy of 50" wide x 90" high. It will fit in a room with standard ceiling heights, but in case I ever needed to use the top and bottom separately, I installed a solid top for the bottom case so it can stand alone (and with the addition of a cushion, it would make a handsome hall bench).

The size did have me fretting about stock costs, so I culled the "shorts" bin at our local lumber store for lower-priced cherry, and found a nicely figured wide piece for the drawer fronts, as well as sufficient stock for the lower case and all the shelves. The shelves are made of some rather homely boards, but because I added a lip to the front for strength and appearance, you can't actually tell – unless you remove the books and take a close look. I did have to go to the regular-price rack for the upper-case face frame and sides, but I saved money by using poplar for the backboards, which I painted to match the trim in the living room.

Bottom's Up First

First, I cut my parts to rough sizes then surfaced and thicknessed all the stock but the drawer fronts, and glued up panels for the sides, lower case top and upper case top, and all the shelves. I never cut my pieces to final size until I need them – and then I mark cuts using the project as a guide, not the cutlist. No matter how meticulous I am with the measuring, things are never perfect. But, once my pieces are cut to size, I plane and finish-sand as much as possible before assembly because it's hard to maneuver around a piece the size of a New York apartment.

Because I didn't have a 7"-wide piece for the lower rail, or two 49"-long pieces with matching grain that I could glue up, I had to scab on a 4" x 14" piece at each rail end for the curved feet (the downside of parsimony).

I then traced my pattern onto each foot, cut it at the band saw and smoothed the cuts on a spindle sander – but had to resort to hand-sanding where the curve met the flat.

After setting up the mortiser with a ¼" bit, I made a 1½"-wide mortise for the 2"-wide center stile dead in the middle of the lower rail, then moved to the table saw to cut 1¼"-long tenons on each end using a dado stack.

Holding the workpiece took a little thought, because the two feet created a not-solid surface on the bottom edge (a good argument for spending a little extra to make the lower rail and feet out of one board – or at least a solid panel glue-up, and cutting the tenons before

cutting out the feet). But no worries – a 3"-long offcut clamped to the sliding table did the trick. I cut each tenon face in two passes, first removing ¾" or so at the end before pushing the end against the fence to remove the remainder of the waste on each shoulder.

The resulting tenon was 6½" wide – on the cusp of too wide to offer sufficient mortise-wall strength – so I split it by sawing out a 1"-wide piece with a coping saw, then chiseled the shoulder flat while removing the remaining waste. I cut 1¼" tenons on the upper rail and center stile at the table saw, marked then cut the mortises on the side rails at the mortiser. After I glued together the face frame and set it aside to dry, it was on to the side pieces.

I marked the curved cutout on each piece, then made the cuts at the band saw. (Note: the apex is not centered; it's ¾" closer to the front.) Because the full dado stack was still in place, I went ahead and added a sacrificial fence, then cut a ¾" x ⁷⁄₁₆" rabbet up the back of each side piece to house the backboards. In retrospect, I should have cut an 11" stopped rabbet, because the backboards don't go all the way to the floor. While the unnecessary 7" portion of rabbet doesn't show, the base would be stronger without it.

I adjusted the dado stack to make a ¾"-wide cut, and made a ¼"-deep dado across each side piece 7" from the bot-

SIMPLE SHELVES. Though it's large, this Shaker-inspired bookcase is fairly simple to make – and three adjustable shelves make it simple to fit books of all sizes.

tom (the top edge of the dado is flush with the top of the lower front rail) to accept the web frame, which is joined with pocket screws. I glued the web frame into the dados on each side, squared it up and tightened the clamps. After the glue dried, I glued on the face frame and attached a rail across the top of the back, flush with the backboard rabbets, with pocket screws.

Upper Case

First, I cut the mortises and tenons for the face frame and glued it together (luckily, no one had adjusted the mortiser from when I did the lower face frame).

I made it about ⅛" oversized on the sides (as I did with the lower case face frame), so I could flush it easily to the sides later with a flush-trim router bit.

Then it was on to the side pieces, and cutting dados for the bottom and middle fixed shelves. Workholding was tricky here, because the side pieces are 70½" long – well over the edge of the saw table. So, I clamped a handscrew around the crosscut sled fence, on which to rest the overhanging part. This, however, meant I couldn't use the stop on the sled, so a stepoff block on the fence solved the problem to locate the ¾" dados for the fixed bottom shelf.

I also cut ¾" dados in each side 30⅜" from the bottom for the center fixed shelf, and marked and drilled holes for the adjustable shelf pins. The locations were figured from a graduated shelf progression – but with the remaining three shelves adjustable, it's unlikely that progression will ever be evident.

Stiff Lips

With the sides done, I cut the bottom and middle shelves to size (note that the widths are different; the bottom shelf has no lip), and glued a 1½"-wide lip across the front edge of the middle shelf, leaving just better than ¼" of the shelf's front edge uncovered at each end to slip into the dados.

After the glue dried and I sanded the lip flush, I ran a bead of glue in each side-panel dado, set the fixed shelves in place flush with the front edge of the side, clamped across, then toenailed the fixed shelves in place. Be careful with the angle of your nail gun and the length of your nails. I blew through the side once. OK, maybe three times.

While that glue-up dried, I added lips to the three adjustable shelves, keeping them just shy of either end to make shelf adjustment easier (the face frame covers the shelf ends, so the gap won't show).

Next, I added the face frame, and got a little help clamping it up square – there was simply no way for me to reach corner

SCABBY FEET. Because I had very little extra stock, and not enough with matching grain to glue up a solid panel for the curved bottom rail, I had to scab on the foot piece at either end.

CUT THE CURVE. I traced my pattern onto each foot and made the cuts at the band saw.

JIGGED UP. Because the feet created a non-flat surface, and the sliding table is shorter than my workpiece, I simply clamped a flat piece of scrap to the fence against which I could hold the rail while I made the tenons.

SPLIT TENON. A 6½"-wide tenon is too big, so I split it using a coping saw then chiseled out the remainder of the waste.

to corner to pull things into place without assistance. Then, I pocket-screwed a rail at the top edge to which I later attached the backboards.

Topping Things Off

I cut the upper- and lower-case tops to size, and rounded over the edges with #80-grit sandpaper until I liked the way it looked, then progressed through grits to #180 until the shaped edge was smooth.

The lower-case top is attached with L-shaped wood buttons, and has a 1" overhang on the front and at each side; the upper-case top (to which the crown attaches) has a 2⅞" overhang on the front and either side. It's screwed to the back rail, sides and face frame.

A Dusty Crown

I dislike making crown moulding. It is incredibly dusty, and my arms get an unwanted (but not unneeded) workout pushing ¾" stock at an angle across the table saw blade. But there's no getting around it. So I had to set up the table saw, suck it up (the dust, that is) and get it done. And then there's the sanding. Lots of sanding.

The simplest way to fit the crown is to invert the upper case, then wrap the moulding around the front and two ends. Secure it to the top, sides and face frame with brads.

Put Your Back Into It

My backboards are shiplapped random-width poplar, and in the upper case they're painted. I did cut a chamfer on the front of each for added visual interest – not that it will show when the case is loaded with books.

FRAMED. The pocket-screwed web frame was glued into the side panel grooves and squared up before I tightened down the clamps.

MORE JIGS. Again faced with secure workholding problems at the table saw, I used a hand-screw attached to the sliding table to support one end, and an stepoff block at the other to safely locate the groove for the bottom fixed shelf.

TOENAILS. Be sure you have 1¼" nails in your gun – or if it's loaded with 1½" nails, make sure you angle your shots enough so that you don't blow through the sides. Or keep the nippers handy.

CROWN MOULDING. To make a simple crown, angle your stock at 45° to the blade and center the blade on the stock (or cut it just off-center so you have a thicker flat on one edge, if you like that look). Then clamp a long offcut beyond the blade to serve as a fence. Make repeated cuts in each piece of stock, raising the blade a little each time. Stay tight against your fence and to the table. Though I'm not wearing one here, a dust mask would be a good idea.

A LITTLE HELP PLEASE. With a big glue-up, it's best to rope a friend into helping. By oneself, it's difficult to tighten all the clamps down quickly without things sliding around – or reach corner to corner should you need to square things up. Or click a camera button from 9' away.

Bibliophile's Bookcase

	NO.	ITEM	T	W	L	T	W	L	MATERIAL	COMMENTS
			DIMENSIONS (INCHES)			DIMENSIONS (MILLIMETERS)				
UPPER CASE										
❑	1	Upper rail	3/4	5 3/4	47 3/16	19	143	1199	Cherry	TBE*
❑	1	Lower rail	3/4	3	47 3/16	19	76	1199	Cherry	TBE
❑	2	Stiles	3/4	2 5/8	70 1/2	19	67	1791	Cherry	
❑	2	Sides	3/4	11 1/4	70 1/2	19	285	1791	Cherry	
❑	1	Bottom fixed shelf	3/4	10 1/2	48 15/16	19	267	1243	Cherry	
❑	1	Middle fixed shelf	3/4	9 3/4	48 15/16	19	248	1243	Cherry	
❑	3	Adjustable shelves	3/4	9 3/4	48 1/4	19	248	1225	Cherry	
❑	4	Shelf lips	3/4	1 3/4	48	19	45	1219	Cherry	
❑	1	Top	3/4	14 7/8	55 11/16	19	378	1414	Cherry	
❑	2	Crown	3/4	4 1/4	54	19	108	1372	Cherry	Rough size
❑	varies	Backboards	5/8	varies	70 1/2	16	varies	1791	Poplar	
LOWER CASE										
❑	1	Upper rail	3/4	3	47 3/16	19	76	1199	Cherry	TBE*
❑	1	Lower rail	3/4	3	47 3/16	19	76	1199	Cherry	TBE
❑	2	Feet	3/4	4	14 1/4	19	102	362	Cherry	TOE**
❑	2	Outer stiles	3/4	2 5/8	18	19	67	457	Cherry	
❑	1	Center stile	3/4	2	10 1/2	19	51	267	Cherry	TBE
❑	2	Sides	3/4	12 3/4	18	19	324	457	Cherry	
❑	1	Top	3/4	14 1/2	51 15/16	19	369	1319	Cherry	
❑	2	Drawer fronts	3/4	8	21 1/4	19	203	539	Cherry	Size sides, bottom to fit
❑	varies	Backboards	5/8	varies	11 3/4	16	varies	298	Poplar	
WEB FRAME										
❑	2	Long rails	3/4	2 1/2	43 15/16	19	64	1116	Poplar	
❑	2	Short rails	3/4	2 1/2	12	19	64	305	Poplar	
❑	1	Center stile	3/4	4	7	19	102	178	Poplar	

* Tenon both ends, 1 1/4"; ** Tenon one end

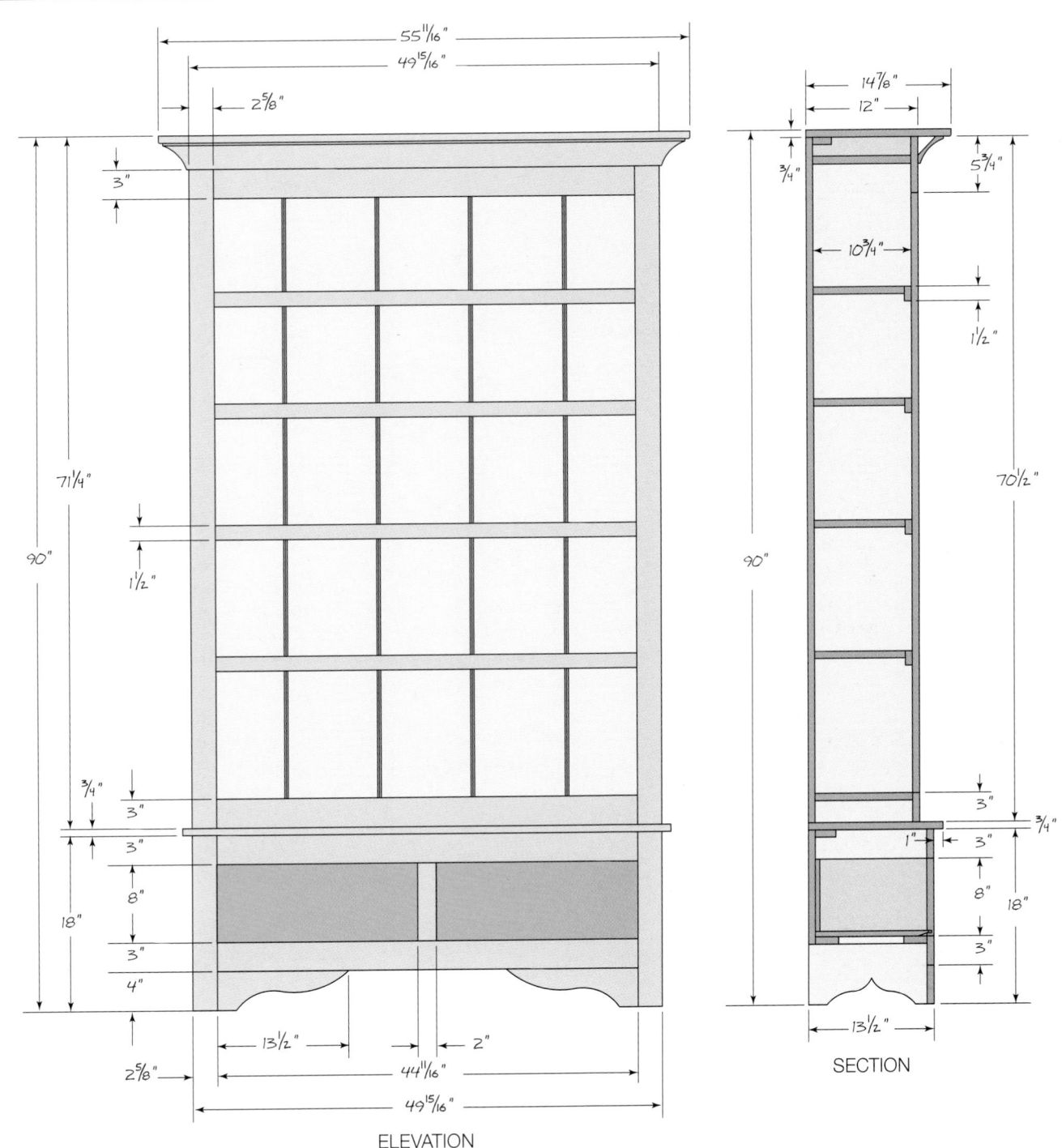

ELEVATION

SECTION

In the lower section, the backboards are unpainted and have no chamfer – but they do run vertically to match the top. (If you have an 11"-wide piece, you could get away with one board, run horizontally. But your co-workers might snicker at the idea.)

Hidden Storage

Last, I fit the inset drawer fronts and constructed drawers with half-blind dovetails at the front, and through-dovetails at the back. The bottom is an upside-down raised panel slid into a groove (the back edge isn't beveled), then secured to the drawer back with a 1½" shingle nail. I suspect these drawers would have originally housed candles and perhaps paper and writing implements; I'm using them to store extraneous cat toys.

The finish is two sprayed coats of amber shellac (with sanding after each) and a top coat of pre-catalyzed lacquer.

Supplies

Rejuvenation
888-401-1900 or rejuvenation.com

4 • square bin pulls in oil-rubbed bronze
   #EC 7004, $7 ea.

Rockler
800-279-4441 or rockler.com

1 • 16-pack of 1/4" shelf supports
   #33902, $4.89

Prices correct at time of publication.

Barrister Bookcases

BY GLEN D. HUEY

Almost everyone likes the look of barrister bookcases. But what makes them so appealing? I think there are a number of characteristics that make the barrister design popular and enduring.

First is that the individual units of the case stack together. And because they are separate units, they can be arranged in any desired height configuration to fit any area of your home or office.

Second, they are elegant as well as functional. The wood-framed glass doors, when lowered, protect your books or other valuables from moisture and dust – not to mention those tiny pudding-laced fingers of the little ones. They also allow you to look through the glass for a specific item without the undo stress of operating the doors. In the open position, with the doors raised and slid back into the case, you have easy access to those leather-bound sources of knowledge.

Third, as you will see, we rethought the construction so these cases can be built with the easiest techniques – without sacrificing any classic design elements. These are the easiest barrister bookcases you will ever build.

We decided to build a stack of three units – each identical in construction and design, with one slightly different in height. There are two larger units for over-sized books and special keepsakes, and one that is slightly shorter in height. Those, along with the top and bottom units, add up to the appropriate design for our bookcase needs.

Your set can be created with only one unit, or it could be a stack of five, along with the top and bottom sections. (More than five units is unwieldy and potentially unstable.)

One Panel Chops into Three

We wanted the grain on each case side to be consistent from top to bottom as we stacked our individual units. This is a matter of aesthetics, not a necessity. (I'm sure somewhere during this case's lifetime, the units will be stacked without regard to the grain.)

What is a necessity, in order to get the units to stack without problems, is to make the width of each unit equal in size. This is best accomplished by starting with one large glued-up panel of the correct width that is then crosscut into the appropriate lengths.

Once the sides are milled according to the plan, there are three rabbets that need to be cut in each side panel. One rabbet goes at the top and bottom of each side panel. Those rabbets are for the full-width case bottom and the front and back rails at the top. You also need a rabbet at the back edge of the side panels that will house the backboards. That rabbet hides the backboards when viewing the bookcase from the side.

A dado blade is the best choice for cutting the rabbets. Install a sacrificial fence, set the blade for the widest cut (at least ¾") and position the blade below the saw top. Adjust the fence to the blade so that ¾" of cutting width is exposed and with the blade running, slowly raise the cutter to a height of ⅛". With this setting, a single pass over the blade will create the ¾"-wide x ⅛"-deep rabbets at the top and bottom edge of the side panels.

Next, again with the blade moving, raise the height to ⁷⁄₁₆". This is to create the rabbet for the backboards. They fit into a ¾"-wide x ⁷⁄₁₆"-deep rabbet. If you are trying to keep the grain aligned, as we have, you need to determine the front edge of the bookcase prior to crosscutting the individual side panels into smaller sections. Or, choose the best edge of your stock for the front face at this time and cut the backboard rabbets into the opposite edge.

SACRIFICIAL FENCE

Using the widest setting on a dado stack along with a sacrificial fence is the best choice for creating rabbets for these case sides. This will ensure that the cut clears the waste entirely.

Raising the blade height is the only adjustment needed to cut the backboard rabbets. The front edge of this side looks as though it is raised from the saw top because of the previous rabbet cut.

Your Groove is Important

Creating the groove in which the doors slide is the most difficult task involved in building these bookcases – but all it takes is a plunge router with a guide fence and a ¼" upcut spiral router bit.

Positioning this groove is the trick. It needs to be located correctly from the top edge of the sides, so the guide fence of the router becomes key. Set the fence so the router bit plunges into the side with 1⅛" of material between the top edge and the groove. The ¼" cut will then be perfectly set for the placement of the centered brass rods in the bookcase doors, and it builds in the necessary ⅛" spacing so the top edge of the door does not bind when opened.

Next, you need to find the starting or stopping point of the cut depending on which side you're working. On each right-side panel you'll plunge at the front edge and finish the cut through the backboard rabbet. On the left-side panels you'll begin coming through that rabbet and complete the cut by stopping at the correct location and removing the bit from the work surface. Attacking the groove this way registers each cut off of the top edge of the side panels and makes the best use of the guide fence.

The location that you need to stop on is ⅜" in from the front edge of the sides to the beginning of the routed groove. Where did this number come from, beside the plan? The ¼" brass rods that are used to hang the doors are located in the center of the ¾"-thick doors. The outer ¼" of door stock along with the design feature of the ⅛" offset of the door to the front edge of the case adds up to that exact location.

With the setup and location locked in, rout the ⁵⁄₁₆"-deep grooves into the sides as shown in the picture at right.

The doors will be held in position toward the front with two brass rods per side. The top rod is centered 1¾" from the top edge of the side and in 1" from the front edge. These two rods act as a pivot for the sliding door.

The second rod location is pulled from the bottom edge of the sides and is also set at a measurement of 1¾". It too is located 1" in from the front edge. This

Creating the groove for the door pins to ride in is the most exacting step of the process. A plunge router with a guide fence makes it short work. Check the layout before routing.

There are pin locations at both the top and bottom that act as guides for the doors. Use the drill press for this step – unless you've a steady hand and good eye.

rod placement gives the door something to close against while holding the door parallel to the case front when closed.

Assemble the Box

Mill to size and thickness the material for the top-front rails, rear rails and the catch rails, as well as the bottoms. You can get away with using a secondary wood for the rear and catch rails, as we chose to do, because these pieces will not be seen as you view the bookcase. All pieces connect to the sides with pocket screws.

Cut three pocket-screw holes on the worst face of the bottoms, leaving the best face for the inside of the piece. Position a hole at 1½" from each edge and one that is centered across the bottoms. The rails used for the top also

attach with pocket screws. Place two holes at each end of both rails.

Now you are ready to assemble the boxes. Position the bottom on your bench and match the two sides to the bottom, making sure that the bottom fits into the shallow rabbets. Next, slide the top rails in place – the oak at the front and the secondary wood at the rear. These rails fit into the rabbets at the top edge. Add clamps as shown below then attach the rails to the sides with the screws. Flip the box then add the screws to attach the bottom.

With the box set on its top, position and attach the catch rail to the bottom. Align the piece off of the front edge of the unit and center the rail from side to side. Each rail lines up with the inside

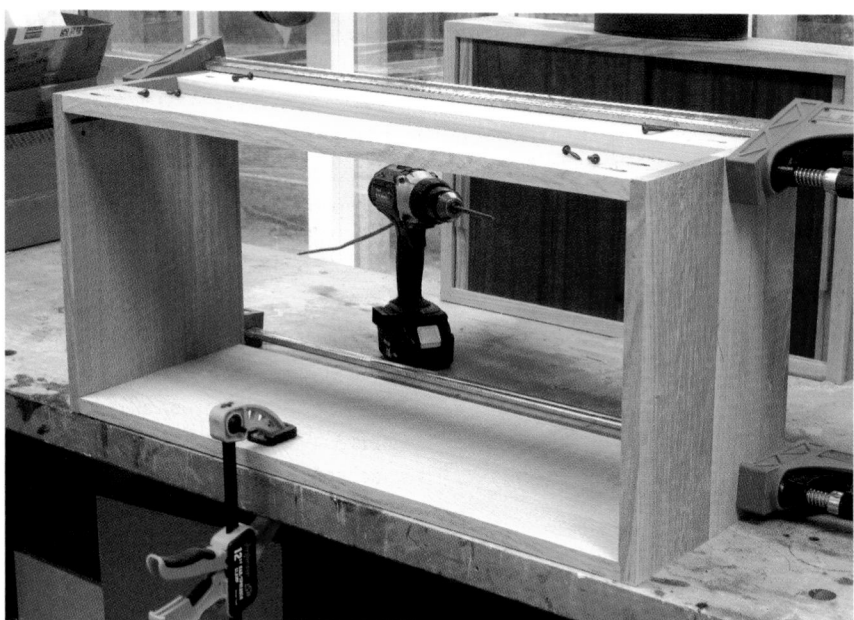

Assembling the boxes is a matter of 14 pocket screws. Clamping the box ensures that it will be square. The opening in the top is for the adjoining catch rail on a second unit.

The catch rail is fastened to the box bottom. It is important to properly align the piece to fit the other units.

The catch rail for the top unit rests inside the end rails. To keep the rail from sliding downward as the screws are installed, rest the piece on a block cut to the correct size.

The 3" rail in the base unit is toward the front while the wider rail is held to the back. Each rail is not only connected to the frame sides, it is also attached to a center support.

The chamfered base moulding is fit to the base frame on three sides. The secondary wood of the frame is hidden when the bookcase is stacked.

face of the side, not the edge of the rabbet area. Attach the rails to the bottom with wood screws.

Creating the frames for the top and base units is next. We found that building the frames and then attaching the mouldings was the best way to approach this part of the project. It also allowed us to use secondary wood for these hidden areas.

Each frame starts with the assembly of a box. The end supports receive the pocket-screw holes and are attached to the rails through that connection. Also, while you have the pocket-screw jig out, add a number of holes to the top frame that you'll use for attaching the top.

With the narrowness of the frames, you should arrange the pieces so the screws are to the outside of the unit. The drill, with the square drive installed, is too large for the inside of the frame.You should also attach the center support, the piece that runs from front to back and is centered along the width of each frame, through the outside with four #8 x 1¼" wood screws.

From this point the construction of the frames differs. In order for the top and base units to fit the design of the bookcase, the top unit must have a catch rail while the base unit receives a front and back flat rail.

The catch rail of the top unit fits between the frame's side rails, with a ¼" extending beyond the side rails, and attaches to the center support with two #8 x 1¼" wood screws.

Make sure that the catch rail is aligned to fit into the top rails of any of the bookcase units – they are all consistently positioned, making them interchangeable.

In the base unit the front and rear flat rails are set flush with the top edge of the frame and attached using the pocket-screw method. Remember that the front rail is only 3" wide, whereas the rear rail is 3¾". Each of these flat rails also attaches to the center support with #8 x 1¼" wood screws.

The mouldings are next. Mill the material for the crown moulding, the base moulding and the bookcase top to size and thickness. The top edge of the base moulding has a ⅜" chamfer. Cut

the edge with a router equipped with a chamfering bit, then fit the pieces to the base. Because there is a solid frame backing the mouldings you can nail the pieces in place with brads. Add a small bead of glue at the mitered corners as you assemble the mouldings for added strength.

Make the Crown Moulding

The crown moulding is a bit more complex than the base moulding. It begins with a cut at the table saw. Tip the blade to 10° and position the fence so that the blade exits the stock about 1" down from the top. This will leave about ⅜" of material at the bottom edge of the stock. This setting will need to be fine-tuned at your saw. Run the cut for both pieces of stock – one for the front and one piece that is crosscut into the two ends.

I elected to make a pass over the jointer to clean up the saw marks on my mouldings. Set a light depth of cut and be sure to use push sticks. If you choose not to use the jointer you can sand the moulding face smooth. Once the piece is cleaned and sanded it can be attached to the top frame.

I work counter-clockwise around the unit to get an accurate fit when wrapping mouldings. This allows for easy marking of cutlines as well as easy positioning of the cuts at the miter saw and it allows me to make my mitered cuts without changing the angle of the saw. Cut and fit the first mitered corner and clamp the pieces to the frame. Slide the third piece, with its end cut square, to meet the back of the front crown piece as shown in the photo below and mark the top edge on the front moulding.

At the miter saw, align the mark with your blade (saw angled to the right) and make the 45° cut. With the top edge up it is easy to match the blade to the layout line. Now to cut your final miter, simply place the end piece at the saw with the top edge pointing down while the face side is out and make the cut. The angle of the saw doesn't change and the cuts are correct. This is also how I would cut the first mitered corner.

Place the top unit, with the moulding now applied, onto the bookcase top, centered from side to side and flush to

While the setup is involved, the ripping of the crown moulding is straightforward. Just make sure to have a push stick handy.

The cutting of the crown moulding can leave saw kerf indications and burn marks. A quick run over the jointer knives works best to clean the face.

SIDE MOULDING

FRONT MOULDING

CUT MITER HERE

The crown moulding is attached to three sides of the top frame. Miter the corners and add a small amount of glue to reinforce the area. Brads will affix the pieces to the frame.

Complete the work on the top unit by attaching the moulded frame to the case top. Pocket screws are quick and easy.

the back edge of the top unit. Use pocket screws to attach the frame to the top then set the completed top unit aside.

The Doors are a Snap

The only easier method that could be used to build doors would be a flat-paneled door and that wouldn't give us the glass panels that we need for these cases. The secret for these doors is accurate cutting of the pieces.

Rip the material to the required width then set stops at the saw to allow for accurate cutting of the required lengths. If the pieces are all cut to the same sizes (two matching sets of the rails and stiles per door) two things will happen – one, the doors will be square

when assembled and two, the assembled doors will correctly fit the openings of the boxes.

Cut the stiles to be $^3/_{16}$" less than the opening of the box and the rails to be $4^1/_8$" less than the total width of that opening. This will build in the appropriate reveal around the doors.

These doors are also assembled with pocket screws placed in the rails, and the location of the holes is important. If the hole is too close to the outside of the rail, as you drive the screws there is potential to crack the end of the stiles. If the hole is set too near the interior of the rails, as you rabbet for the glass, you have the possibility of cutting into the screw area. The best location is at $^5/_8$" from both edges.

With the pocket-screw holes cut you can now assemble the doors. Place a clamp over the intersection of the two pieces, a rail and a stile, and drive the screws. Work the four corners of each door in the same manner.

Rabbeting the doors for the glass and glass-retainer strips is another router operation. Install a rabbeting bit, set for a $^3/_8$" rabbet, and cut the interior of the frame. It is necessary to position the door hanging over the edge of your table or bench so the bearing screw does not rub the bench.

If you try to make the entire cut by running the router in the standard manner, into the bit rotation, you're likely to have areas, especially in quartersawn

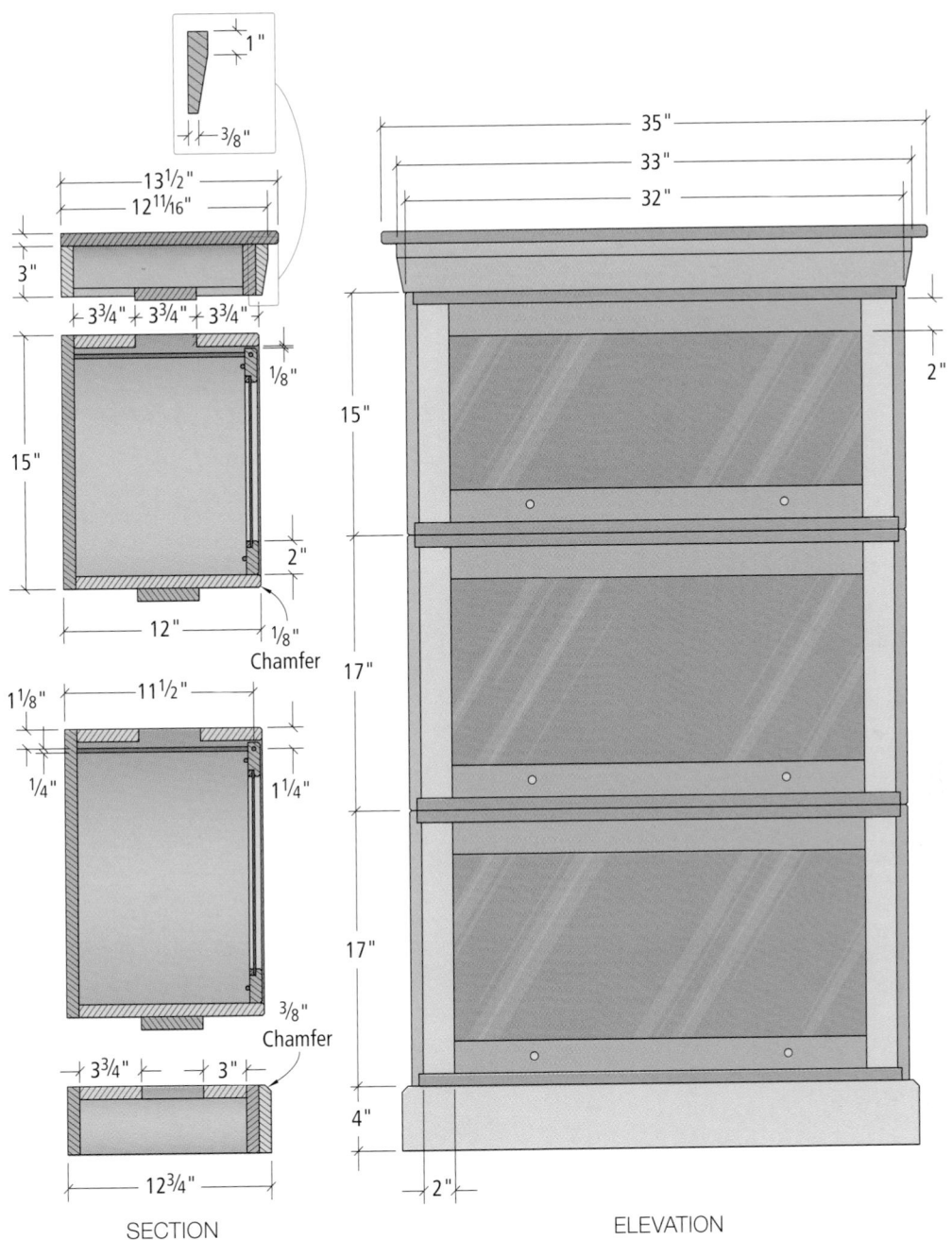

SECTION

ELEVATION

white oak, that will splinter and tear out. To remedy this you must climb cut during a portion of this process.

Start by climb cutting the first ⅛" of the rabbet then reverse the routing procedure and complete the rabbet. By having a small shelf of routed area from climb cutting, the removal of the balance of the waste material will shear off at that point and prevent most tear-out.

To complete the rabbet you'll need to square the rounded corners left from the router bit. Use a straightedge to continue the lines to reveal the exact corner and use a sharp chisel to bring the rounded corners to square. Clean the corners until you're level with the bottom of the rabbet.

Before moving forward now is the time to create the small bevel on the edges of the doors as well as the edges of the boxes themselves. Chuck a chamfer bit in a router and set it to cut ⅛" and run the profile around the doors outside edge and along the top and bottom of the boxes, including both sides and the front.

Each door edge, at the top of the door, needs to have a hole drilled to accept the short brass rod (available at any hardware store) on which the door will hang and travel in the groove as it is opened. A shop-made jig is just the trick to complete this step quickly and accurately.

Build the jig using a scrap of the cutoff material from your door pieces. Locate the center of the piece, which will be ⅜" from the edge, and also mark a line that is ⅜" in from the end. At that crossing is where you need to drill the

Barrister Bookcases

	NO.	ITEM	DIMENSIONS (INCHES) T	W	L	DIMENSIONS (MILLIMETERS) T	W	L	MATERIAL	COMMENTS
❏	2	Case sides	3/4	12	50	19	305	1270	QSWO*	Cut to length shown in drawing
❏	3	Bottoms	3/4	11 1/4	30 3/4	19	285	781	QSWO*	
❏	3	Top front rails	3/4	3 3/4	30 3/4	19	95	781	QSWO*	
❏	3	Top back rails	3/4	3 3/4	30 3/4	19	95	781	Poplar	
❏	3	Box catch rails	3/4	3 3/4	30 3/4	19	95	781	Poplar	
❏	2	Top frame rails	3/4	3	32	19	76	813	Poplar	
❏	2	Top frame sides	3/4	3	10 1/2	19	76	267	Poplar	
❏	1	Top frame center support	3/4	2 1/2	10 1/2	19	64	267	Poplar	
❏	1	Top frame catch rails	3/4	3 3/4	30 1/2	19	95	775	Poplar	
❏	1	Front crown moulding	3/4	3	36	19	76	914	QSWO*	
❏	1	Side crown moulding	3/4	3	26	19	76	660	QSWO*	Makes both sides
❏	1	Case top	3/4	13 1/2	35	19	349	889	QSWO*	
❏	2	Base frame rails	3/4	4	32	19	102	813	Poplar	
❏	2	Base frame sides	3/4	4	10 1/2	19	102	267	Poplar	
❏	1	Base frame center support	3/4	3 1/4	10 1/2	19	82	267	Poplar	
❏	1	Base frame front flat rail	3/4	3	30 1/2	19	76	775	Poplar	
❏	1	Base frame back flat rail	3/4	3 3/4	30 1/2	19	95	775	Poplar	
❏	1	Base moulding/front	3/4	4	36	19	102	914	QSWO*	
❏	1	Base moulding/sides	3/4	4	26	19	102	660	QSWO*	Makes both sides
❏	6	Door rails	3/4	2	26 3/8	19	51	670	QSWO*	Rails for three doors
❏	4	Door stiles/tall	3/4	2	15 1/16	19	51	383	QSWO*	Stiles for two doors
❏	2	Door stiles/short	3/4	2	13 1/16	19	51	333	QSWO*	Stiles for one doors
❏	9	Glass retainer strips	5/16	5/16	28	8	8	8	QSWO*	For three doors
❏	1	Short unit back	3/4	14 7/8	31 7/16	19	378	798	QSWO*	Plywood
❏	2	Tall unit back	3/4	5/16	31 7/16	19	8	798	QSWO*	Plywood

* QSWO=Quartersawn White Oak

Positioning the pocket-screw holes in the door rails is important. Too close to either edge can cause problems. Don't forget to add glue at the joint.

The 3/8" x 1/2" rabbet for the glass and the retainer strips requires that you climb cut a portion to eliminate any tear-out.

Aligning the holes for the doors to pivot becomes easy work with the use of this shop-made jig.

Squaring the corners left rounded from the router bit is a job for the chisel. It works best to begin with a cut across the end grain and to then take small cuts with the grain, removing the waste.

Adding a small bevel to the edges of the piece will help hide the joints between the separate units. This edge work also allows the doors to flip up and slide back into the case without binding.

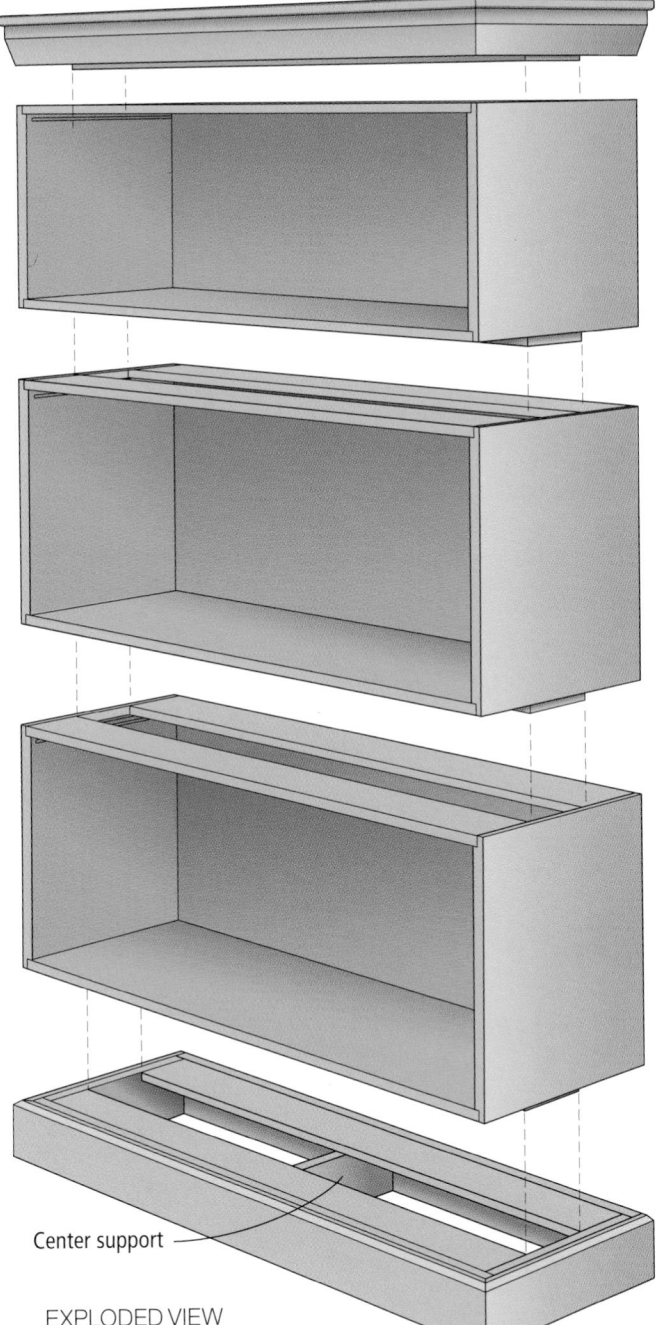

Center support

EXPLODED VIEW

Supplies

Horton Brasses
800-754-9127 or
horton-brasses.com

6 • knobs, ³⁄₄" semi-bright
#H-42

Call for pricing.

to work carefully around the end grain. All that's left is to cut the plywood pieces that comprise the backs of the individual units and mill a number of pieces to use as the glass retainers from some scrap.

Finish as Easy as the Project

This finish technique was developed by *Popular Woodworking* Senior Editor Robert W. Lang. If this method had been around years ago when I was working with oak, I would have built many more projects from this hardwood. You will not find an easier finish anywhere that I know of.

To begin, don't waste a huge amount of time sanding. I know you like the sound of that! Bring the piece to #120 grit with the random-orbit sander and finish sand by hand using #150-grit sandpaper. Done! Now you are ready to stain the bookcase.

The staining process continues in the easy category. Rag on a coat of Olympic oil-based "Special Walnut" stain. Apply an even coat and allow it to sit for 15 minutes before wiping any excess away. That coat needs to dry for 24 hours before moving on.

Next up is one coat of Dark Walnut Watco Danish Oil. Apply this in the same fashion as the stain. Rag a coat onto the stained bookcase and allow that to cure for 15 minutes, then wipe away any extra oil with a clean rag. In this process the oil acts as a toner that will even the shading as it adds color to the project. Again, let the oil coat dry for a day.

The rags used in both of the previous steps can become a fire hazard if not disposed of properly. You can lay the rags out on the floor of your shop or put them into a bucket of water. Combustion is a result of these rags thrown into a pile either in the trash can or a corner of the

¼" hole completely through the block. Use the drill press because you need the hole to be straight.

Next, add two pieces of Masonite, or other thin plywood-type material, to both sides of the block. To use the jig, slide it over the long grain of the stile, keeping the ³⁄₈" space toward the top edge of the door. Add a clamp to hold the jig and drill the hole using the jig as a guide. Set the drill bit to cut to a depth of ³⁄₄".

Drill two holes per door, install a 1" piece of brass rod using no glue (we need to be able to remove them over the remainder of the project). Once the rods are in place you can test the door to the opening. If you have a problem it will most likely be binding at the top or bottom.

In either case you will need to remove a sliver of material to allow the fit. This can be done at the jointer or with a plane. Both solutions require you

The barrister bookcase gets an Arts & Crafts look with the simple finishing method described for this project. It works great for oak – both white and red.

With the finish complete, an easy way to install the glass for the doors is with matching retainer strips. They are cut and fit then attached with a 23-gauge pinner.

No glue is used to hold the brass rods in place. They can be removed if the door should ever need to be taken out of the bookcase.

shop. Always dispose of rags properly.

The final step in the finishing process is to apply a coat of amber shellac. Can you guess how this is applied? You bet: Rag it on. Keep a wet edge on the wide-open areas and on any other areas simply coat them. That's it. Once the shellac is dry (the next day) add a coat of paste wax after knocking down any nibs with a non-woven abrasive pad.

The Finishing Touch

Attach the plywood backboards to the back of the units with screws after the finish is complete. All that is needed is to run four screws, one at each corner, through the pieces and into the unit bottom and the rear rail of the unit top. Use a countersink and wood screws for a professional look.

Installing the glass and knobs will complete the bookcases. Have $\frac{1}{8}$" glass cut to fit the openings of the doors and fit a glass-retainer strip around the inside of the rabbet holding the glass in place.

The knobs are like the rest of the project; simple and elegant. What would finish this project better than a simple brass knob? Find the location and drill a pilot hole to make installing the knobs

a snap. A bit of wax on the threads will ensure easy installation.

Sliding the doors into the boxes is the last step before filling the bookcase with your books. Slide the door into the case on a slight angle to the front, lift the brass rod on the side toward the rear of the case into the groove and position the other rod to move into the groove as you bring the door square to the front.

Lift the door so it is perpendicular to the case and slide it to the rear of the case. Holding the door up to the top of the unit, install $\frac{3}{4}$"-long brass rods into the remaining holes. Your barrister bookcase is ready to use.

The great thing about this barrister bookcase design is that as your collection grows, and you know it will, so can your bookcases. You can add to the existing stack or start another bookcase. They are easy to build and adding to the stack is something you will enjoy.

Bent Laminations

BY ROBERT W. LANG

Most of the time when a piece of wood has a bend or a curve, it means trouble: Your stock is warped or bowed. But sometimes a bent part can add an interesting design element. The curved supports in these shelves transform what might be plain and ordinary into an interesting and contemporary design.

I usually like to keep things simple, which to me means using as few parts as possible. But when it comes to curved parts, such as the supports for these shelves, I form the curves by gluing together several thin strips rather than steam bending one piece of wood. This technique of bent lamination is faster and the results are more predictable than steam bending.

With steam bending, you need a boiler, a steam box and a way to quickly clamp a scalding-hot piece of wood to a form. Then you need to wait several days for the part to dry. With bent lamination you need only a form and a way

to clamp the thin strips of wood to it. You don't need to wait an hour or more for the wood to get ready to bend and you don't need to race like a madman to get a hot piece of wood clamped in place. Once the glue is thoroughly dry, the parts are ready to use.

The techniques I used to build these shelves can be employed many different ways. Table aprons and chair backs are common uses for curved parts. Once the shape and size of the curve is determined, you build a form for gluing, and decide what thickness of strips to use to make the curved parts.

Make an Educated Guess

I like to use the thickest strips possible to minimize the number of parts and glue lines. The more strips in the lamination however, the stronger it will be, and the likelihood of the curve springing back away from the form will be minimized.

To get the finished thickness of ¾",

I could use four strips ³⁄₁₆" thick, six strips ⅛" thick, eight strips ³⁄₃₂" thick or a dozen pieces ¹⁄₁₆" thick. It all depends on what wood is used and how tight the radius of the curve is.

I make a good guess at a thickness, and resaw a piece of the material to that size. I then bend the piece to roughly the curve I want. If it's difficult to bend, or I hear any popping or cracking noises as I make the bend, I try again with a slightly thinner piece. For this project, which uses ash, I started at ³⁄₁₆" thickness but ultimately decided to use ⅛" for the strips to make the shelf supports.

The next step is to build the form used for bending the curved parts. The shelf supports finish at 2" wide, but the laminations are glued together at 2½". The extra width means I don't have to worry about keeping all of the edges perfectly lined up during gluing. After the glue has dried overnight, I can get a clean edge on the jointer, and achieve

Instead of making a giant compass, I draw the curve by bending a thin strip of wood across the layout marks. Finish nails hold the shape while I mark the curve with a pencil.

After smoothing the first piece, rough-cut parts are then added to the form. A flush-trimming bit is used in the router to make identical curves for the bending form.

the final width by ripping the part on the table saw. One more light cut on the jointer will remove any saw marks. A few quick swipes with a card scraper leave the edges ready for finishing.

To get the 2¼" thickness for the form, I used three layers of ¾"-thick birch plywood cut to the inside radius of the curve, and a fourth piece as a base plate. It doesn't matter what the form is made

from; I used material that was left over from another project. I would have used particleboard or medium-density fiberboard (MDF) if I had found a piece of that first.

The radius is 56¹¹⁄₁₆", which would require a long trammel to draw and cut the curve. Instead, I simply marked the end points and centerline of the curve, and marked off the 4" rise at the center.

I then drove a 4d finish nail at each of these points, and bent a thin strip of wood across them.

It takes three hands to bend and mark the curve. If you don't have someone to help you, drive finishing nails at an angle close to the points used to define the curve. With the midpoint inside the nail, and the ends outside, the thin piece will hold its shape. You can bend the nails to position it exactly where you want it. I cut the curve on the band saw, being careful to saw just outside the pencil line. Then I used #80-grit sandpaper wrapped on a block of wood to get the curved edge smooth.

The First Part is the Pattern

The first layer of the pattern is the only one that requires this much work. The remaining pattern pieces can be marked by tracing the first one. After cutting them slightly oversize, they are attached to the first piece with half-a-dozen #8 x 1¼" screws, and the edges are trimmed with a flush-cutting bit in the router.

After attaching the base plate, the surfaces of the form were given a couple coats of paste wax to keep glue from sticking to them.

Now make the strips for the laminations. They can be ripped on the table saw, but it can be dangerous to work with parts that thin, and nearly half of the material will be lost to the saw kerf. By using the band saw, the operation is much safer and less material is wasted.

Resawing strips on the band saw is safer and less wasteful than using the table saw. I cut them a little thicker than necessary, clean up the saw marks, and bring them to final thickness with the planer.

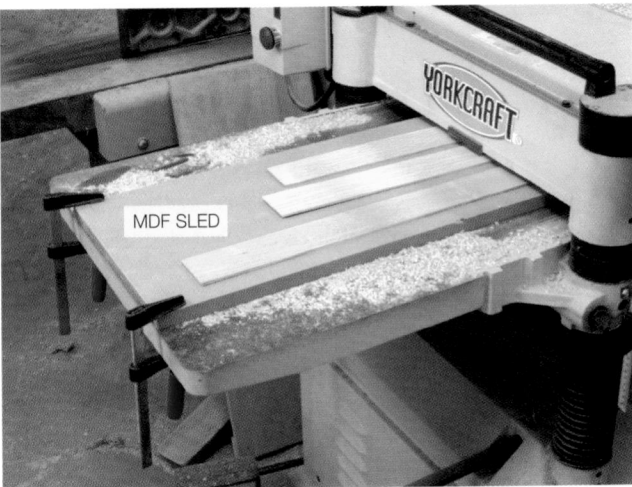

Thin pieces can be sent through the planer on a sled, a piece of ¾"-thick MDF that extends past the feed rollers and is clamped to the planer bed.

Polyurethane glue can be messy as it cures. I use a thin bead of glue and spread it out with a putty knife to avoid this.

American Cabinet

BY TROY SEXTON

Besides a table and chairs, no piece fits the dining room better than this quintessentially American country-style cabinet with storage behind doors and a flat surface for serving food. This project fills both needs perfectly and is a study in simple construction. Build a face frame, attach that frame to a four-panel carcase, then add a top and a few simple details and you're set to store and serve.

Start the Cabinet Face First

Prepare the face-frame pieces according to the cut sheet, but add $^1/_{16}$" to the width of the stiles so they can be trimmed flush to the frame later. This ensures the assembled face frame overhangs the case when following the cut sheet. Locate and lay out the mortise-and-tenon locations on the rails and stiles.

Because a bead wraps around the inside edges of the face frame (it's not an integral part of the frame) there is no need to leave shoulders on the tenons. In fact, with the center and upper rails

being narrow, I like to use the entire width of the rails as a tenon, which adds strength. The mortises are $^3/_8$" wide and $1^1/_{16}$" deep.

Cut the mortises into both stiles of the face frame. I use a dedicated mortise machine for this task, but you can also chop them by hand or use the drill press to start the mortises then square and clean out the slots with a chisel. The mortise for the top rail is open on the top edge of the stiles. These are the only mortises for the project.

Next, create the matching tenons on the ends of the rails. I set up a dado stack and hog away the waste material, leaving a snug-fitting tenon. With these tenons, because they are the width of the rails, cut only the face cheeks of each end.

Set the dado stack for a $^3/_{16}$" deep cut. Set the fence to create a 1"-long tenon, then make passes for each face to form the tenon. The last pass is with the end of the rail tight against the fence. This ensures that all tenons are the same length. And that extra $^1/_{16}$" of depth in the mortise is just a glue reservoir.

Check the fit of the first tenon and make any necessary small adjustments. Finish the tenons and assemble the face frame. Apply glue in the mortises and on the tenons then add clamps and allow the glue to dry.

Wrapping Up the Frame

The added beading gives the face frame a "pop" and is so simple to make. Start with a piece of stock surfaced on four sides and milled to $^3/_4$" thick. Next, chuck a $^1/_4$" corner-beading bit into the router table. My setup looks different because I position my router horizontally. With the setup in a standard router table you'll run the stock vertically to form the bead.

Run the profile on both edges of one face of the stock and rip those pieces off

A SMOOTH FACE. Flatten the edge of the stock with a handplane or jointer before milling the bead. This guarantees a "show" face on the bead. Make certain to install the smooth face outward.

ADDING A "POP." The bead is installed into the openings in the face frame. Careful measurements are key to a proper fit while glue and brads hold the bead in place.

EASY ON THE EYE AND SIMPLE TO BUILD. Combine a face frame with a bead detail and simple case construction to build a cabinet that affords copious amounts of storage and easily fits into many places in the home.

SPRING TENSION. If the fit is correct, you should need to bow the bead in order to slide the piece into the face frame.

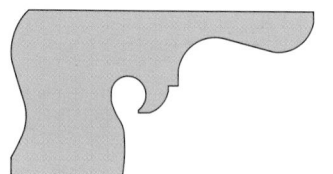

1 grid square = $\frac{1}{2}$"

FOOT PROFILE

at the table saw to a $\frac{5}{16}$" width. Then, after running the edges over the jointer to get a clean surface, it's back to the router table to make two more pieces. Make enough beading to wrap the door and drawer openings.

Before adding the bead, finish sand the face frame. If you do more than touch up the face frame by sanding after the bead is in place, you'll flatten the bead profile.

The beading is mitered to fit into the corners. The miter saw is the best tool for the job. Cut the pieces so they need to be bowed out just a bit in order to fit them in place. Too tight a fit won't work and too loose makes the job look sloppy.

With the bead pieces cut to fit, add a thin line of glue along the beading (the edge with saw marks) then tack the bead in place with small brads. The brads act as clamps until the glue sets.

The Case is Nailed

Begin the carcase by milling to size the panels for the sides, fixed shelves, adjustable shelf and the top. That's a good amount of work, but they are the only panels needed for the cabinet. You could

forego the milling for the top and adjustable-shelf panels at this time if you want to divide the job. These two panels are needed later.

At the table saw, set a dado stack for a $\frac{3}{4}$"-wide x $\frac{1}{4}$"-high cut. Position the fence to cut dados in the side panels for the fixed shelves. Locate the fence so the top face of the bottom panel ends up a $\frac{1}{4}$" above the top edge of the bead on the lower face-frame rail (the $\frac{1}{4}$" step acts as a door stop). Then set the fence so the top face of the top shelf is flush with the top edge of the bead on the face frame's middle rail. Gather these measurements from your assembled face frame.

Once the dados are cut, add an auxiliary fence to the table saw and bury the dado stack $\frac{1}{4}$" into the extra fence. The $\frac{1}{2}$" that's exposed is the amount needed for the rabbet that will house the cabinet's backboards. Rabbet the back edges of both case sides.

Before starting any assembly, drill $\frac{1}{4}$" holes for the adjustable shelf. I have a jig for this task, but I've seen woodworkers use pegboard and a $\frac{1}{4}$" drill bit, too. Clamp your hole-drilling jig against either fixed shelf, but make sure to use

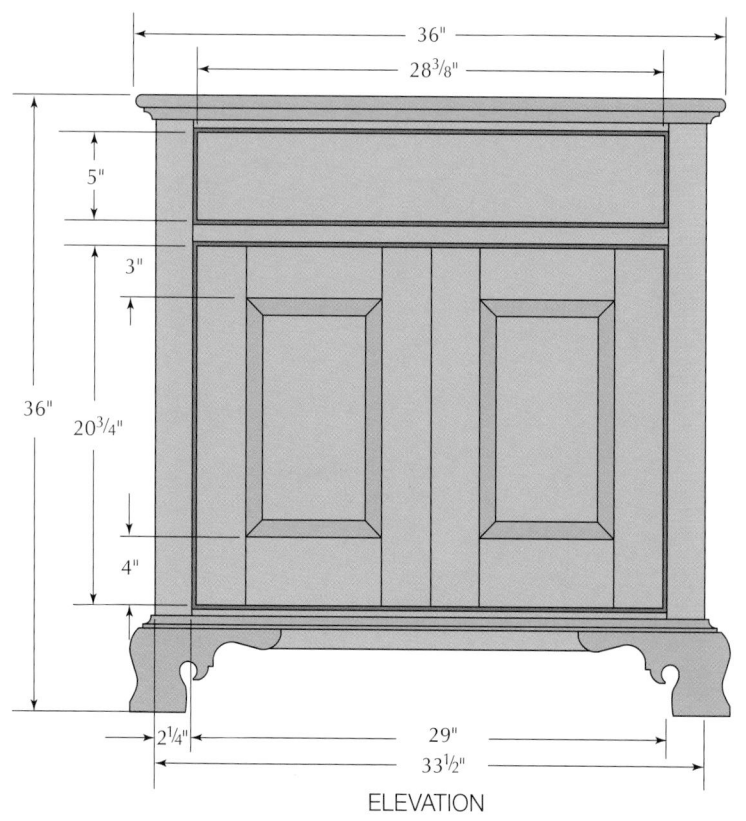

ELEVATION

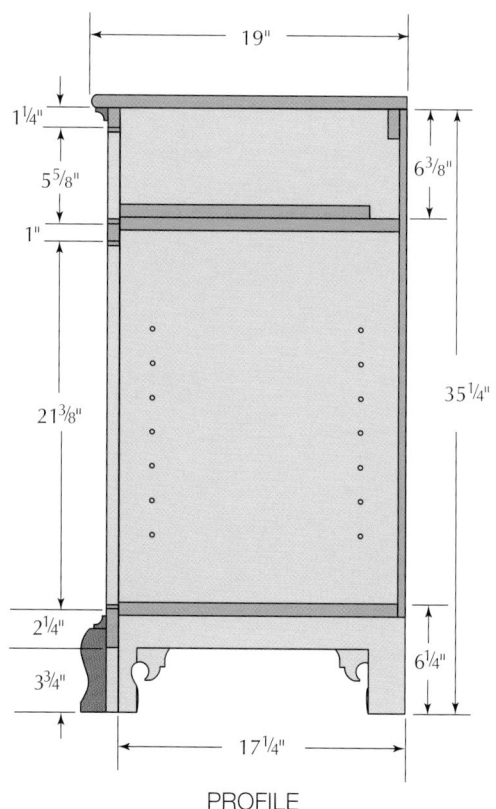

PROFILE

NO TIME TO SPARE. To keep the glue from running out of the dado joint you'll have to move quickly. Any hesitation with the case side inverted results in a lengthy glue clean-up.

A SIMPLE CONNECTION. What could be easier than connecting the sides to the shelves with brads? Drawing a line at the center of the joint provides a nailing location and translates into efficient work.

GET YOUR FACE ON. Check the fit of the face frame. If everything is correct, add a bead of glue to the case's front edge and position the frame on the case. You can add clamps if you like, but brads should hold the frame tight.

American Cabinet

	NO.	ITEM	DIMENSIONS (INCHES)			DIMENSIONS (MILLIMETERS)			MATERIAL	COMMENTS
			T	W	L	T	W	L		
❑	2	Face frame stiles	3/4	2 1/4	35 1/4	19	57	895	Cherry	
❑	1	FF top rail	3/4	1 1/4	31 1/8	19	32	790	Cherry	1" tenon both ends
❑	1	FF middle rail	3/4	1	31 1/8	19	25	790	Cherry	1" tenon both ends
❑	1	FF bottom rail	3/4	2 1/4	31 1/8	19	57	790	Cherry	1" tenon both ends
❑	6	FF bead stock	5/16	3/4	30	8	19	762	Cherry	
❑	2	Sides	3/4	17 1/4	35 1/4	19	438	895	Cherry	
❑	1	Top	3/4	19 1/4	36	19	489	914	Cherry	
❑	2	Fixed shelves	3/4	16 3/4	32 1/2	19	425	826	Poplar	
❑	1	Adjustable shelf	3/4	16 1/2	31 3/4	19	419	806	Poplar	
❑	3	Door stiles	3/4	3	20 3/4	19	76	527	Cherry	
❑	1	Door stile (wide)	3/4	3 1/2	20 3/4	19	89	527	Cherry	
❑	2	Door top rails	3/4	3	9	19	76	229	Cherry	Cope/stick joint
❑	2	Door bottom rail	3/4	4	9	19	102	229	Cherry	Cope/stick joint
❑	2	Raised panels	5/8	8 7/8	14 1/2	16	225	369	Cherry	
❑	1	Drawer front	3/4	5	28 3/8	19	127	721	Cherry	
❑	2	Foot stock	1 1/4	5	30	32	127	762	Cherry	3 feet per piece
❑	1	Moulding stock	3/4	5	30	19	127	762	Cherry	All cove mouldings
❑	1	Cleat	3/4	1 1/2	32	19	38	813	Poplar	Attach to underside of top
❑	2	Drawer guides	1/2	3/4	17	13	19	432	Poplar	
❑	1	Back	1/2	33	29 3/4	13	838	756	Poplar	Shiplapped boards
❑	1	Thumb-turn	1/2	3/4	1 3/4	13	19	45	Cherry	

TRIMMING THE FAT. The extra ¹⁄₁₆" added to the face frame stiles ensures the frame overhangs the sides of the case. Any remaining material must be removed. A flush-trim router bit with a bottom-mount bearing is the perfect solution.

the same shelf throughout the process; that keeps the holes aligned. I place the holes 2" in from the front edge and the same distance in from the rabbet at the back edge.

With the adjustable-shelf holes drilled, it's time to assemble the case. Place a bead of glue into the dados of one case side before slipping the fixed shelves into position. Now comes the

Supplies

Woodworker's Supply
800-645-9292 or woodworker.com

2 • Amerock non-mortising hinges
#891-749, $3.69

1 bag • plated steel shelf pins
#857-330, $4.09

Horton Brass
800-754-9127 or horton-brasses.com

1 • cupboard turn
#H-97, call for pricing

1 • solid brass knob
#P-97, call for pricing

Prices correct at time of publication.

tricky part of the case construction. Add glue into the dados of the second case side and position the shelves so they slip into those dados. This is tricky because you need to get the joint assembled before the glue drips from the dados.

Align the shelves flush with the front edge of the case sides. Use a framing square to mark the location of the center of the shelves on the exterior of the sides, then with a brad nailer add five 1½" brads through the case sides and into the fixed shelves. Flip the case then install brads in the opposite side.

Putting a Face to the Cabinet

Dry-fit the face frame to the case checking both for overhang at the sides and that the fixed shelves line up with the beaded rails. If everything's a go, add a bead of glue to the front edge of the case then carefully position the frame. Tack it to the case with brads, again making sure to align the shelves to the rails. Allow the assembly to dry.

The next step is to trim the face frame to the case. This is where having the extra ¹⁄₁₆" on the frame makes life simple. Use a router with a flush-trim bit to flush the frame to the sides. I always climb-cut (work against the rotation of the router bit) as I trim. The last thing you want to have happen is to catch the grain and rip the face frame causing irreparable damage.

If you haven't milled the top to size, now's the time. With the top prepared, use a ⅜" roundover bit to profile the front and ends of the panel; shape both top and bottom. Take time to sand the edges before affixing the top to the case. Then, position the top on the case so that there is equal overhang on either end and the top piece is flush at the back. This time use a 2" brad through the top and into the sides and front top rail. A small bead of glue along the front rail reinforces the joint.

Flip the case onto the top to install the ¾" x ¾" cove moulding. Make enough for the transition moulding for the base at the same time. Finish sand the intersection of the case to the top before adding the cove; you won't be able to get to this area easily after the cove

is in place. Fit the moulding to the case with miters at the corners, then attach it to the case with brads. A bit of glue along the front and the first 4" back on each side adds strength as well as keeps the miters tight. At this time, add a cleat for the backboards. It is attached to the underside of the top and flush with the rabbets in the sides.

Fascia Feet

The ogee bracket feet are a facade. They are fit to the cabinet and look great, but they do not carry the cabinet's weight. Instead hold them slightly off the end of the face-frame stiles and the ends of the case sides as they're installed. If you want to simplify the building process even more, use a bracket-style foot in place of the ogee. Both designs work identically.

If you plan to forge ahead and create the ogee feet, begin by laying out the profile on the ends of the stock. Next cut a cove at the table saw just as you would to make a piece of cove moulding. Match the size of the cove to the foot profile. (For more information on making ogee bracket feet, see Lonnie Bird's article in the August 2005 issue, #156.)

With the cove profile complete, place the stock at the table saw fence with the top edge on the table. Adjust both the fence and the angle of the blade to remove as much of the profile of the curved top edge as possible without touching the lines. Make a couple passes adjusting the fence to remove more waste material with each pass. From here you should be able to finalize the shape of the feet with a rasp or power sander.

Next, cut the foot stock to length and create a 45° bevel on four of the pieces; you'll need two matching sets. The rear feet are simply cut square. Lay out the scrollwork on each foot, then at the band saw or scrollsaw cut to the lines and clean up any rough edges with a spindle sander or hand tools.

Adding the Feet

Position the feet on the case and remember to hold them about ¹⁄₁₆" off the bottom edge. You'll notice there is material showing behind the feet. Trace the

ONE FOOT AT A TIME. Place the feet on the case and mark the profile. Cut away the waste material after connecting the top edge of the feet across the case, both front and sides. Don't be too concerned with the task; the feet and transition moulding cover any raw edges.

MAKE COVE MOULDING SAFELY. The small cove moulding is made using a wide board at a router table. Next, rip the moulding to its final width at the table saw. Fit the cove to the case then attach with brads.

profile of each foot, then remove that waste with a jigsaw. Don't worry about the look; just get the waste out of the way. All the edges are covered with the feet and the cove moulding that wraps the case.

Nail from the back of the case to attach the feet. Add glue to the miters to help hold them tight. Next, install the remaining cove moulding at the top edge of the feet. The cove is attached to the case with brads. These miters should be reinforced with glue as well.

Drawer, Doors and Back

The drawer for this cabinet is made in a traditional method. The sides join the back with through dovetails and the front is attached to the sides with half-blind dovetails. The drawer bottom is slid into grooves in the sides and in the drawer front. It is secured in the drawer with nails that extend through the bottom into the drawer back. The drawer rides on the fixed upper shelf. Drawer guides, butted to the face frame and held with brads, keep the drawer running straight.

The door joints are cut with a cope-and-stick set at my router table. The right-hand door in the photo has a rabbet cut into the rear of the left stile. That rabbet fits over a matching rabbet cut in the right

stile of the left door. That stile is the 3½"-wide stock.

With the door frames dry fit, measure the raised-panel openings then make two raised panels using either a table saw or router bit. Check the fit of the panels then assemble the doors using glue in the rail-and-stile joint only. No glue is used in the raised-panel area. Install pegs to give the cabinet an antique look.

Once dry, carefully hang the doors to the opening with simple butt hinges. The left door is held to the case with a wooden thumb-turn located behind the right-hand stile. It catches the middle rail.

The backboards continue the bead detail from the case front. Create the shiplap joint then add the bead detail to the individual pieces. As always, I spaced the boards using Popsicle sticks and nailed them to the case – all after finishing the cabinet. The finish is a mixture of aniline dye with three coats of spray lacquer.

While this piece usually sits mainly in dining rooms, it is a great project for anywhere you need storage. If you build it, I'm certain you'll find a place to show it off and use it.

Leaning Shelves

BY CHRISTOPHER SCHWARZ

It was about 1 a.m., and I was at the grocery on a bleary-eyed run to buy orange juice for the family's breakfast. The only other shopper that hour was a woman tooling through the frozen food aisle. Perched atop her mound of food was a box that contained the disassembled parts to some shelves much like these.

At that moment it became official; these shelves are now everywhere – even among the pork rinds and toaster pastries at the corner store.

And so this begs a question: Why would we tackle such a ubiquitous design for the magazine?

Simple. We can make them better than the stuff at the store.

Many of the so-called leaning shelf designs I've examined have flaws. Some rack unacceptably. Some use a lot of extra material to become sturdy. Many have top shelves that are too narrow (3" in some cases). Others have lower shelves that cantilever too much out the back.

It was time to fire up the CAD software and start drafting.

After numerous experiments and revisions, I discovered that these shelves actually are more of an engineering equation than a woodworking project. The leaning angle and the height of the units work together to determine the depth of the shelves. Getting these factors to work together to produce sensible shelving is trickier than it first appears. So take care if you want to modify this design – small alterations make big differences.

I also sought to squeeze out the maximum amount of shelf space from the minimum amount of material. After

additional work in CAD, I squeezed it down to this: To build two shelf units and one desk unit, you'll need to buy:
- One sheet of ¾" plywood
- Six 8' 2 x 4s
- 35 linear feet of 1 x 4s
- 70' of edge tape

For this investment in material, you'll get 30 linear feet of shelving and a desk – not bad.

Construction is simpler than any bookcase I've built. The shelves rest in dados in the uprights. The uprights are prevented from racking by braces that

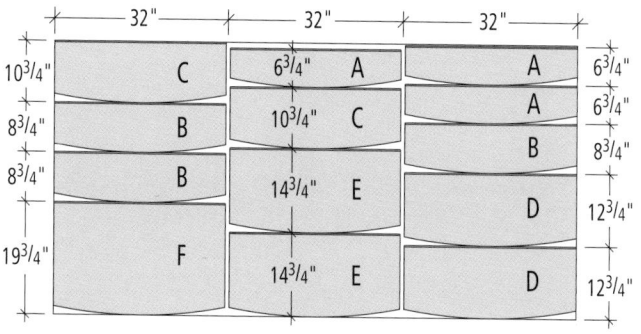

CUTTING DIAGRAM

Take care when cutting your plywood because every kerf counts. Shown is my stack of finished shelves. That little pile on top of the shelves is the waste that was left from an entire sheet of plywood.

Cutting 85"-long pieces all to the same size is impossible on most table saws. So I gang-cut the pieces on my miter saw. Clamp your mating uprights together and crosscut them simultaneously. This way if they're a little off, they'll still match.

We've acquired a few straight bits throughout the years. After testing a few I found that the Woodline plywood bit cuts a dado that was closest in size (.714" wide) to the particular sheet of plywood I bought. (Woodline: 800-472-6950 or woodline.com; item# wl-1028-1, $9).

To build a dado jig, draw a 7° angle on your scrap and then build the jig around that line and your router's baseplate using scraps, glue and nails.

are pocket-screwed into the shelves and uprights. There's no back, no top and no bottom.

It was so simple, in fact, that I decided to add some visual interest by cutting curves on the braces and front edges of the shelves.

Begin Construction

I always like to begin a project that uses plywood by first breaking the 4' x 8' sheets into smaller sizes – plywood takes up a lot of room in small shops.

Using the cutting diagram at left you first want to crosscut the full sheet into three equal-sized pieces that are 31¾" long. These are a bit oversized so you can trim them down on your saw and remove the factory edges from the plywood. Then you can easily rip the shelves to their finished widths using the diagram as a guide.

Now you need to work on the uprights. Dress your stock as true as possible and then cut it to its finished length.

Now lay out the locations of all the dados on the uprights. Because these dados are cut at a 7° angle I recommend you mark out every joint to avoid a blunder.

Now you should make a few test dados in a scrap piece to find the best bit for the job. Plywood varies in thickness from sheet to sheet. And straight bits

designed for plywood come in slightly different diameters, too. Your best bet is to mill a ¾" x ¾" dado in a scrap and see how the plywood shelves fit into it.

Different Diagonal Dados

You need to make two router jigs to cut the angled dados in the uprights – one for the left-hand uprights and one for the right-hand. I know that it seems like you should be able to make just one jig and flip it around, but the geometry doesn't work that way.

I like dado jigs that capture the router's base on both sides. This ensures the router won't wander, and it allows me to make the occasional climb cut without the tool jerking severely.

Also note that a router with flat edges on its base will make your dado locations more accurate. With some round-base routers, the bit isn't always in the dead center of the baseplate.

I'm sure that some of you will figure out a way to do this on the table saw, but the band saw is far quicker for me. A roller stand holds the bottom end up while I make the cut at the top end.

With the angle cut, clamp two mating uprights together and plane down to your line. The longer the plane the straighter your surface will be.

I used poplar for my uprights, which is easy to plane. After removing any bow with my jointer plane, a pass or two with a smoothing plane is all this forgiving wood needs to be ready to finish.

upright at 1¾". Now make a second mark. This one should be where the bottom edge of the top shelf hits the back edge of the upright. Join those two marks with a line.

Finish up your work on the uprights by routing a ¼" x ¼" rabbet on the outside corner of each upright – this adds a shadow line and gives you a bit of forgiveness when lining these units up against your wall. Now sand or plane your uprights to prepare them for finishing.

Clamp the jig to an upright and your workbench, and rout all the dados – I like to use three passes (increasing depth) to keep from taxing the router or the bit.

Matching Angles

With the dados routed, you can now cut the angles that allow the shelves to tip back against your wall. Set your miter saw to make a 7° miter. Clamp two mating uprights together and trim the feet simultaneously.

Now you need to cut the long miter on the top of the uprights. The best way to do this is mark your cut line, cut it close on the band saw and clean up the cut with a hand plane.

Marking out this angle looks like a challenge, but we have made it easy for you. At the top of the upright, make a mark halfway across the width of the

Shelves and Braces

Because the braces need to fit tightly between the uprights, I cut them each about ½" longer than necessary at first and trim them to fit the assembled unit.

The first step on the braces is to cut a 7° bevel on one long edge of each part. To accomplish this, I beveled the blade of my table saw to 7° and ripped one long edge of a spare brace. I then placed it up against an upright to make sure the geometry worked.

If you're going to add a curve to your braces and shelves, you should make two routing templates to ensure the curves are consistent – one template is for the shelves and the other template is for the braces.

With the 7° bevel cut on one edge of a brace, check it against an upright. You've hit the right angle when the brace fits in perfectly where the dado meets the back edge of the upright.

To make the two templates, bend a flexible scrap between two nails as shown. Bend the scrap 1½", hold it in place and trace a line on both sides of the scrap. Now you've marked lines for both the inside and outside curves. Band saw between these lines and clean up the sawn edge of the two templates.

When routing the braces, you might have to climb cut some sections because the grain is likely to reverse on you in the curve. If you take a light cut and hold the tool securely, this is a generally safe operation. But do take care.

Magic Shelves

BY STEVE SHANESY

Go ahead. Take a guess. Just what do you think one of these shelf units weighs? I'll give you a hint. The thickness is 1⅜", the length of the longest part is 78" with the other leg 61". The height is 24" and the depth is 11". Some serious cherry timbers, you think? Say 40 or 50 pounds? Well, guess again friend 'cause you're off by a factor of two. Yes, 23 pounds for the big unit and just 20 pounds for the smaller one.

What you're looking at are three torsion boxes for each unit that use a solid cherry front edge, a top and bottom of

¼" cherry plywood and several pine ribs that run cross grain to the cherry ply, or perpendicular to the front edge. It's all glued together to make a strong, flat and lightweight panel.

So how is it fixed to the wall? I'm not revealing that trick until the second act!

And by the way, if you think you've seen these shelves before, chances are you have. Our version was inspired by those shown in an Ace Hardware advertisement. I wasn't surprised to learn from Ace that they'd had hundreds of requests for plans to build this project. When I suggested we feature it here, they jumped at the chance.

Torsion (or anti-Torsion) Boxes
Before heading to the shop, understand that what you are essentially making are

a series of torsion boxes. Now why they are called "torsion" boxes and not "antitorsion" boxes I'll never know (unless one of you would be kind enough to help me). To me, "torsion" means "twisted, or twisting," and what this construction technique does is prevent that from happening. Everything from aircraft wings and fuselages to hollow-core doors use this principle to keep their shape, even under a lot of stress. If you do much woodworking, you'll find torsion boxes a terrific solution to construction "problems" that come up from time to time.

After looking over the drawings and collecting your materials, begin by cutting the parts. Cut the plywood to length and width and mill the solid cherry for the front edges. At this stage, leave the solid cherry just a little long and keep the edges square, but do cut the ½" x ¼" rabbet where the plywood will be joined to the solid front edge. You should make sure that the rabbet's depth leaves the solid edge flush or just proud of the plywood.

Build the Ribs
Now cut the pieces you'll need to provide the build-up between the two plywood faces. It should be exactly the thickness of the dimension created by the two rabbet cuts. Note there are, how-

The shelf panel torsion box is made up of a solid cherry front edge, a top and bottom ¼" cherry plywood skin, and a series of built-up ribs. All the parts are glued together to make a strong, lightweight, torsion-resistant panel.

ever, two different widths and lengths. The pieces that are assembled at each end are both longer and wider than the intermediate ones. Lastly, cut out four strips of plastic laminate to the dimen-

After gluing and pinning the cherry plywood skin to one side, flip the partial assembly and glue all the parts. Then pin together both sides. If you don't have a pinner, you can clamp all the parts, although this method should be done in several stages.

sions given. If you don't have a plastic laminate such as Formica handy, you could substitute $\frac{1}{16}$" x 1" pre-cut strips of aluminum or steel.

Before starting assembly of the shelf panels, glue the plastic or metal strips to the inside back edge of the plywood that will be the top side of the four long shelves. This material will reinforce the plywood when you attach the shelves to the wall. If you use plastic laminate, use either white or yellow woodworking glue. If you use metal, use an epoxy or polyurethane glue.

Panel Assembly

Depending on how your shop is equipped, assembly could go relatively quickly, or it could take a while. It'll be quick if you have a pneumatic pinner/nailer; slower if you have to rely on clamps exclusively. Regardless, the process will be the same.

First, glue one plywood piece to one of the rabbets in the cherry edge. Make sure you have a nice tight joint. For this, white

or yellow glue is fine. Next, glue the end and intermediate ribs in place, spacing them about a foot apart. For this cross-grain gluing, use polyurethane glue. Also, use glue where the end of each rib butts to the solid cherry. Lastly, glue the second piece of plywood as before.

Even if you use a pneumatic pinner, clamp the ends and the rabbet joints. Also, keep your nails out of the way of the 45-degree end cuts to come later. Don't forget to pin or clamp the pine pieces on both sides of the shelf.

Continue assembling panels until all four horizontal and two vertical panels are done.

After the glue has dried, sand or use a scraper to flush up the surfaces where the plywood and front edge meet. Now you are almost ready to cut the big chamfer on the front edge of each panel. Carefully mark each panel so that the reinforced plywood back edge is facing up for correct orientation to the chamfer. Next, use your router to form a $\frac{1}{4}$" radius on what will be the outside edge

After the glue has cured and a $\frac{1}{4}$" radius has been routed on the correct long edge of the front, cut the big chamfer detail on the table saw.

Each of the six panels must be mitered on both ends. Take special care to make sure your cuts are properly oriented to the panels' final assembly position.

of each panel's front edge. When done, cut the chamfer using your table saw so the cut blends into the radius detail.

The ends of each panel now get a cross-grain miter cut. Again, before cutting, note the orientation of the cut relative to the reinforced plywood. It's best to put the three parts that make up one unit together, mark the edges to be glued later and — for the horizontal pieces — the end which is strictly decorative. Make the cut with a table saw, sliding compound miter saw or a radial arm saw.

The last bit of preparation before assembly is to cut biscuit joints in the miters that will be glued together.

Assembly

Dry assemble the parts to check fittings and figure out a clamping strategy. I fashioned an "I-beam" type piece from ¾" plywood that 1) held the long panels up and in position while assembling; 2) gave me a surface to clamp to that didn't require long clamps; and 3) went a long way toward holding the entire assembly square during the process.

After the glue has set up and before removing the "I -beam" brace, make a simple support that attaches to the back side that will support the long "legs" through the rest of the work and until you install the units. Just make simple

blocks that can be screwed into one of the interior pine pieces, then screw a brace between them.

Now cap the other long ends that are chamfered with some homemade cherry "veneer." Slice four pieces that are about ¹⁄₁₆" thick off a piece of cherry of sufficient width. Size the pieces so that there is about ⅛" extra all around when applied. A simple way to attach these is to use contact cement. Trim and sand off the overhang after applying.

In preparation for installation, cut lengths of a sound hardwood, such as oak or maple, milled to the exact thickness of the opening in the back of each

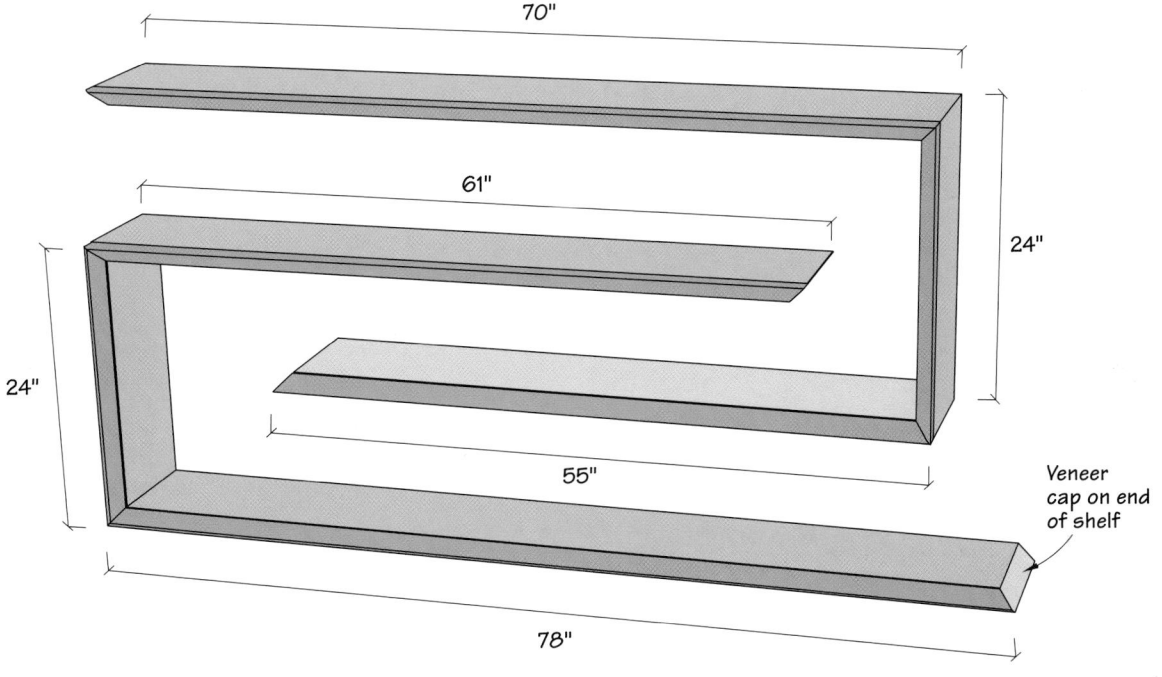

Magic Shelves

	NO.	ITEM	DIMENSIONS (INCHES)			DIMENSIONS (MILLIMETERS)			MATERIAL	COMMENTS
			T	W	L	T	W	L		
❏	2	Front edges	1³⁄₈	2	24	35	51	610	Cherry	
❏	1	Front edge	1³⁄₈	2	78	35	51	1981	Cherry	
❏	1	Front edge	1³⁄₈	2	70	35	51	1778	Cherry	
❏	1	Front edge	1³⁄₈	2	61	35	51	1549	Cherry	
❏	1	Front edge	1³⁄₈	2	55	35	51	1397	Cherry	
❏	2	Shelf skins	¼	9½	55⁵⁄₈	6	242	1413	Cherry ply	
❏	2	Shelf skins	¼	9½	70⁵⁄₈	6	242	1794	Cherry ply	
❏	2	Shelf skins	¼	9½	78⁵⁄₈	6	242	1997	Cherry ply	
❏	2	Shelf skins	¼	9½	61⁵⁄₈	6	242	1565	Cherry ply	
❏	4	Shelf skins	¼	9½	24⁵⁄₈	6	242	676	Cherry ply	
❏	12	End bldups	⁷⁄₈	2½	9⅛	22	64	232	Pine	
❏	30	Bldups	⁷⁄₈	1½	7⁵⁄₈	22	194	194	Pine	

Approx. 22' hardwood cleat material ⁷⁄₈" x 2⅛".

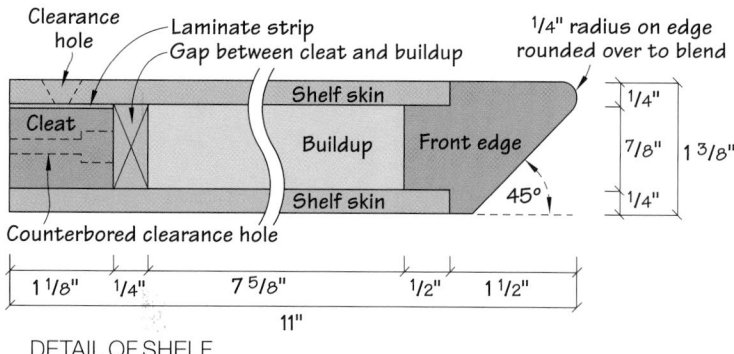

Clearance hole

Laminate strip
Gap between cleat and buildup

1/4" radius on edge rounded over to blend

Cleat

Shelf skin

Buildup

Front edge

Shelf skin

1/4"

7/8" | 1 3/8"

1/4"

45°

Counterbored clearance hole

1 1/8"   1/4"   7 5/8"   1/2"   1 1/2"

11"

DETAIL OF SHELF

long shelf. The width should be about 1/8" less than the depth of the opening. These pieces will be securely fastened to the wall studs and positioned so that the openings in the rear of the shelves will sleeve over them. Screws will then be used to fasten each shelf to its wall cleat. You can pre-drill and countersink holes in the top rear edge of shelf, spaced about 14" apart. Now you understand why the plastic laminate or metal was used to reinforce the thin plywood. Wait until you are ready to install the shelves before drilling pilot holes in the cleats. That way, you can mount the cleats on the wall, then position and mark the locations for pilot holes.

To complete the shop portion of this project, thoroughly sand and be careful to remove any dried glue, especially near the miter joints. Sand to 150 grit. For this project, I clear coated the units with lacquer. Just take the time to sand between coats to help achieve a nice, smooth finish.

Ultimately, this is a simple project that is a terrific primer on torsion box construction and produces a striking end result. You might say that for all but beginning woodworkers, it's a project you can ACE.

The long panels are joined to the short vertical panels using biscuits in the miter joint. The biscuits strengthen the joint and help hold alignment during glue up.

What could be an unwieldy glue-up is simplified using an "I-beam" shaped plywood fixture. The fixture clamps to the long panels, holding them in place, provides a clamping surface for pulling the end in position and helps keep the whole assembly square.

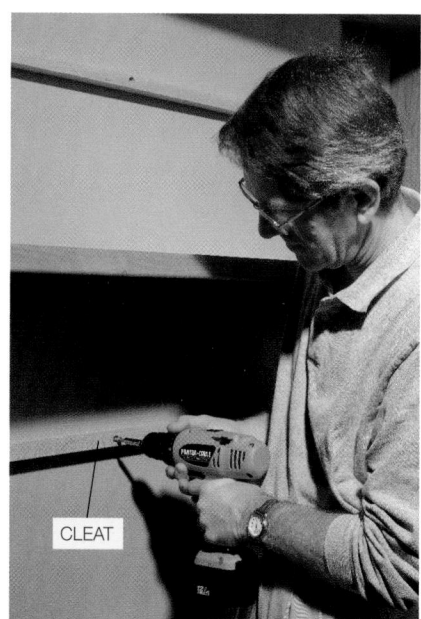

The shelves hang on cleats that are carefully positioned and then screwed to the wall.

Monticello's Stacking Bookcases

BY CHRISTOPHER SCHWARZ

I like to think of Thomas Jefferson's personal library as America's first "book-mobile."

When the British burned down the nation's capitol in 1814, the inferno took with it many of the books owned by the government of our young nation. Lucky for us, Jefferson had a personal library of about 6,700 books – an astonishing accomplishment for the time.

And after some negotiations, Jefferson agreed to cede his entire library at Monticello to Congress for the sum of $23,950. The question was, how to transport 6,700 books from Virginia north to Washington, D.C., with horse-drawn wagons.

Lucky for us, Jefferson was a clever man. He stored his precious library in pine boxes that were designed specifically to travel. While it isn't known if Jefferson designed the book boxes (or "book presses" as they are sometimes called), they do bear the mark of his cleverness.

For when the day came to transport this massive chunk of knowledge, the process was straightforward. Scrap paper was stuffed among the books to protect them, then a lid was nailed over the front of each unit and it was loaded onto a wagon and carted to Washington.

Jefferson's collection of books (which continues to make headlines even today) was the foundation for our Library of

STACKED TO MOVE. This modular system of stacking book boxes allowed Thomas Jefferson to easily expand and move his enormous library.

THE DESIGNER? While we might never know if Thomas Jefferson designed these book boxes, he designed many clever devices at Monticello.

Congress. His method for organizing his books (memory, reason and imagination) pushed us into a more modern classification system. Until that time it was common to organize books by height or color.

But What About the Boxes?

While a good deal is known about the books in Jefferson's collection that he sold to Congress, far less is known about the stackable boxes that he used to store his library at Monticello. By examining the written records, officials at Monticello built six bookcases for the museum in 1959 that are a good guess at what would have housed Jefferson's library (though he could have had as many as 20 of these units, if you do the math).

Since the day I started woodworking, I have been concerned about amassing information on the craft. For me, the written word enhances my personal experience in the shop, and it is a way to stay in touch with the craft while I am on the road, in bed or sitting on the couch.

As my library got out of hand sometime about 2005, I decided I needed to build something to store all my woodworking books. I also wanted something that would allow them to be easily transported when my wife and I leave our house after the kids are off to college, and we launch the next phase of our lives.

And so I became interested in Jefferson's book boxes. I read the original letters that describe how the books were transported. I used the standard measurements for books of the day to help fill in the blanks when it came to designing the three different case sizes Jefferson describes in his correspondence.

Oh, and what was the joinery on these boxes? Who knows. Perhaps the boxes were nailed together, as there were as many as 150 individual book boxes to hold the nearly 6,700 books. But I prefer to think that our third president, who was familiar with the principles of joinery, would insist on something more substantial.

And so, despite the fact that no surviving examples of these book boxes exist, I built each of these units using through-dovetails with mitered shoulders at the corners. The backs are shiplapped and nailed on to the carcases. This approach to building a box is typical for the time, and I bet that my modern book boxes would easily survive a wagon journey from Monticello to Washington, D.C.

A Discussion of Sizes

After researching Jefferson's book boxes and the history of 18th-century publishing, I found that these original book boxes would not be as friendly to the modern library. The largest book box is taller than necessary, and the smaller two boxes are shallower than necessary for some modern titles that are squat. But I decided to build my book boxes to suit old books – you can alter yours as you see fit.

Here are the old dimensions. Jefferson said the bottom cases were 13" deep, the middle cases were 6¾" deep and the top cases 5¾" deep. As to the heights, we can turn to the standard sizes of books at the time (according to the American Library Association). The lower cases were designed to hold "quartos" and "folios." A folio is 15" high x 12" deep. A quarto is 12" high x 9½" deep (the typical size of a modern woodworking book).

The middle cases were designed for "octavos," which are 9" high x 6" deep.

The top cases were for "duodecimos," which are 7⅜" high x 5" deep.

So I designed the three different book boxes around these three sizes. As I mentioned above, the lower cases are a little taller than necessary, and the middle cases are a little shallow. But it actually works, and I like the way the boxes step gracefully up my wall.

About the Joinery

I chose to use through-dovetails with mitered shoulders at the corners. This was the same joint the joiners at Monticello used in the 1959 reproductions of the book boxes. I like this joint because it dresses up the front edge of each box with a miter. Also, it is strong and easy to make. Yes, you read that right: easy to make.

You might be wondering if you can cut a mitered through-dovetail joint. The answer is: Yes. It is as easy as a regular through-dovetail, once you let go of your fear of miters and cut the joint freehand and use the joint's natural compression to help you fit it so it's airtight. Of the 24 mitered dovetails in this project, only one is less than airtight. And it was the first one I cut.

The rest of the joinery for these boxes is cake. The ½"-thick backs rest in ½" x ½" rabbets cut into the end pieces and are nailed to the top and bottom of the boxes, which are ½" narrower than the end pieces.

The only other thing to build is the plinth that supports the book boxes. Jefferson's papers don't mention a plinth, but the joiners at Monticello in 1959 built plinths for their cases, and I think it's a fine idea.

The profile I chose for the plinth is a typical late 18th-century foot that you can find on furniture made in both the North and South of the United States. Feel free to select another profile for your plinth, especially if your bookcases will reside in a more modern setting. After all, when old furniture started to look unfashionable, the owners would change the plinth and the hardware to update it. So you can alter your plinth to reflect Shaker, Arts & Crafts or even Scandinavian aesthetics. It's your library.

Building the Shelves

These shelves are 48" long without any center supports. This sounds like a recipe for sagging. But if you nail in your back pieces (which add strength) and use beefy, ⅞"-thick stock, you will find that your book boxes are nigh on indestructible.

You could get away with ¾" stock throughout without too much of a visual compromise, so don't think that you have to find 4/4 rough stock to build these shelves.

Begin by dressing all your stock to thickness. I was lucky enough to score some Eastern white pine boards of unreasonable widths. So I had to dress the boards for my bottom cases by hand before I could run them through my powered planer.

After dressing my stock to size, I cut a shallow rabbet on the ends of the tail boards. This rabbet is ¹⁄₁₆" deep and the width of the mating pin board. This shallow rabbet makes it quite easy to mate up the two pieces when transferring the marks from my tail board to my pin board.

If I had only a couple boxes to build, I'd make this rabbet with a moving fillister plane. But because I had 28 of these

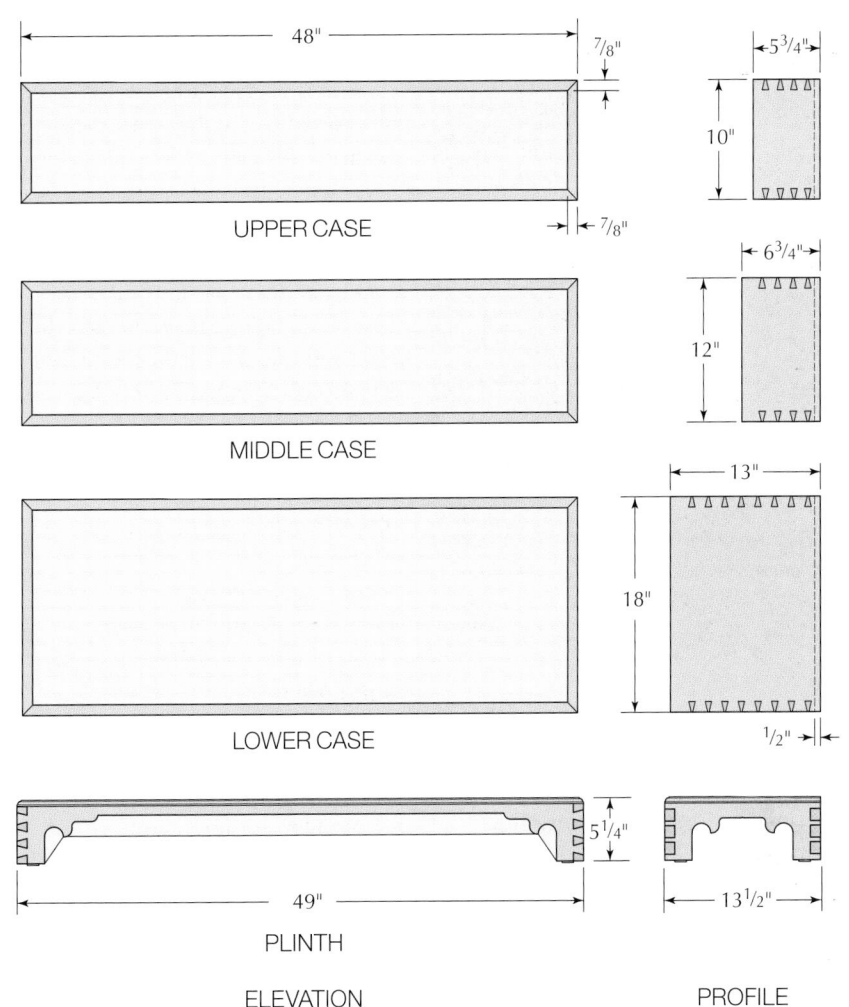

Monticello's Stacking Bookcases

	NO.	ITEM	DIMENSIONS (INCHES)			DIMENSIONS (MILLIMETERS)			MATERIAL	COMMENTS
			T	W	L	T	W	L		
LOWER CASE										
❏	2	Ends	⅞	13	18	22	330	457	Pine	
❏	2	Top & bottom	⅞	12½	48	22	318	1219	Pine	
❏	1	Back	⅞	18	47½	22	457	1207	Pine	
MIDDLE CASE										
❏	2	Ends	⅞	6¾	12	22	171	305	Pine	
❏	2	Top & bottom	⅞	6¼	48	22	158	1219	Pine	
❏	1	Back	⅞	12	47½	22	305	1207	Pine	
UPPER CASE										
❏	2	Ends	⅞	5¾	10	22	146	254	Pine	
❏	2	Top & bottom	⅞	5¼	48	22	133	1219	Pine	
❏	1	Back	⅞	10	47½	22	254	1207	Pine	
PLINTH										
❏	2	Ends	⅞	4¾	13½	22	121	343	Pine	
❏	2	Front & back	⅞	4¾	49	22	121	1245	Pine	
❏	1	Interior support, front	¾	3	47¼	19	76	1200	Pine	
❏	2	Interior support, ends	¾	3	11¾	19	76	298	Pine	
❏	4	Glue blocks	1	1	4⅛	25	25	108	Maple	
❏		Moulding	½	½	72	13	13	1829	Pine	

WORTH THE EFFORT. I dressed the concave face of my wide boards with my jack plane then ran them through my powered planer. By jacking one face before planing the other, I avoided having to rip the boards down and re-glue them.

UNDER PRESSURE. Press the stock down hard to ensure that the cut is consistent across the width of your boards. The dado stack will try to turn your board into a hovercraft. Don't let it. Press down.

rabbets to cut, I set up a dado stack in my table saw and cut them all using the table saw.

While this might seem like a no-brainer technique, it requires finesse. You need to really press the top of your work hard against the table when making these rabbets. Anything less, and the rotation of the cutterhead will lift the work off the table. No lie.

With all your shallow rabbets cut, you can cut the ½" x ½" rabbets in the inside back edge of the end pieces. I again use a dado stack for this.

Now you can begin to lay out your dovetail joints. This is tricky to explain, but once you cut one mitered dovetail joint, you will laugh loud and hard. It's flipping easy. If you are skeptical, then please give it a try using some scrap first, then you can come crawling … .

Tail Layout

When you lay out a traditional through-dovetail joint, you will lay out a number of full tails on the tail board. The pin board has full pins – plus half-pins at the ends. Not so with this project.

Because of the miters, the tail joint at the front of the case has one of its corners that mutates into a miter. It looks like a half-pin in one direction and a full tail from another. I know, I know. It seems confusing. Stick with me.

At the rear of each case, I used a half-tail at the back edge so that I could easily conceal the backboards with simple through-rabbets. The half-tail conceals the ½" x ½" rabbet on the inside back edge. As a result, the completed end pieces look a little weird to the traditional eye. But you'll get over it.

So here's how you should proceed: Figure out a tail width at the rear of the case that will hide the backboards and remain strong. Lay out that tail.

At the front of the case, things are a little more complicated. The miter should begin ⅜" from the front edge. So mark a line ⅜" from the front edge of your tail board. Make this mark on the end grain. But don't mark it down the face grain of the outside face of your tail board, which would be typical. Instead, make this sloping tail mark on the inside face of the board. It's weird, I know. But do it.

Lay out the rest of your tail cuts between these two tails, leaving a gap between your tails that is about ⅛" wide at the top.

Now make your tail cuts with a dovetail saw. When you are done with one face, it should look like you have a board with two half-tails at either end. Turn the board around so the rabbeted face is facing you. Take your dovetail saw and make the compound cut at the front of the case that defines the face of the miter. This cut is 45° to the front edge. It looks tricky. It ain't. If you can see the line, you can cut the line.

Now position the board so the front edge of the corner faces the ceiling. Take

HERE'S THE DEAL. You can see almost all the trickiness here. Note how the tail on the left doesn't go through the face of the board, so it looks like a half-tail. On the right, you can see how the half-tail conceals the rabbet for the back.

AN INSIDE JOB. Turn your tail board around and cut the front tail on the inside of the corner. It's a 45° cut.

SLICE THE WACKY WASTE. Then turn the board on its side and saw the miter on the front edge. This looks like a complex cut, but just follow the line. It makes sense when the waste falls away.

THE RESULT. See? Here's the miter at the front, which intersects the sloping tail. Once you see it, you'll get it.

a miter square (or your combination square) and use it to lay out the miter from the tip of the case to the baseline. When I mark this miter, I use a thin-lead (.3mm) mechanical pencil.

Cut this miter freehand to free the waste at the front of the corner. You'll need to angle the saw at 45° to make this cut. Again, try this once on scrap and you will be a pro.

When that waste has fallen away you can clear out the waste between the other tails. I use a coping saw. But feel free to bang it out with a chisel.

Pin Layout

When the waste is clear, you need to transfer the pattern of the tail board onto the pin board. The shallow $1/16$"-deep rabbet makes this a cakewalk. Clamp your pin board upright in a vise. Place the tail board's rabbet on top of the pin board and press the two together. When the two are mushed together, trace the shape of the tail board onto the pin board with a marking knife.

The little mitered section at the front is tough to get a spear-point knife into. Depending on the acuteness of the tip of the knife you can do a fine or a lousy job. Do your best and then "infer" (read: guess) the remainder of the slope with a ruler and a knife.

With the lines marked out on the end grain of the pin board, I take the extra step of dropping those lines down the face of my pin board to my baseline. It slows me down, but it's a habit I have yet to break from my first dovetail class.

Slice all the pins with your dovetail saw. But before you remove the waste between the pins, cut the miter at the front of the pin board.

Clamp the pin board on its side and lay out the miter from the tip of the board to the baseline – just like you did with the tail board.

Saw the pins and remove the waste between the pins using a coping saw and chisel. Then saw the miter (on the waste side) freehand. If you are sloppy, clean up the cut a bit to the line with a shoulder plane.

TAILS, MEET PINS. I have my tail board resting on a scrap to keep it in position as I press its shallow rabbet against the pin board. Knife in the joint. Use light strokes at first, followed by heavier ones.

MORE WACKY MITERS. Here's the completed pin board layout, with the waste marked with "X"s. Clear out the waste between the pins, then cut the miter.

THE PIN BOARD RESULT. This board looks a little more straightforward than the tail board. It's basically a standard-looking pin board with a miter cut on its front edge.

Fit & Slice

When you have the pins and tails cleaned up to your satisfaction, it's time for the fun part: fitting the miters.

Drive the tail board onto the pin board. What is likely to happen is that the tails will seat everywhere but up by

NEEDS A FIT. You can see how the tail isn't fully seated in its socket. The way to fix that is to saw through the miter.

SAW RIGHT THROUGH. Use a thin-kerf saw and cut right through the miter. The joint might pinch the blade a bit. That's OK. It means the process is working.

the miter. The miter is what is preventing the tail from landing home at the bottom of the pin socket.

When the parts are driven together, they will generate some pressure right at the miter – a good thing. Place the joint on your workbench so the miter faces the ceiling. Take a thin-kerf saw and cut through the miter freehand.

Yes, you read that right. Saw through the miter freehand.

The set of the teeth will remove the excess wood on either side of the saw plate. As you saw, you should feel the wood pinch the blade. Keep sawing. When you reach the bottom of the joint, slide the saw out and the miters should draw closer together. The evidence of this will be that the tail will seat more deeply in the pin socket.

If the miter is tight and the tail is fully seated, you are done. If the tail isn't fully seated, saw through the miter again.

Sometimes the pressure from the joint isn't enough to pull the miters together as you are sawing. If this happens, clamp the joint and then saw it.

Make all the boxes using these techniques. Yes, it takes some time, but by the end you'll be able to make this joint without hesitation, and it's a fine one to have in your arsenal.

The Backs

The backboards for these boxes are nothing more than ½"-thick pine boards that are shiplapped, beaded then nailed on the back of the boxes after the bookcase is finished. You can make your backs now or later.

The Plinth

A traditional plinth looks delicate but will support the entire weight of the book boxes above without any problem. The trick is to design it correctly.

The corners of the plinth should be dovetailed before you cut the scrollwork to create the feet. If you cut the scrollwork first, the plinth boards will be too fragile for dovetailing.

After dovetailing the corners, trace your foot design onto the front, back and ends. I drew my shape freehand and it was based on a typical design of the period. Once the shapes are laid out, cut the scrollwork and clean up the saw cuts with rasps or an oscillating spindle sander.

Assemble the four plinth pieces with glue, clamps and lots of care. This is when the pieces are fragile. I destroyed one foot while clamping things together. Luckily, I was able to glue it back on.

With the outside of the plinth complete, work on the inside guts that offer brute strength. I glued a mitered three-sided frame inside the plinth to give it strength. I used 3"-wide boards that were scrap. Really, anything wider than 2" will be fine here.

Once you glue in the mitered frame, flip the plinth over and glue in 1" x 1" maple blocks in the corners. These glue blocks reinforce the corners of the plinth and carry the weight of the entire bookcase. When made properly, the maple blocks should extend ⅛" from the bottom of the plinth.

Moulding & Finishing

Trim all the dovetails and prepare the plinth, backs and book boxes for finishing. When that is done, place the lowest book box on the plinth and glue and nail a small moulding around the lowest

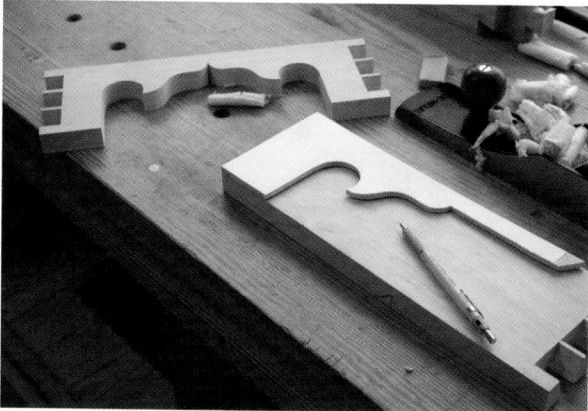

CLEAN THE CORNERS. I use a block plane to dress the long straight run on the front. But when it comes to the corners, a chisel plane is handy for getting right up against the scrollwork.

case. I use a small square ovolo profile here, which matches the period.

To finish the bookcases, I applied two coats of orange shellac, followed by one coat of dull-sheen lacquer. The versions at Monticello are dark brown.

After the finish was dry, I nailed on the backboards using clout nails then stacked the book boxes in place on top of the plinth. To keep the boxes from sliding around, I screwed each box to its neighbor using #8 x 1¼" wood screws. And to keep the bookcase from tipping forward should a toddler attempt to scale it, I attached the whole thing to the wall with an anti-tipping kit.

Then came the best part – loading the bookcase with my woodworking books. These book boxes added 24' linear feet of storage for my books, which have been piling up in my office.

But joy turned to defeat. I have more books than I thought. When loaded, this case holds only half my books. I need to build a second set.

Hmmm, perhaps Jefferson's book boxes were just nailed together.

TRACE, CUT, SHAPE. The plinth design is where you can alter the design to suit your house. Like Shaker stuff? Look at Shaker feet and draw something similar on your feet.

MITERS THAT WON'T SHOW. This will be covered by the lower case and moulding, so it doesn't have to look pretty. It just has to be strong.

GLUE BLOCKS. These maple blocks do almost all the work. They are ⅛" proud of the foot of the plinth and support all of the weight of the book boxes. They also strengthen each corner to protect them from swift kicks.

Line & Berry Chest of Drawers

BY GLEN D. HUEY

In southeastern Pennsylvania, just northwest of Philadelphia, is Chester County. It was one of the original three counties formed by William Penn in 1682, under a charter signed by King Charles II. In 1729, a large portion of the western county was split off to become Lancaster County, and in 1789, the southeastern townships closest to Philadelphia were organized as Delaware County. That left Chester County as we find it today.

Throughout the 1700s, Chester County furniture makers produced pieces with unique surface decoration, such as the line and berry inlay shown on this chest. Furniture makers of the period scribed inter-connected half-circles into the surface. The design was scratched using a compass, which is why the process is often referred to as "compass inlay." Sometimes, at the termination of those circles, small groupings of round

INLAY GETS NOTICED. This arresting, seemingly complex inlay is accomplished using a router and series of patterns.

berries completed the design. This decoration reached a popularity peak in the 1740s.

Where to Begin?

The striking feature on this chest is the inlay on the drawer fronts – but the chest, on its own, has attributes not often seen in furniture construction.

Begin by prepping the panels for the case sides and bottom. Notice that there is a difference in the widths of these components. The $5/16$" offset allows for the added double-bead moulding on the case sides and drawer blades, a common feature during the William & Mary period. That offset is at the front of the chest, so when transferring your dovetail layout, work with the rear edges of the panels aligned.

There is quite a bit of work needed on the case sides. Dovetails join the sides to the case bottom and single sockets hold the support rails, both front and back. From a pins-first point of view, set your marking gauge to $5/8$" and scribe the two case sides along the bottom edge. Why $5/8$" when the thickness of the bottom is $3/4$"? It's to hide the dovetail joints when the base pieces wrap the chest. Lay out and cut the pins in the case sides.

With the pins complete, mark the case bottom where the front edge of each side ends. Chuck a straight bit into your router, set the depth of cut for a shallow rabbet that leaves $5/8$" of material and clamp a fence even with the inside layout line. Now make the cut from that mark to the back edge of the bottom on both sides. The rabbets help register the sides to the bottom and provide a more accurate transfer of the pin layout. Cut the tails at both ends of the bottom and fit the joints. Tweak the fit as necessary.

After the dovetail joints are fit, lay out and cut four sockets at the top of the sides, along the front and rear edges. The tails for the support rails slip into the sockets from the top down. The front support rail fits $7/16$" behind the front edge of the sides; the rear support rail is set flush to the backboard rabbet, or $3/4$" in from the rear.

Slide-in Blades

The drawer blades attach to the case sides with sliding dovetails. Lay out the sockets along the front edge of each case side and on the back edge for the one rear blade, making sure that each location matches its counterpart in the opposite side – you want the blades to be level across the front of your chest. Slide a $3/4$" dovetail bit through a $3/4$"-outside-diameter guide bushing, then chuck these in your router. Position the platform to the left of the socket area as shown in the top right photo, then cut the $1/2$"-deep x $2\frac{1}{4}$"-long sockets. (Read more about this technique in the November 2008 issue of *Popular Woodworking*, #172.)

For the backboards, cut a $7/16$"-deep by $3/4$"-wide rabbet along the rear edge of the case sides. Now the work on the sides is complete.

Next, mill your drawer blades, front top rail, support rails, vertical divider and drawer runner stock to thickness and size. To get exact lengths, measure off of your assembled case. The blades'

DISAPPEARING JOINERY. Form the tails in the case bottom after you cut a rabbet $1/8$" below the inside surface. This allows the base moulding to cover the dovetail joint.

MORTISE BOTH ENDS OF LOWER DRAWER BLADES

STRONG CONNECTIONS. The top and rear blades are mortised for the housed and center runners. The lower drawer blades have a single mortise cut at each end to hold the runners in position.

lengths includes the two dovetails, as do the support rails. The top front rail runs from outside edge to outside edge.

Dry-fit the sides and bottom, position the support rails to the sockets cut in the sides, then transfer the layout onto the rails. Trim the ends then fit the rails to the case – be sure to mark front or rear. The drawer blades get the tail portion cut into both ends. Do this with the same dovetail router bit used to create the sockets. Install the bit in your router table and adjust the cut height first, then set the fence to cut the sliding tail to fill the socket. (It's best to test the setup using a scrap of the proper thickness of stock.) To complete the work on the blades, lay out and cut mortises for the runners.

A Runner to Ride On

The next step is to assemble the case. Apply glue to the bottom, sides and dovetails, and slip the joints together. For the front blades (leave the rear blade floating), apply a dollop of glue at the front of each dovetail slot then add a thin coat on the tail before slipping the blade into position. A light touch with a mallet should set the blade flush with the front edge of the case sides – that's a correct fit.

In the center of the front support rail, cut a through-mortise that's ¼" wide and 1¼" long (oriented front-to-back) for the center divider. Take a look at the photo above. The divider has a unique shape because the top notches around the front top rail as the tenon fits through the support rail. The divider is joined at the bottom with a ¼"-thick dovetail that slips into the top blade. That's a lot of work. If you want to simplify the process, a couple screws through the rail and blade make this quick.

With the center divider ready to install, add glue to the joinery, including the sockets in the case sides and the dovetails on the support rails, then slide it all together. The front top rail fits tight to and is glued to the support rail and wraps over the case sides, building out the ⁵⁄₁₆" to match the case bottom. The notches are cut at the table saw.

Cut tenons where needed on the ends of the runners. The housed and center

BEST ROUTER SETUP. A platform jig, ¾"-dovetail router bit and a ¾"-outside-diameter guide bushing are used to create the sliding dovetails that attach the drawer blades to the case. It's simple.

WANT TO MAKE IT EASY? All the joinery work on the center divider is hidden – covered by the mouldings or the top. To make quick work of the divider, attach the piece to the blade and support rail with screws.

tenons each get a ¼" tenon at the front and a 1" tenon at the back. Glue the tenons in position (the rear tenon is not glued, which allows for seasonal movement) square the runners, then nail them to the case side.

Keep Your Bevels Sharp

Except for the bottom and front top rail, the front face of the chest is covered with a double-beaded moulding. Use a traditional beading bit to form the twin beads. The setup for the beaded moulding requires accurate adjustment to get

BUILT OUT TO MATCH. Here you can see exactly how the front top rail fits with the support rail to bring the front edge equal with the case bottom. The notches at the ends of the rail are nibbled away at the table saw.

the beads evenly spaced without the second pass cutting into the first bead. Once set up, create the profile on a wide board that's milled to the proper thickness. Slice the moulding from the board then produce another set of mouldings until you have the pieces needed.

Use blue tape to hold the moulding pieces to the case sides then use a chisel to mark the exact location where the blades meet the sides. From those marks, draw lines along the back of the moulding at a 45° angle to show the waste area that's removed to accept the end of the blade mouldings.

Saw as much of the waste out as you can without working past the lines then pare exactly to the lines. To keep the

Supplies

Ball & Ball
ballandball.com or 610-363-7330

8 • A69 backplate with A72 drop on post
#A000-000, $26.47 each

5 • 1¾ x 1¾ Wm & Mary chased, cast escutcheon
#L61-002, $17.12 each

Prices correct at time of publication.

SET FOR CHANGE. The bottom drawer runs on the case bottom and the top bank of drawers rides on housed runners. The middle runners, to allow for seasonal changes, are attached to the case side with cut nails.

LEFT-HAND STOP. The magnetic stop set to the left of the material is used to precisely align the moulding profile with the saw blade. Push the stock tight to the auxiliary stop then pull the table saw fence tight to the stock before ripping.

edges square and the angle correct so the perpendicular moulding fit is tight, use a simple V-shaped guide block. Pare the V-shape until the chisel rides the guide block.

The bead mouldings that cover the blades have pointed ends to fit the V-shaped cutouts. Form the ends just as you did on the side mouldings. That's easy. The trick is to get an accurate cut length. It's best to cut it long then pare to a good fit. The center-divider moulding is cut square, to fit against the front top rail.

To attach all the mouldings, add a thin bead of glue to the back of each then secure the pieces to the case with blue tape. Add a few inconspicuous 23-gauge pins to help keep pieces from moving.

Simple & Solid Base

The base for this chest is as simple as it gets. Mill the pieces to thickness and size before adding your favorite profile along the top edge. Next, miter the pieces to length using the chest as your guide. The top edge of the base is flush with the top edge of the case bottom. After the pieces are fit, trace the cutout profile at each end of the three pieces and draw a line connecting the profiles.

The base pieces have a thin bead of glue along the top edge and are attached to the case using cut nails. To keep glue squeeze-out to a minimum, cut a shallow groove on the back face of the base approximately ¼" down from the top. Align the front piece to the chest then add a couple clamps to hold it in place and tight to the chest. Add glue along the front 6" of the base side, position that piece to the front piece and tack it in place with a 23-gauge pin. Work the second side, too.

Next, remove the front piece, add glue along the top edge and on the miters, then clamp it back in place. Pin the mitered corners to keep them aligned until the glue sets. For an authentic look, drill pilot holes and install cut nails in the base, with the nails set just below the surface.

To complete the base, slip the rear feet in position and reinforce the corners with glue blocks. The chest actually stands on the blocks, which extend slightly beyond the base. Glue blocks should also be installed along the base/bottom intersections behind the feet.

The top is attached to the chest with #8 x 1¼" wood screws through the support rails (screws in the rear rail should be in oversized holes) and two wooden clips per end that are evenly spaced between the rails. I cut the ¼" slots for the clips with a plate joiner; screws hold the clips in place.

The underhung moulding is made at a router table with the lower portion of a specialty moulding router bit (Rockler

ACCURACY IS IMPORTANT. A sharp chisel marks the beaded moulding exactly at the place the V-shape is to be cut.

BACK UP THAT CUT. The V-shaped notches that accepts the drawer blade bead moulding need to be perfectly cut, as do the mouldings. Use a backer with a 45° opening cut made at the table saw to pare them.

FORM THE FOOT. Use a 1¾" Forstner bit to clean out the rounded portion of each design that forms the spur. Then at your band saw, cut away the remaining waste.

WORK ON YOUR BENCH. Use scrap 8/4 to raise the chest off your bench and make fitting the base that much easier. One piece at each corner does the job.

91881). With a wide board stood on its edge, create two profiles then rip the mouldings at your table saw. The moulding is attached to the chest just as the base is – glue and square-head nails.

Patterns Make Repeating Easy

With the chest assembled, mill and size the drawer fronts to fit the openings – these are flush-fit drawers so keep the reveals at a minimum (¹⁄₁₆" or less). Depending on your preference, at this time either build the drawers or work on the inlay for the drawer fronts.

The drawers are built using 18th-century construction techniques – half-blind dovetails at the front and through-dovetails at the rear. The drawer backs are sized so the drawer bottoms slide under the backs. The bottoms are beveled to fit into ¼" grooves in the drawer sides and front – the tops of those grooves are cut ¾" above the edge. Cut a slot in the drawer bottoms even with the inside edge of the drawer back. Nails driven through the slot and into the drawer back secure the bottoms and allow for seasonal movement.

Patterns for the string grooves can be created from a design you already have in mind – or use the plans included here on page 111. To make your own patterns, create a design in a full-size drawing (Google SketchUp is great for this step). Next, select a guide bushing size (for this piece, I used a ³⁄₈"-outside-diameter bushing) and offset the lines to compensate for the bushing. Transfer your new lines to ¼" plywood then cut out the patterns. Plywood thicker than ¼" causes problems with the bit length when cutting the grooves.

For this project, three patterns were developed. The included patterns are sized for the top drawers. Because the drawers are graduated, make a second set of patterns (20 percent larger) for the lower three drawers.

Each of the inlay designs is created around a center point. That point is established using one of the top drawers. Find the exact center of the drawer front then measure from the edge of the drawer front to that center point. Each drawer inlay design, whether on the right or left of the drawer, is set to that measurement – all the designs line up vertically on the chest.

For the top drawer, draw vertical lines that are equally spaced 2⁵/₁₆" off the center point (the line spacing for the larger drawers is 2¹¹/₁₆"). Also draw a line horizontally as shown in the photo below.

Begin with the twin-bump-shaped pattern. Set the pattern square to the drawer front with the valley of the bumps set at the intersection of the horizontal centerline and one of the 2⁵/₁₆" lines. Point the bumps toward the drawer center.

With the guide bushing and a ¹/₁₆" straight bit chucked in the router, and the bit set to cut a strong ¹/₁₆" into the fronts, locate the bushing at the top end of the pattern, plunge the bit into the drawer front then rout the design. Stop when the bushing hits against the pattern's flat step, completing the pattern. Repeat the steps with the pattern set to the opposite lines, again facing the center.

The second pattern is the tulip design. Place this pattern squared to the drawer front with its top-to-bottom center aligned with the drawer front's centerline. The pattern is also aligned with the outer edge of the twin-bump routed line as shown in the bottom right photo on the opposite page. Begin with the bushing located at one of the corners. Plunge into the wood then rout through the tulip shape until the bushing nestles into the opposing corner.

The next two steps of string routing are the most difficult. To locate the wave pattern, you need to lay out a couple lines as shown in the top right photo below. The first line is squared off the drawer front and aligned with the ends of the tulip design. The next line toward the center is half the width of the guide bushing being used. It's used to set the wave pattern square to the drawer front and just at that inside line.

This time, fully plunge the router off the pattern then place the router bit to

PROPER LAYOUT. The design of the drawer fronts is dependent on getting your layout right. Space the lines off each drawer's center to keep the designs aligned.

KEEP IT STRAIGHT. The jigs used in this project are all held square to the drawer front. Proper placement is essential to the task.

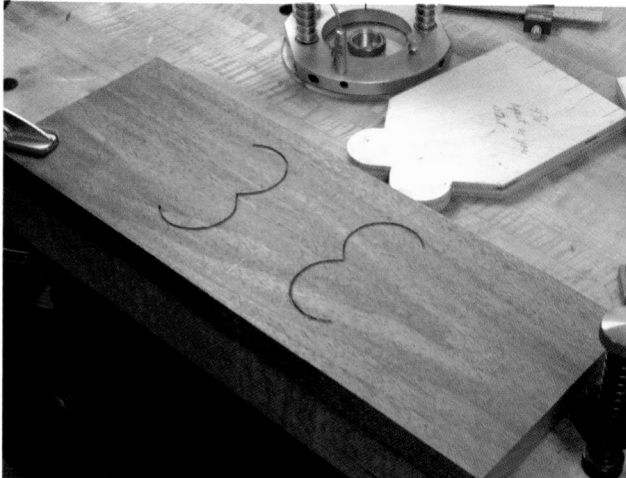

THAT'S STEP ONE. These are the first set of lines in the design. The depth should be a strong ¹/₁₆" for a secure fit that's easily trimmed after installation.

ACCURATE PLACEMENT. After the jig is properly placed, the two flat steps at the top of the tulip are where the router guide bushing begins and ends. The bushing snaps into the corner.

drop into the tulip line, right at the end. Hold the bit out of the wood and the bushing against your pattern as you start the router then allow the bit to settle into the tulip line. Rout to the center of the pattern then back out toward the second end of the tulip design. When you get to that second line, stop your movement and release the plunge on your router. As you repeat this process for each inlay design, you'll develop a feel and ear for it – you'll hear a different sound as you break into the second line. But on the first couple passes, watch the router bit as you move.

The last bit of pattern work is to reverse the wave pattern and cut in the pointed end. To locate the pattern, measure along the drawer centerline out from the valley of the wave line and place a mark at 1" for the top drawers and 1¼" for the other drawers. Again, the valley of the wave sits at the intersection. Routing the line is a repeat performance, but on a smaller scale.

The center grooves are cut with a circle-cutting setup. Drill an ⅛" hole at the center of the inlay design. Due to the diameter of the circle being so tight, I simply drilled a ⅛" hole in the router's base plate, set to cut from pattern to pattern. For the top drawers, the radius is $1\frac{11}{16}$" and on the other drawers the radius is $1\frac{15}{16}$". Rest the bit in one of the routed grooves, start the router and rotate it to cut the arced groove. Stop the cut as you reach the opposite string groove. Repeat the steps for the second arc.

Finally, String & Berries

There are straight grooves for inlay, too. The small section between the bumps and the tulip can be routed or you can use a regular screwdriver to punch the surface just deep enough for stringing. The other straight grooves are around the entire perimeter of each drawer. This line is routed using a fence attached to your router. Space the grooves ⅞" from the outside edge of the drawers.

Traditionally, string used in Chester County furniture was made of holly for its white appearance, but I have oodles of scrap maple lying around my shop. That's what I chose for my string. (You can also purchase string material.)

String inlay needs to be sized to fit your grooves. Mill a piece of scrap

STEP TWO. The completed tulip design faces away from the drawer center and is spaced just outside the bump design.

PLUNGE TO BEGIN. The tulip top string groove is the first of two grooves that require that you see the bit as you work – or develop a feel for when to stop at the line.

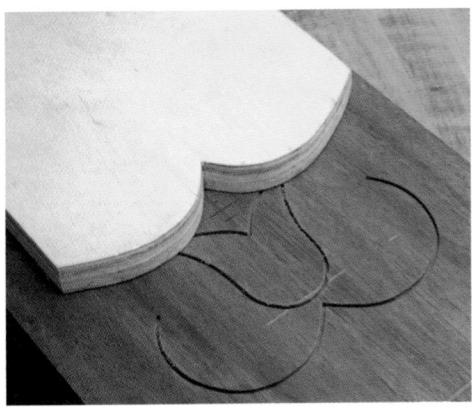

A SIMPLE REVERSAL. Flip the wave pattern then set the distance between the pattern and the previous groove at 1" for the two top drawers and 1¼" for the lower drawers.

IT'S ALL IN THE BASE PLATE. The arcs around the center of the design are cut using the router base plate as a circle-cutting jig. Place a dowel into the drawer front's centered hole, slip the router plate over the pin then cut the groove from bump to bump.

Working With Inlay Bits

A 1/16" router bit is used to create the grooves in the line and berry design found on Chester County furniture and elsewhere. Bits available through most suppliers have 1/4" shanks and the cutting length is a short 1/4" at most.

Two potential problems arise when using these bits in string inlay work. First, the cutting length is too short so as not to allow ample depth of cut for your stringing if you push through a guide bushing and beyond a plywood pattern, as we're doing with this project.

Second, the 1/4" shank, when extended enough to reach through the above-described scenario, requires that you use a larger guide bushing than the 3/8" bushing used for the chest – the inside diameter of the bushing is only slightly larger than the shank diameter, so without spot-on setup, the bit has the potential to rub the bushing. What to do?

The first and most simple fix is to use a larger-diameter guide bushing.

Working with a larger-diameter bushing reduces the crispness of the design, but allows the bit's shank to easily pass through the guide bushing as the router bit tip reaches your drawer front.

You can also use thin pattern material. With less thickness to pass by, your bit doesn't have to extend as far to cut the grooves. (Remember, it's OK to shorten the length of the guide bushing to make everything work.)

Another option is to use a 1/8"-diameter router bit in conjunction with a collet reducer. This setup (as shown in the photo) allows you to extend the collet reducer beyond the router's collet and if you pull the 1/8" router bit out of the reducer to its fullest extent, the bit's reach is enough to create the grooves without adjustments to either the bushing or your pattern.

One source for the 1/16" straight bit is inlaybandings.com; collet reducers can be found at IMService (cadcam cadcam.com).

STRETCHING THE POINT. Collet reducers, chucked into regular collets, can help to lengthen a router bit's reach.

HOT PIPES. The heat from the torched galvanized pipe steams the water and dries the string at the shape needed to fit into the grooves. It's always good to have pipes of various sizes on hand.

Heat the pipe until it's hot but not scorching hot – a couple test pieces should clue you to what temperature is best. Lightly wet the string then, using a backer strip such as a piece of pallet banding, bend the string around the heated pipe.

Fit the string to the grooves and don't sweat the areas where the string ends. Those spots get berries to cover the raw ends. The place to work meticulously is where two pieces of string meet. The tighter the fit, the nicer the look. However, as with dovetails, a few imperfections says "handmade."

A few small dabs of glue along the groove keep the string in place. As you tap in the string, the glue chases around the groove. Wipe off any excess when all the string is placed.

The berries are where you become the artist. On the original, each berry cluster – most likely made from red and white cedar – was set with the two berries that touched the vine perfectly aligned with the length of the drawers.

TAKE YOUR TIME. With the stringing bent to closely match the grooves, begin at one end of the run then work to the opposite end. String left in the groove tends to hold its shape better. As you glue the pieces in place, work again from end to end of the groove.

BERRY NICE. The placement of the berries is left to your discretion. I think it's best to have the berries overlap and appear like clusters of grapes on the vine.

A third berry was placed directly at the center while just touching the other two berries. The symmetrical look was very regimented.

My take is to lighten up. I randomly located the berries that touched the vine, and made sure the two lapped, as did the third when it was installed. To do this, you have to install a single berry at a time. Drill an ⅛"-deep x ⅜"-diameter hole at each berry location.

The berries themselves are face-grain plugs, either shop-made or store-bought. Dab glue in the hole then tap in the berry. Use a chisel to flush the berry to the drawer front prior to drilling and installing the second and third berries. I used two cherry berries and a single maple berry for each of my clusters. The choice is yours.

At the Finish Line

With the drawers and drawer front inlay complete, the only woodworking left is the chest back. The backboards run from side to side and fit one another with a tongue-and-groove joint. Each board is nailed with a single nail at each end; the top board has two nails per end.

As for the finish on the chest, stain or dye would reduce the contrast of the string against the walnut background. So, to achieve a deeper color in the walnut while highlighting the string,

IT'S A PERFECT MATCH. The face-grain plugs that become berries are fit into holes drilled with a ⅜" drill bit. Because of the flat-grain to flat-grain gluing surfaces, the berries will stay put.

apply a coat of boiled linseed oil. Follow that with a layer of clear shellac once the oil is dry. From there, I sanded the clear shellac then added multiple layers of amber shellac – the amber color warms the walnut, but also colors the other woods – sanding between coats to smooth the walnut grain. Once I achieved the color I wanted, I returned to clear shellac in order to build a smoothed surface. I thoroughly sanded the shellac before spraying a layer of dull-rubbed-effect pre-catalyzed lacquer to dull and further protect the surface.

After the hardware is added to the drawers (I ordered post-and-nut equipped pulls instead of snipe pins), the chest is ready for use. Mine is going into my bedroom, but you might just want this piece in a high-visibility area. It commands attention.

Classic Six-Legged Huntboard

BY GLEN HUEY

My dad has been making this six-legged huntboard for a number of years now, and it's always sold well at the furniture shows we attend. One year he built one for a woman who requested glass knobs on the piece. As most business people know, the customer is always right. Though we weren't sure the glass knobs were right for this piece, we took that huntboard with us to a show to solicit sales anyway. Our first sale that day was for the huntboard. But there was one request: "Could you put some different handles on it?" I'm happy to present here a classic six-legged huntboard with the handles we usually put on the piece.

Quick Tapers for the Legs

The joinery on the huntboard is predominantly mortise and tenon, with all the rails and panels attached to the legs with tenons. The inner partitions are dadoed into the solid back and tenoned into the center legs. Start construction by cutting the legs to size according to the Schedule of Materials.

Each leg is tapered to 1" at the floor, starting 16" down from the top of the

leg. The four corner legs are tapered on the two inside edges, but just to make it so you can't use one tapering jig setup (and because it's historically correct) the two middle legs are tapered on the back and both sides. I use a simple tapering jig on my table saw for the four corner legs. Rather than make a new jig for the middle legs, I mark their tapers, cut them $\frac{1}{16}$" proud on the band saw, then run them over the jointer to clean up the cut.

Many Many Mortises

With the legs tapered, take a couple of minutes to glue up panels for the back, ends and partitions. Set them aside to dry. Next, mark each leg for mortises. Where the panels meet the legs there are three $\frac{1}{4}$" x 3" x 1$\frac{1}{4}$"-long mortises, evenly spaced along the top 15$\frac{1}{2}$" of the leg and set so the ends will be flush to the outside face of the outer legs and the partitions flush to the inside edge of the two interior legs. Where the dividers and rails meet the legs, use $\frac{1}{4}$" x $\frac{1}{2}$" x 1"-long mortises, again orienting the mortises to keep the rails and legs flush to the outside.

With all the mortises cut, unclamp your panels and trim them to final size. Then mark the tenon locations to match your mortises, and go ahead and form the tenons. If you use your table saw for this step, you'll notice that the back is a little difficult to mount in your tenoning jig without taking out a section of your ceiling. I'd recommend setting your rip fence for the 1$\frac{1}{4}$" length of the tenon (don't forget to include the thick-

My tapering jig is simply a couple of pieces of $\frac{3}{4}$" pine screwed to a $\frac{1}{2}$" piece of Baltic birch. It is built to cut one particular taper, in this case the taper for a huntboard leg, and is inexpensive enough to be one of many tapering jigs I use. Unlike some tapering jigs, the leg is carried on the $\frac{1}{2}$" piece, supporting the leg from bottom and side.

ness of your blade), set the blade height to $\frac{1}{4}$" and run the back flat against the table using the miter gauge (or a sled) to support the panel's back edge. Nibble away the rest of the tenon length with repeated saw passes. The rest can be cut with a hand saw.

If you haven't noticed, I'm a fan of solid wood — even on my backs, partitions and bottoms. Along with that

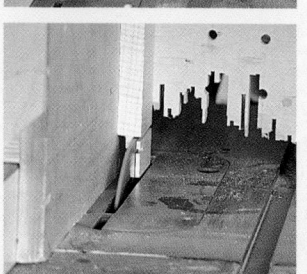

Haunched Tenon Doors

The joinery used in the doors is a little complicated when you look at it, but makes so much sense that once you've done a set, you'll use this method without question.

1. With the rails cut to size, the first step is to define the shoulders of the tenon. With your rip fence set to cut $1\frac{1}{4}$" (don't forget the blade's thickness), cut $\frac{1}{4}$" deep on the two wide faces for the rails, and on one edge of the rail. On the final edge, reset the fence to cut 1" and make the cut. This is the haunched part of the joint and will be the outside edge of the door.

2. The next step is to use a tenoning jig (you can see mine has seen a little bit of use) to cut the cheeks of the tenons.

3. The third step is to reset the fence to define the width of the tenon. First cut the full-depth side of the tenon, then reset the blade height and cut the haunched side of the tenon (shown).

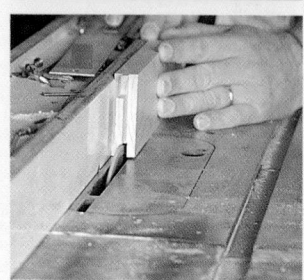

4. The last step is to run the groove for the door panel. This same groove process works for the panels in the door section bottoms. When running a centered groove like this, I first make a cut approximately in the center of the piece. Then I adjust the fence and, with a scrap piece, test my cut. By running first one face against the fence, then flipping it and running the other, I am guaranteed the $\frac{1}{4}$" x $\frac{1}{4}$ groove is centered on the door piece.

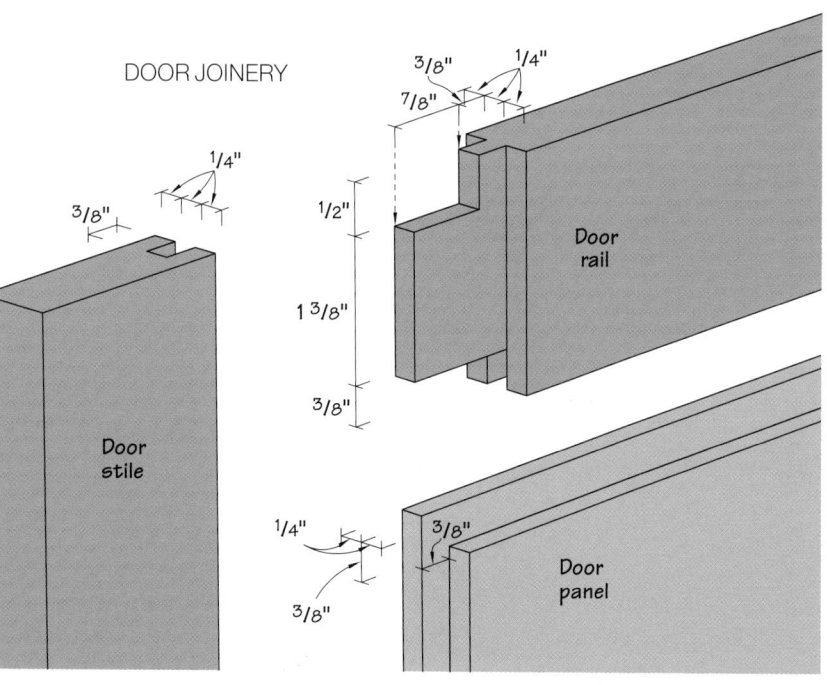

When the stiles and rails are assembled, the haunch left on the tenon hides the groove on the stiles, making it unnecessary to make stopped grooves.

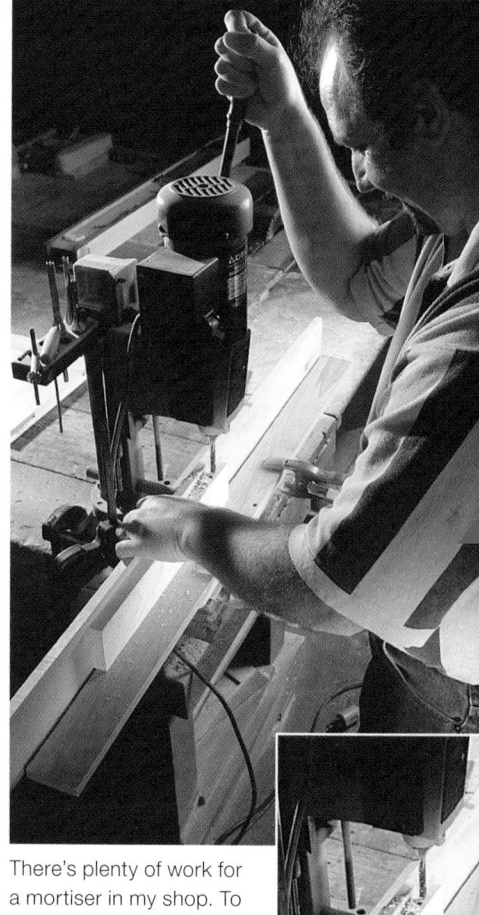

There's plenty of work for a mortiser in my shop. To avoid taxing (or damaging) the mortising chisel, make your first two cuts one at either end of the mortise. Then skip a chisel-width space moving toward the center of the mortise, and come back to clear the space you skipped. This keeps the chisel from being bent.

DOOR JOINERY

appreciation of solid wood comes an appreciation of what solid wood can do when it moves with the seasons. Because of this, trim the width of your tenons on the panels as much as $\frac{1}{8}$" per tenon. This should allow room for wood movement. In addition, when you get to the assembly stage, it's prudent to glue primarily the center of the panel, which will allow the ends to expand.

While you're milling the back, set your saw to cut two $\frac{1}{4}$" x $\frac{3}{4}$"-wide dadoes in the back to accept the ends of the partitions. Other necessary pre-assembly joinery includes mortises in the back of the drawer dividers for the drawer runners. Mark and cut the two $\frac{1}{4}$" x 1" x $\frac{3}{8}$"-deep mortises in each drawer divider.

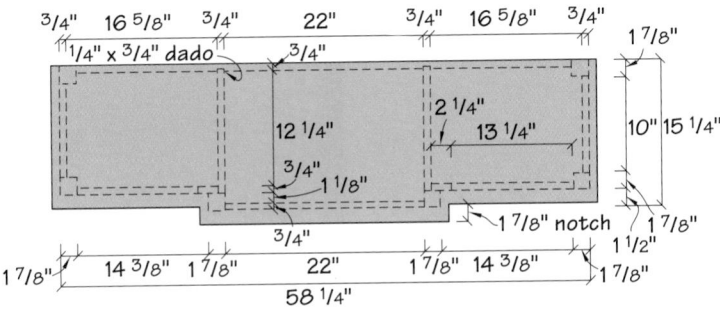

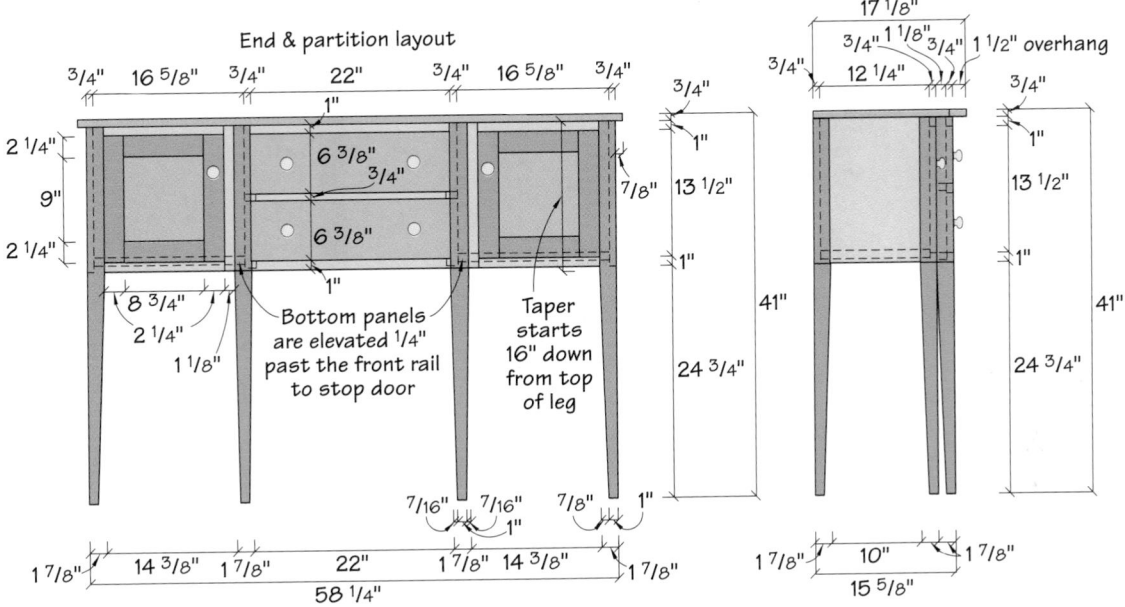

End & partition layout

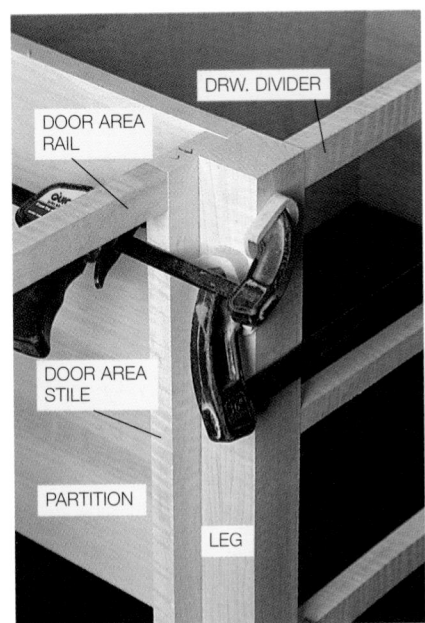

The most complicated joinery location on the piece. Shown here is the intersection of the left, middle leg, with the partition, top drawer divider, and left door section stile and top rail. Once you get a good look, you can see it's simple.

How Many Clamps Do You Have?

You're now ready to assemble the case. You're going to need at least four clamps; more if you want a quick assembly. Start by attaching the three drawer dividers between the two center legs. Next attach the partitions between the drawer face assembly and the back piece. Clamp this up and set it aside to dry. If you own enough clamps to continue, glue up the two end panels between the front and rear corner legs. The final step is to glue the end assemblies to the back piece, and to attach the door area rails to the mortises in the legs, and the door area stiles. Screw the stiles in place to the back of the middle legs. Pre-drill a clearance hole and pilot drill the leg to avoid splitting.

Doors and Drawers

With the case assembled, turn to making up some frame-and-panel pieces — the doors and the bottoms of the door sections. I used a half-lapped frame and panel assembly for the bottoms in the door sections. The panel is rabbeted and rests in a $\frac{3}{8}$" x $\frac{3}{8}$" groove in the rails and stiles. By using a frame-and-panel bottom, I again help alleviate any problems caused by wood movement, while still using solid wood throughout the piece.

The doors are frame-and-panel as well, but are assembled with haunched mortise-and-tenon joinery, again with a rabbeted panel, with the recessed face showing to the outside of the cabinet. For both the bottoms and the doors, glue only the rail and stile joints, allowing the panels to float in the grooves.

While the doors and bottom panels dry, move back to the case and remove the clamps. To add strength and to enhance the appearance of the piece, I peg each of the mortise-and-tenon joints with squared oak pegs. Sharpening one end of the peg in a pencil sharpener

allows me to start the peg in a round hole and end up with a visible square peg. After the joints are pegged, cut them flush and give the entire case exterior a thorough sanding.

When the doors are dry, use the same pegging technique, then sand the doors and bottom panels.

Next make the two drawers. They are constructed using half-blind dovetails on the front and through-dovetails at the back. The bottoms are solid panels raised on the table saw to fit into 1/4"-wide x 1/4"-deep grooves in the drawer sides, fronts and backs. The groove is cut 1/2" up from the bottom of each piece. If

When the door section bottoms are installed they must be notched to fit around the legs. They're attached using 3/4" x 3/4" cleats attached to the partition and end. Position the cleats so the bottom panel is proud of the door area rail. This allows it to act as a door stop. Screw the cleats in place. Then peg the bottom in place through the ends and partition.

Classic Six-Legged Huntboard

	NO.	LETTER	ITEM	DIMENSIONS (INCHES) T	W	L	DIMENSIONS (MILLIMETERS) T	W	L	MATERIAL	COMMENTS
CASE											
❏	1	A	Top	3/4	17 1/8	60	19	435	1524	P	
❏	6	B	Legs	1 7/8	1 7/8	40 1/4	47	47	1022	P	
❏	2	C	Ends	3/4	15 1/2	12 1/2	19	394	318	P	1 1/4" TBE
❏	2	D	Partitions	3/4	15 1/2	14 1/2	19	394	369	S	1 1/4" TOE
❏	1	E	Back	3/4	15 1/2	57	19	394	1448	P	1 1/4" TBE
❏	2	F	Drw. dividers	3/4	1	24	19	25	610	P	1" TBE
❏	1	G	Center divider	3/4	3/4	24	19	19	610	P	1" TBE
❏	4	H	Drwr runners	3/4	1 1/4	14 3/8	19	32	366	S	3/8" TOE
❏	2	I	Door area stiles	3/4	2 1/4	15 1/2	19	57	394	P	1 1/8" Exposed
❏	4	J	Door area rails	3/4	1	15 1/4	19	25	387	P	1" TBE
DOOR AND DRAWER PARTS											
❏	4	K	Door stiles	3/4	2 1/4	13 1/2	19	57	343	P	
❏	4	L	Door rails	3/4	2 1/4	11 1/4	19	57	285	P	1 1/4" TBE
❏	2	M	Door panels	1/2	9 3/8	9 5/8	13	239	245	P	3/8" TAS
❏	4	N	Drw. sides	1/2	6 1/8	13 1/2	13	155	343	S	
❏	2	O	Drw. backs	1/2	5 3/8	22	13	137	559	S	
❏	2	P	Drw. fronts	7/8	6 3/8	22	22	162	559	P	
❏	2	Q	Drw. bottoms	5/8	13 3/4	21 1/2	16	349	546	S	
DOOR SECTION BOTTOMS											
❏	4	R	Stiles	7/8	3	16 5/8	22	76	559	S	1/2 lap BE
❏	4	S	Rails	7/8	3	12 1/4	22	76	559	S	1/2 lap BE
❏	2	T	Panels	7/8	6 7/8	11 3/8	22	174	559	S	3/8" TAS
❏	4	U	Cleats	3/4	3/4	12	19	19	305	S	

TOE=tenons one end, TBE=tenons both ends, TAS=tenons all sides • P=maple, S=poplar

The door section bottom is a half-lapped frame and panel. Seen from the ends, the two frame pieces show the center groove for the panel, and the half-lap cut. Seen below the pieces is the assembled frame.

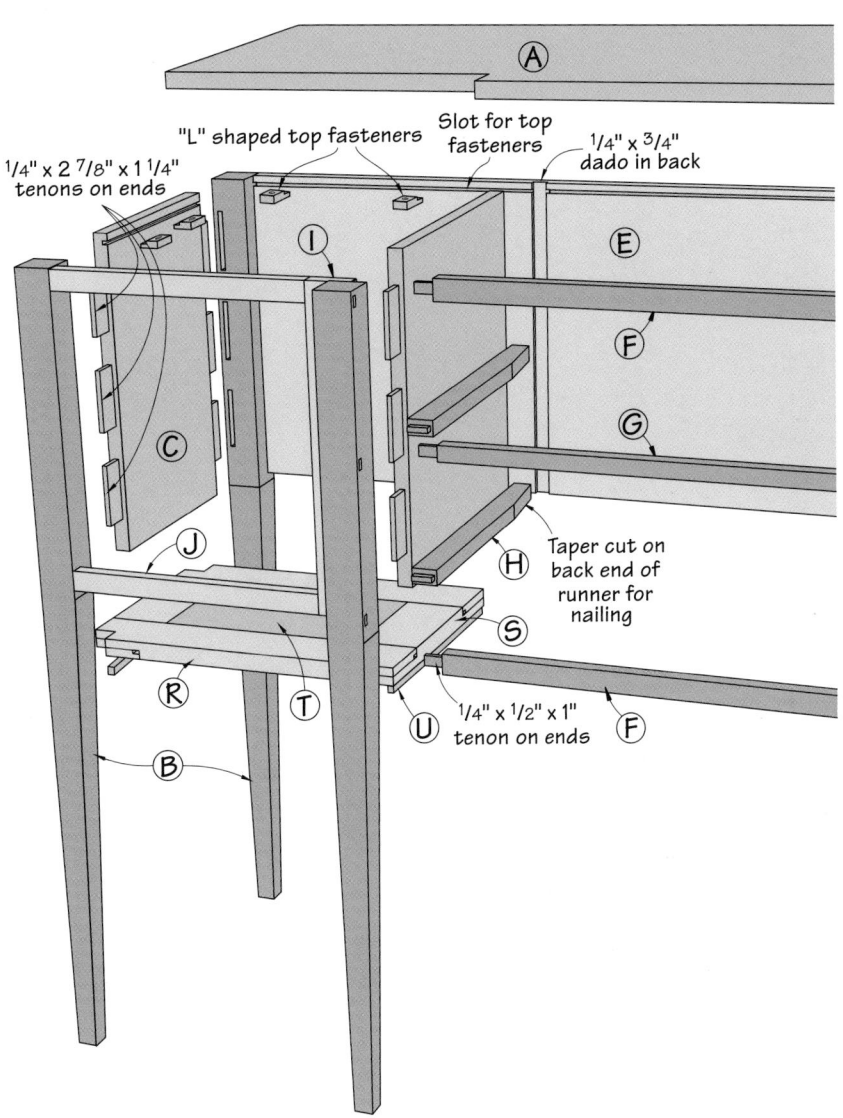

"L" shaped top fasteners

Slot for top fasteners

¼" x 2 ⅞" x 1 ¼" tenons on ends

¼" x ¾" dado in back

Taper cut on back end of runner for nailing

¼" x ½" x 1" tenon on ends

Happy that I got everything glued up on the case by myself, I'm ready to mount the drawer runners on the inside of the center drawer section.

you do this on your table saw, make sure the groove is aligned properly with the dovetails to hide the groove at the joints.

The drawers ride on runners attached to the inside surface of the center partitions. Each runner has a tenon on one end that fits into the mortises cut earlier in the back of the middle and lower drawer divider. I taper the back end of each runner to make it easier to nail the back end in place to the partition, once the proper alignment is achieved.

Across the Finish Line

The last piece is the top itself. Glue up the pieces necessary, leaving them slightly oversized until dry, then cut the top to finished size. To attach the top to the case, I use "L"-shaped fasteners that I make myself. One end of the fastener is screwed to the underside of the top, and the other fits into slots cut on the inner surface of the case with a router and spline cutter. Don't push the tongue of the fastener all the way into the groove to allow for wood movement in the top from front to back. The front edge of the top is attached by screws run up through the top rails in the door and drawer sections.

Before finishing, attach the hardware for the doors, mortising the doors to accommodate the hinges. Test the doors and trim to fit if necessary.

The finish itself is one I use on all my pieces. I start with a water-based aniline dye. I used Moser's Early American Cherry (Woodworker's Supply, 800-645-9292, item #W14304, $11.70) on the piece shown here. Once the dye is dry, lightly sand the entire piece to remove any raised grain, then spray the piece with sanding sealer and five coats of lacquer.

The hardware that I like for this piece is simple brass (unless someone wants glass.) I used two H-97L 1¼" knobs for the doors and four K-12 1¼" knobs for the drawers. All are available from Horton Brass (800- 754-9127). Of course, if you prefer a nice glass knob, there's nothing wrong with that. The customer is always right.

Contemporary Shelves

BY JIM STUARD

It's rare that bookshelves look as interesting as the objects you display on them. After all, how much can you decorate the edges of your shelves and sides? This unit is unusual because the shelves and sides are beefier than you would normally see, and the two bevel cuts on the front edges give these shelves nice visual interest.

Best of all, perhaps, is that this piece is simple and quick to build.

Dividers and Shelves

Start by cutting out the sides and shelves. The $1\frac{1}{2}$"-thick sides are made by gluing two pieces of $\frac{3}{4}$"-thick plywood together. The $1\frac{1}{4}$"-thick shelves are made by gluing $\frac{3}{4}$"-thick plywood to a $\frac{1}{2}$"-thick piece. Note that the finished sides have a $\frac{3}{4}$" x $\frac{1}{4}$" rabbet for the back that's formed by gluing a narrower piece to a wider one. The adjustable and fixed shelves in the side openings are all the same width. The center shelves are $\frac{1}{4}$" wider to account for the lack of a back.

To cut the sides, crosscut a whole sheet of plywood to the length of the sides first, then rip them to width (11" and $11\frac{1}{4}$"). Cut the sides a little wide ($\frac{1}{16}$"), initially, to give yourself a little room to saw off a square straight edge. This will give you a clean edge for attaching a piece of maple later. Now nail and glue the dividers together, remembering to offset the back edge for the rabbet. Place your nails so the shelves will hide them.

Here's an easy way to cut the shelves. Rip them to width from a full piece of plywood, then nail and glue up a length

of shelving. Then crosscut the shelves to length from the long pieces. You can get five 16" shelves out of a 96" rip. For even less work, cut the shelves to length after attaching the edging.

Edges and Angles

The edges for the bookshelves are solid maple. Because the thickness of $\frac{3}{4}$" and $\frac{1}{2}$" plywood is considered "nominal," you will end up with finished thicknesses about $\frac{1}{16}$" less. Rip your edging stock a little wide and attach it with biscuits and glue. With a flush-cut bearing bit in a router, trim the edging flush to the sides and shelves, then clean up your work with a plane or scraper.

The last step is to bevel the edging. The photo on the left-hand side of page 123 shows how I did this on the table saw. Remember that the setup must change for the different width pieces.

Making it a Stand-Up Unit

The next step is to mill stopped grooves in the topmost and bottommost shelves to accept the tapered sliding connectors that attach the sides together. The grooves in the ends of the shelves are $\frac{3}{4}$" wide by approximately $\frac{3}{8}$" deep, and milled with a dado set on the table saw. It helps to make a practice joint because the depth of the groove is critical to a snug fit using this style of connector.

After cutting the slots in the shelves, lay out and mount the small part of the tapered connector to the side. The large connector will mount to the shelf groove

FACE-GLUE THE PARTS. Once you've got your parts cut to size, glue and nail them together leaving the rabbet at the back. Set and putty the nails, then rip the dividers to their final width.

with the wide end towards the shelf front. Do a test fit on the shelves. The shelves in the side units should be flush to the rabbet in the back edge of the sides. The center shelves should be flush with the back.

The next step is to cut the stopped grooves in the rest of the shelves for the hidden wire shelf supports. If your blade is too narrow, take two cuts to get the ⅛" groove necessary to slide the shelf onto the wire supports. Some drill and chisel work will be necessary to lengthen the kerf to accept the entire 9¾" length of the shelf wire. This requires drilling and chiselling into the end of the front edge. Lay out and drill the locations for the wire supports in the side and center

sections so the shelf heights will match across the bookcase.

Now it's time for all the parts come together. Begin by assembling the two outside units of the bookcase. Tip them onto their backs and attach the aprons to the bottom shelf using cleats and screws. Next attach the side units together forming the center section. The best way to do this is to assemble with the front facing up. Use a handscrew clamp to hold up the sides while you're assembling. The apron on the center bottom can be screwed onto the shelf and braced with corner blocks prior to assembly. Push the lower shelf into place and mark the location of the apron, also called a "kick"

or a base. Then remove the shelf and add two stop blocks to the sides to support the center apron from behind.

When you're happy with the fit of the parts, disassemble the bookcase and finish. I applied a coat of light stain to give the maple an aged appearance. (I used about two ounces of linseed oil and colored it with Olympic stains, one-half Early American #41552, and one-half Red Oak #41567. ¼ teaspoon of each.) Wipe on an even coat of oil. Wipe off the excess and let it dry for 24 hours. The next day, lightly sand the surfaces and clean them with a tack rag. Finish with two or three coats of a clear finish.

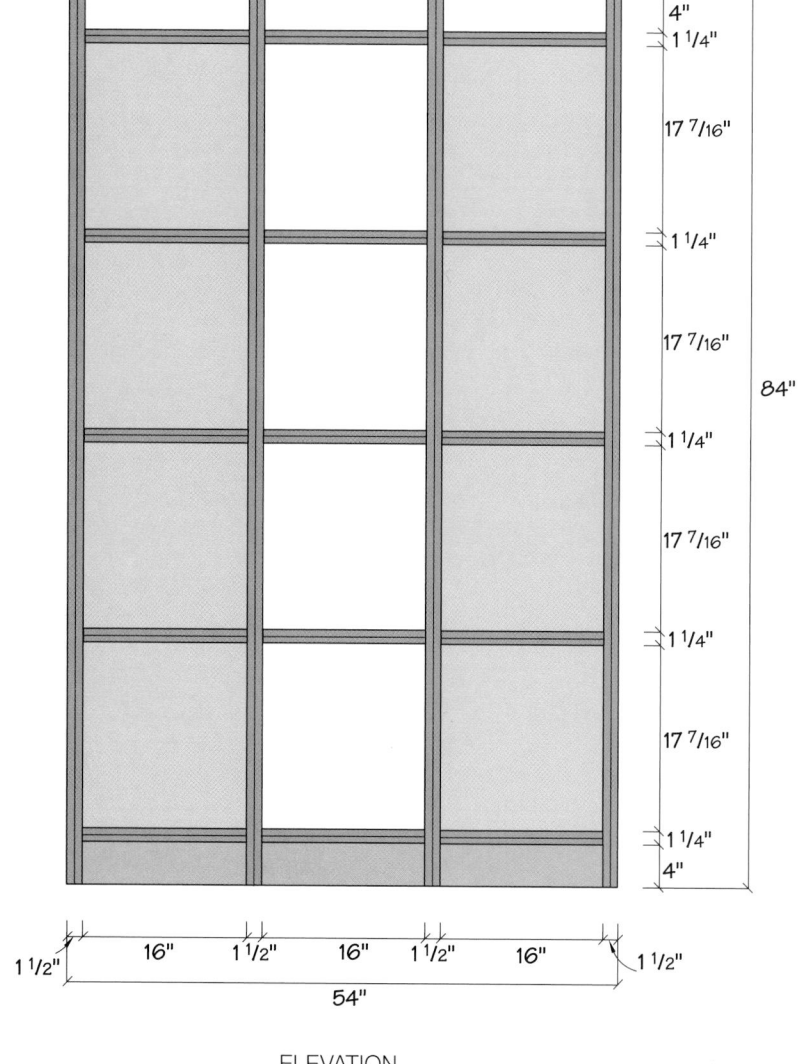

ELEVATION

PROFILE

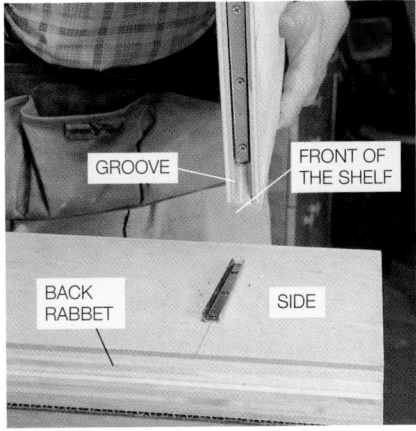

PROFILE. The bevels on the edges are basically a "V" shape on the entire edge. See the diagram at right for the details and cutting angles. Clean up your saw marks with a plane.

MOUNT KNOCKDOWN HARDWARE. Use a dado stack to cut a ¾" x ⅜" groove from the joint where the edge attaches to the shelf to the back of the shelf. The knockdown hardware is mounted in about the middle of the shelf. It pulls together pretty tightly, so you might want to sand any bumps or ridges off the ends of the shelves to keep from scratching the sides.

MAGIC WIRE. After cutting the ⅛" grooves in the shelf sides, assemble the case. Tap the wire shelf supports in and slide the loose shelves in place.

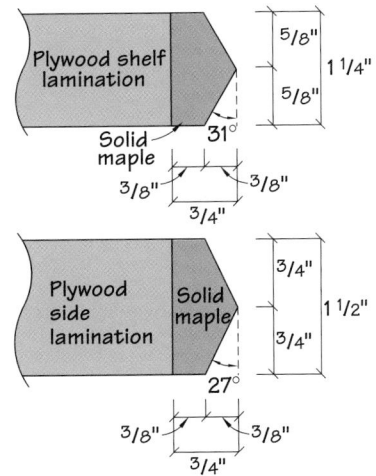

DETAIL OF BEVEL PROFILES

Contemporary Shelves

	NO.	ITEM	DIMENSIONS (INCHES)			DIMENSIONS (MILLIMETERS)			MATERIAL	COMMENTS
			T	W	L	T	W	L		
❑	4	Sides	¾	11¼	84	19	285	2134	Plywood	
❑	4	Sides	¾	11	84	19	279	2134	Plywood	
❑	10	Outr. shelf tops	¾	10⅛	16	19	257	406	Plywood	
❑	10	Outr. shelf bottoms	½	10⅛	16	13	257	406	Plywood	
❑	5	Cntr. shelf tops	¾	10⅜	16	19	264	406	Plywood	
❑	5	Cntr. shelf bottoms	½	10⅜	16	13	264	406	Plywood	
❑	2	Backs	¼	17½	76	6	445	1930	Plywood	
❑	3	Aprons	¾	4	16	19	102	406	Plywood	
❑	4	Side edging	¾	1½	84	19	38	2134	Maple	
❑	15	Shelf edging	¾	1¼	16	19	32	406	Maple	

Supplies: Woodworkers' Supply (800-645-9292), 12 6" taper connectors, # 928273 $4.95/pkg. of four. 18 wire shelf supports, # 826028, $1.45 apiece for 10+.

Frame & Panel Dresser

BY JIM STUARD

Stylistically, this dresser is a bit of a chameleon. It tends to take on the look of the environment you put it in. Dress it up or dress it down, it will work in either a country or city setting. Even if you don't plan to build this piece, read on to learn how to build a case piece with web frames, a sturdy way to build furniture with drawers.

I built this project using yew, a beautiful wood with pin knots that add character. It's dense, strong, tight-grained and finishes spectacularly. That said, it will be tough to find if you don't live in the Pacific Northwest. Because you're unlikely to find yew at a traditional lumberyard, you might want to use alder or cherry instead. And if you do find yew for sale, bring your moisture meter to ensure it has been dried properly.

Begin construction by cutting out the parts according to the Schedule of Materials. Glue up a top and set it aside. If you're using yew, it would be wise to make the top from three or four boards to reduce warping.

End Assemblies

The next step is to make the legs. While the legs finish out at $1\frac{1}{2}$" square, they need to start out close to 2" square to accommodate the curved foot. Using $\frac{8}{4}$ lumber should yield 2" x 2" stock for the legs. If not, don't worry, a little smaller than that is OK. Follow the photo and caption at right to first shape the foot on each leg and pare the leg to $1\frac{1}{2}$" square.

Next, rout $\frac{1}{4}$" x $\frac{1}{2}$" rabbets in the back inside corners of the legs to receive the back. With that step complete, lay

Make full-size patterns of the leg profiles in the diagram. Lay out the pattern on the leg ends. Use a table saw to cut the straight sections of the legs to $1\frac{1}{2}$" square. Use a hand saw to cut off the waste and finish the cuts on a band saw. Clean up the curved feet with a spokeshave and scraper.

out the stopped-groove and dowel locations for the side rails and panels according to the diagram. The grooves are made with a router, and they are a little deeper than required to let the panel float in the frames created by rails and legs. The dowel locations (two per rail) are directly in the center-line of the rails.

The easiest way to make the rails for the sides is to run out longer rail lengths, then cut the $\frac{1}{4}$" x $\frac{1}{4}$" panel groove according to the diagrams. The top and bottom rails only get a groove on one side of the rail, so make one length for the top and bottom rails, and another length for the center rails with two grooves. Before cutting the rails to length, glue your drawer guide stock to the rail stock. Then cut this assembly to consistent lengths according to the schedule. The rails are positioned flush to the inside of the legs, so lay out the dowel locations accordingly and begin drilling the $\frac{1}{4}$" dowel holes into the rail

ends and the legs. To run the grooves, set up a $\frac{1}{4}$" mortising bit in a plunge router. Using a fence on your router, plunge rout the $\frac{1}{4}$" x $\frac{1}{4}$" grooves in the legs, between the dowel locations.

To form the panels, first cut them to size, then simply rout the edge profile on a router table. I used a $\frac{1}{4}$" cove bit, running the panels up on edge and taking off just enough material to leave a $\frac{1}{4}$" lip that fits into the grooves in the legs and rails. Incidentally, the drawer fronts are routed in the same manner, so don't change the setup yet. I found that a curved-edge scraper works well for cleaning up the profile.

You're now ready to glue up the two ends. Make sure that the inside of the rails and drawer guides are flush with the inside face of the legs. This makes for tighter joints when the web frames are attached.

Web Frames

The web frames pull the entire carcase together and also serve as drawer runners. They're attached between the two end panels using screws run into pocket holes on the underside of the web frames.

To build the web frames, attach the front and back rails to the web ends and center support using biscuits.

First cut the web frame pieces to size. Then drill three pocket holes into each frame end. These accommodate screws to attach the frames to the panel ends.

It's important for the web frames to be square, or the whole carcase assembly will go badly. Try this simple trick. Make the front and back rails $\frac{1}{8}$" long. After

What You Should Know About Yew

Yew (Taxus brevifolia) is also called Pacific yew or Western yew and grows all the way from southeastern Alaska down to central California, according to Woods of the World. It's commonly used to make bows, furniture, musical instruments, paddles and in turning.

Yew has a close grain that varies from straight to irregular. The heartwood is bright orange after it's cut, and the wood polishes nicely. Avoid using oil finishes on yew because oil is reported to turn the wood a chocolate tan, instead of the deep orange achieved with film finishes, according to Woods of the World.

Yew takes a screw well, but it tends to split when nailed. The wood is weather-resistant and can be used in outdoor projects that are left unfinished.

Sawdust causes nose irritation and swollen hands in some woodworkers. Most parts of the tree are poisonous, including the seeds and foliage. Ingestion can result in death.

European yew (Taxus baccata) grows in Europe, north Africa and the Himalayas. It was used for centuries by the bowmen of England. Its veneer is prized for paneling, cabinetwork and marquetry.

Now you're ready to dry-assemble an end panel. After checking the fit of the panels, do it all over again with glue. Make sure to check the assembly for square after it's clamped together.

assembly, the web frame can be squared-over and then cut to length by crosscutting on the table saw. This ensures consistent widths and squareness and won't affect assembly.

Carcase Assembly

With the web frames glued up and the end panels ready to go, you're ready for assembly of the carcase. Mark the locations of the web frames on the end assemblies as shown on the diagrams. Then follow the photos on the next page to glue and screw the carcase together. Set the carcase upright and check for square. Any adjustments can be made by placing a clamp across the carcase at an angle that will pull it square. When the carcase is dry, clean up any glue that may have collected in the corners next to the drawer guides and tack in the back to hold everything square.

The Top

After cutting the top to size, radius the front corners with a ½" roundover bit. With a ¼" cove bit, rout a ¼" x ¼" cove in the top edge, on the ends and front.

When you attach the top, you'll see that the web frames don't allow enough room to get at the screws easily. So turn the carcase over and drill three ½" clearance holes each in web end and center piece of the second web frame down from the top. You'll only be able to drill your clearance hole at an angle, but that's OK because the hole is used only to get at the screws that attach the top to the web frame.

I used a couple four-way screwdrivers to run the screws in. The trick is to remove the barrel from one screwdriver and attach it to the bit from the first, making a extra-long screwdriver. Use this "super" driver to mark a point on the top

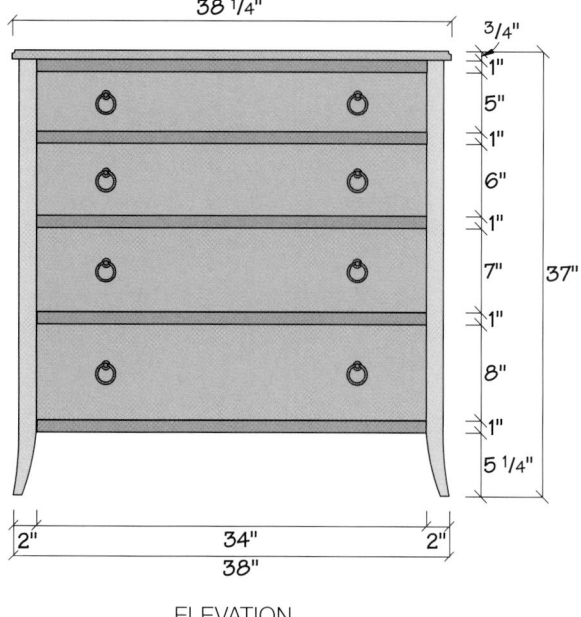

ELEVATION

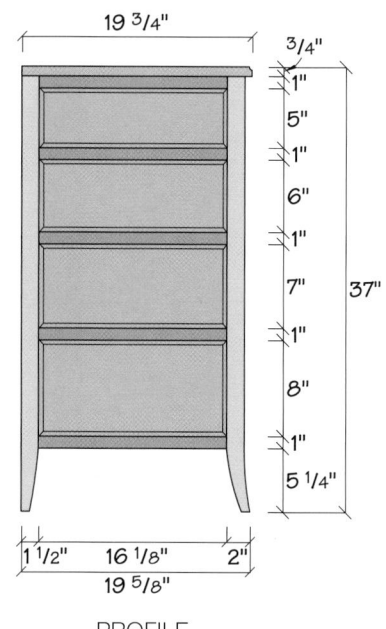

PROFILE

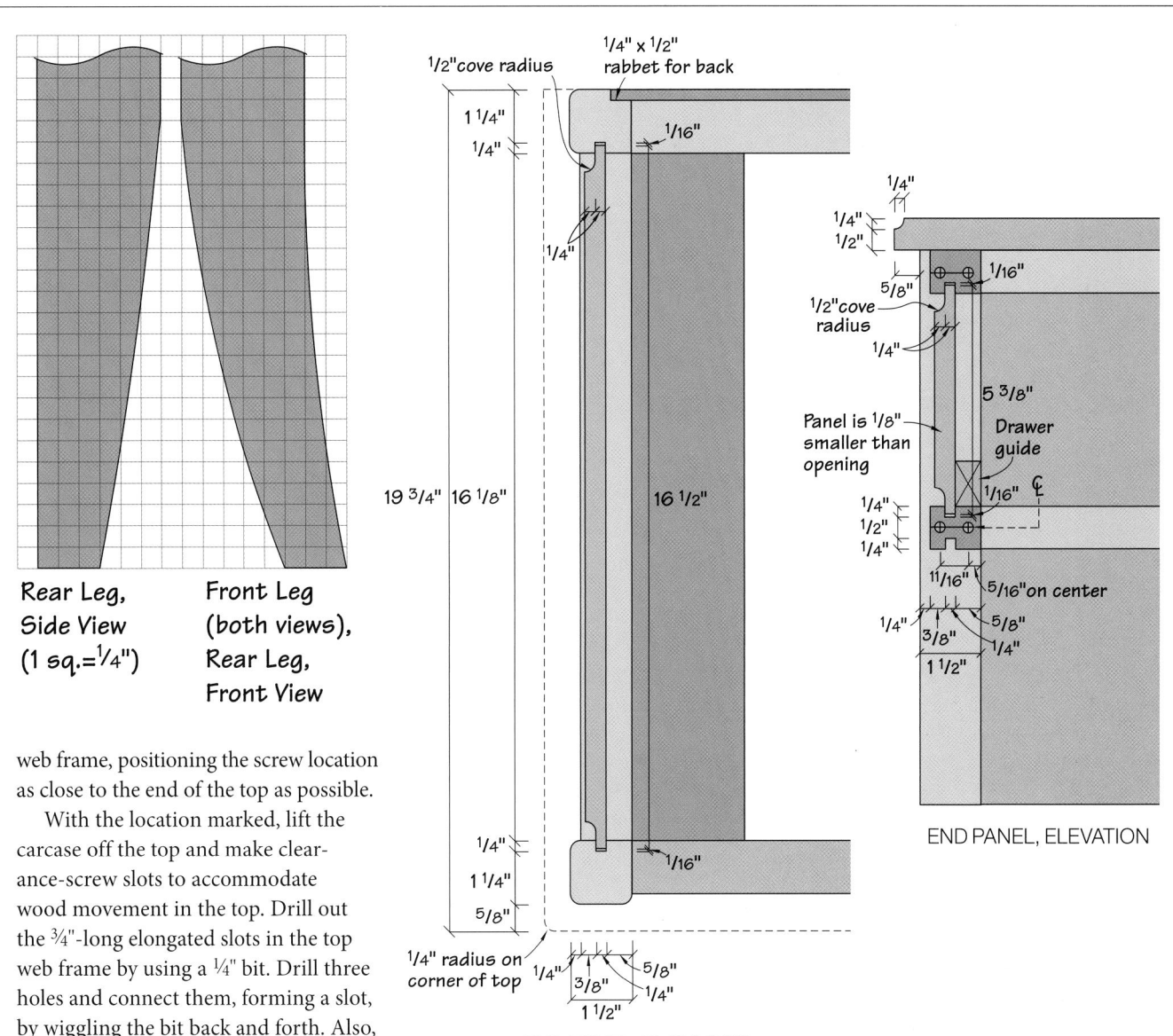

Rear Leg, Side View (1 sq.=¹/₄")

Front Leg (both views), Rear Leg, Front View

¹/₂"cove radius

¹/₄" x ¹/₂" rabbet for back

1 ¹/₄"
¹/₄"
¹/₁₆"
¹/₄"

19 ³/₄" 16 ¹/₈"

16 ¹/₂"

¹/₄"
1 ¹/₄"
⁵/₈"

¹/₄" radius on corner of top

¹/₄" ³/₈" ⁵/₈" ¹/₄" 1 ¹/₂"

¹/₁₆"

END PANEL, PLAN VIEW

¹/₄"
¹/₄" ¹/₂"
⁵/₈" ¹/₁₆"
¹/₂"cove radius
¹/₄"

5 ³/₈"
Drawer guide

Panel is ¹/₈" smaller than opening

¹/₄" ¹/₁₆"
¹/₂"
¹/₄"
¹¹/₁₆" ⁵/₁₆"on center
¹/₄" ⁵/₈"
³/₈" ¹/₄"
1 ¹/₂"

END PANEL, ELEVATION

web frame, positioning the screw location as close to the end of the top as possible.

With the location marked, lift the carcase off the top and make clearance-screw slots to accommodate wood movement in the top. Drill out the ³/₄"-long elongated slots in the top web frame by using a ¹/₄" bit. Drill three holes and connect them, forming a slot, by wiggling the bit back and forth. Also, drill four countersunk clearance holes

Frame & Panel Dresser

	NO.	ITEM	DIMENSIONS (INCHES)			DIMENSIONS (MILLIMETERS)			MATERIAL	COMMENTS
			T	W	L	T	W	L		
❑	1	Top	³/₄	19³/₄	38¹/₄	19	502	971	P	
❑	2	Front legs	2	2	36¹/₄	51	51	920	P	
❑	2	Back legs	1¹/₂	2	36¹/₄	38	51	920	P	
❑	10	Web ends	1	2³/₄	16¹/₈	25	70	409	S	
❑	5	Frt web rails	1	1¹/₄	34	25	32	864	P	
❑	5	Bk web rails	1	1¹/₄	34	25	32	864	S	
❑	5	Web centers	1	4	16¹/₈	25	102	409	S	
❑	10	Dividers	1	1¹/₄	16¹/₈	25	32	409	P	
❑	10	Drwr guides	⁵/₈	1	16¹/₈	16	25	409	S	
❑	2	Panels	¹/₂	5³/₈	16¹/₂	13	137	419	P	
❑	2	Panels	¹/₂	6³/₈	16¹/₂	13	162	419	P	
❑	2	Panels	¹/₂	7³/₈	16¹/₂	13	188	419	P	
❑	2	Panels	¹/₂	8³/₈	16¹/₂	13	213	419	P	
❑	1	Back	¹/₄	35	31	6	889	787	Ply.	

P=primary wood; S=poplar

Assembling the carcase is a simple matter of setting an end panel on its side and screwing the web frames in place with glue. Make sure the back edge of the frame is flush with the inside of the rabbet on the panel leg. The bottom edge of the web frame end is also flush with the bottom edge of the rails on the end panel.

Lay the top, bottom side up and place the carcase, upside down, on the top. Line up the carcase, flush to the back and centered on the top and mark the location. Tap a nail into the screw slot centers, marking the screw location. Remove the carcase and drill pilot holes into the top. Place the carcase on the top again and attach the top with #10-1½" pan-head screws.

in the front rail of the top-web frame. This keeps the top indexed to the front of the dresser. Now attach the top.

Drawers

Measure the drawer openings in the carcase and compare them to the drawer front sizes in the Schedule of Materials. If all went well, your drawer openings shouldn't be more than ¹⁄₁₆" larger than the length and height of the fronts. The drawers are held together by dovetail joints, and unless you want to hand cut the drawer dovetails, I recommend Troy Sexton's method for cutting half-blind pins that uses a router and a custom template you can make quickly with your table saw (September 1999 issue of *Popular Woodworking*). After cutting and fitting the tails, cut a ½" x ¼" rabbet in the back end of the drawer sides to accommodate the back piece, which will be nailed between the sides. Then cut a ¼" x ¼" groove ⅝" up from the bottom edge of the drawer sides and front, to accept the bottom.

To make the drawers match the side panels, rout a ¼" cove profile on the drawer fronts. The final preparation before assembly is to take a ¹⁄₁₆" jointer cut on the top edge of the drawer sides and back for clearance in the drawer opening.

Assemble the drawers by gluing the dovetail joints together and nailing the backs between the sides into the rabbets. Fitting is a matter of taking material off the sides or the edges of the front with a sharp plane. When the drawers are fit and the stops installed (see story below), remove the back. Sand everything to 150 grit and apply two or three coats of clear finish. Clear finish produces a distinctive warm, orange tone. Oil finishers beware. Oil finishes can turn yew a chocolate brown. So you might want to try a sample board and make sure it's what you want.

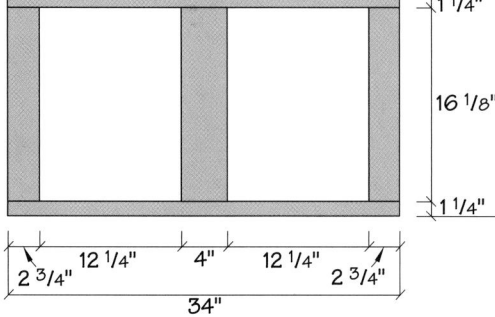

WEB FRAME, PLAN VIEW

1¹⁄₄"
16¹⁄₈"   18⁵⁄₈"
1¹⁄₄"

2³⁄₄"   12¹⁄₄"   4"   12¹⁄₄"   2³⁄₄"
34"

Placing and Installing Drawer Stops

Where you put your drawer stops is critical. Here's the right way to do it.

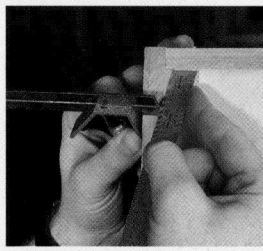
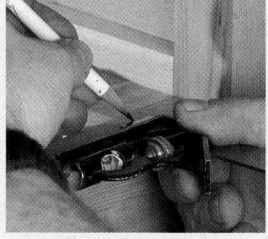

Set the drawer stops by measuring the thickness of the front at both sides of the drawer.

Mark these distances on the web frames with a sharp pencil. Make an additional mark ³⁄₄" away from the drawer guide to provide clearance for the drawer side.

Apply glue to the stop and set it on the web frame up to the pencil marks. Nail it in place and check the location by sliding a drawer up against it. If it's too far forward, do some fitting with a chisel. If it's too far back, it's not too soon after shooting it into place to remove it and try again.

Supplies

Van Dyke Supply Co. Inc.
800-843-3320

Traditional 1⁵⁄₈" x 1⁷⁄₈" pull • set of eight • item # 60030 • $4.45 each

Tri-fold Storage Cabinet

BY GLEN HUEY

Electronic entertainment is a permanent reality in almost every home. Unfortunately the media used to store that entertainment changes quickly. From 8-track to CD and VHS to DVD, our entertainment storage continues to be a tricky proposition.

If these media were as attractive as leather-bound books, that would call for an open bookcase-style solution. But most modern media are, well, pretty ugly. This is especially true if you've gone to the trouble of building attractive period furniture for your home.

After wandering through a home center store and noticing a clever pantry cabinet design, I carried the thought a step further and realized the same multi-layered storage could work next to my entertainment center.

Once the cabinet was finished, I recognized even more uses for this versatile cabinet. It would actually make a very nice dry bar, or you could certainly place it in the kitchen and use it as a pantry. What an idea!

If you would like to see more photos of the construction steps for this cabinet, visit my web site at hueyfurniture.com.

Conception

I went to work deciding what type of storage I'd need. DVDs and CDs were at the top of the list, but I've still got some VHS tapes and LPs sitting around that I wanted to store out of sight as well. I decided a free-standing cabinet would give me ultimate flexibility. And because much of the furniture in my home is early American, I used all these guide-

lines to work up the storage cabinet shown here.

The main door is capable of holding 150 DVDs, while the interior door will store 125 CDs. The drawer can hold VCR tapes or anything else that might need storing. If you have some LPs in your home, skip the drawer and the lower section will hold them.

Overall Construction

The cabinet is essentially a box with two layers of doors. I simply added a period-appropriate base and crown to dress it up. The outer door is of raised-panel construction to continue the look of finished furniture.

Because of the weight the cabinet would be supporting, I used torsion-box design for the top and dado joinery to hold everything tight and square.

Box First

Construction starts with the box of the cabinet. I built the piece out of solid cherry and poplar, with one exception – a plywood back to add even more rigidity when compared to a solid-wood shiplapped back.

Start with the two sides. The left side is a normal rectangle, but the right side is L-shaped to allow space for the second door. To save a bit of lumber, create the right side of the cabinet by gluing the short piece to the long piece with the top of the short piece held 15" up from the bottom edge.

Because it's always a good idea to leave some room for trimming in a glued-up panel, that 15" mark may actually be 15½". After the glue is dry, all you need to do is clean up the seam and trim the panel to size.

The other panels that create the exterior box are the sub-top and the bottom. To join these panels together, you need to first cut a ½" x ¾" rabbet at the bottom and top edges of both sides. I use a straightedge and a router bit with a top-mount bearing for this step.

While you're routing, cut a ½"-wide x ¼"-deep rabbet on the back edge of both sides to accept the plywood back. As you work, make sure that you end up with a mirror image in the sides, except for the notched area.

Because of the depth of the two doors, the base and sub-top of the cabi-

net extend forward beyond the sides of the cabinet. To make these pieces look and fit right I notched both the top and bottom pieces to fit around the sides.

To set up the table saw to notch the sub-top and bottom, you need to locate where the blade moves below the table and ends the cut. To do this, raise the blade to ensure that it will cut the required thickness, then with a square against the fence and the blade, slowly rotate the blade toward you by hand until the square stops traveling. Mark the location.

To make the notches, mark the location on the pieces where you want the cut to stop (12¾" in from the edge), then run the piece into the blade until the lines meet. Finish the cut with a hand saw and chisels, then cut a ½" x ¼" rabbet on the back edges of the sub-top and bottom for the back.

Solid Shelving

The shelves for the inside of the case are permanently mounted in the case using stopped dados. The same alignment and routing set-up as is used for rabbeting the bottoms and the sides is used to produce the ¼" x ¾" dados for the shelves in the case.

There's one last dado to cut, the one for the drawer. I used a drawer design that allows the ¼"-thick drawer bottom to extend beyond the width of the drawer. When the bottom is slid into

Cutting a full board into the above L-shape is wasteful, so I simply glued two boards together to provide the necessary shape for the right side.

these ¼" x ¼" dados in the cabinet sides, no drawer slides are necessary.

Because the shelves are 5⅝" wide (the full depth of the narrow part of the case) and the dado is stopped at 5⅜", you need to notch the front corners of the upper shelves. Set the table saw fence to cut a ¼" width, including the blade thickness, and raise the blade to ¼" height. Two passes over the blade with the shelves on their front edges (using your miter gauge) will produce this notch.

With all the notches and grooves cut, you're ready to assemble the case. Align the sub-top and bottom into position. Use a pilot bit with a countersink and fasten the sides to the top and bottom with screws. Then glue and nail the shelves in place.

Live, On Stage: The Doors!

Set the case aside to dry and begin the doors by milling the parts to width and length according to the cutting list. Both doors begin with a 45°-bevel cut at the corners. I cut these on my table saw with the blade tipped over to a 45° bevel.

After the bevels are cut, you can then assemble the front door frame by adding glue to the joints and clamping everything together with a band clamp. Then set it aside and we will return to it later.

The second door requires a couple of other operations before assembling. Cut a ¼" x ¼" groove along the back edges of all the frame pieces for the back .

Next, cut a ¼" x ¼" groove, ½" in from the front edge of the door bottom and the two shelves. These grooves will hold the retaining strips that we'll get to in a minute.

Now lay out the position of the two shelves in the second door. I used biscuits to attach the shelves to the sides. Cut the slots for two #20 biscuits in each end of each shelf. Glue the two shelves between the sides. After this is dry, glue the top and bottom of the door in place and clamp with a band clamp.

To make the dados for the shelves in the case itself, set the bit to cut a ¼" in depth and run the groove in 5⅜" from the back edge of the cabinet for the upper shelves, and all the way through for the full shelf that is at the 15" mark produced in the first step.

If you choose to add the drawer, cut one other dado in the sides. Set up a dado blade to run a ¼" groove that is a ¼" deep. The drawer bottom will slip into this groove and serve as a drawer slide.

After notching the front edge of the shelves, slide them into the stopped dados in the case. Then nail them through the outside of the case with a small finish nail.

As you attach the sub-top and bottom with screws, notice that each piece is notched to extend past the width of the sides and fits into a rabbet.

GROOVE FOR RETAINER STRIP

GROOVE FOR BACK

Use biscuits to attach the narrow shelves in the inside door. Add glue to the biscuits and assemble the unit. Clamp, check for square and allow the glue to dry.

Tapered Retainers

In building this piece, I challenged myself to find different methods to use in construction. After using the jointer many times to make tapered legs, I decided to use the same process to make the retainer strips that fit into the grooves in the shelves of the second door.

The retainer pieces are called out in the cutting list as ¾" x 1¼" x 21½". Each piece will yield two retainers, so you need to run the tapers on two pieces.

Begin by setting the jointer depth to cut one-half the height of the total taper.

In this case a ¼" (half of the ½" taper), and mark a line that is one-quarter of the length of the retainer (I wanted the piece to peak at the center). Run the board over the jointer up to that line on both ends. Then start with either end and rock the piece until the corner rests on the infeed table and run the final pass to complete the tapering of the retainer. Reverse the piece and repeat the last step.

To finish off the retainer strips, run a bead detail on both sides of the top, tapered edge, using a ¼" corner bead bit. Then resaw the piece to the needed ¼" pieces, leaving the center section as waste. The strips are then glued into the grooves created in the bottom and two shelves of the door.

Spline Reinforcements

The corner miters for both doors, as well as the drawer box, are reinforced with glued-in spline keys to add strength.

I created the slots for the splines on the table saw, using an auxiliary fence set up. You can arrange the splines in a design or simply fit the cuts to the mitered end. Then, make the spline keys to fit and install them with glue.

Front/Back for the Door

The next step is to create the front of the cabinet, which is also the back of the front door. The front is a twin raised-panel facade. Begin by cutting mortises for the intermediate vertical frame piece (or muntin) in the top and bottom rails as well as the needed mortises at both ends of the stiles that will accept the rails. Then, begin the process of cutting the tenons.

While all four shoulder cuts for the muntin are cut at 1¼", the rails need to have a haunched tenon as shown below. Complete the cheek cuts with the tenon jig on the table saw and the edge cuts at the band saw.

To create the groove for the panels I like to use a three-wing ¼" slot cutter on my router table. Assemble the frame

QUARTER-LENGTH LINE

DJ-20

To form the "peaked" retainer, run the piece over the jointer to the quarter-length line on both ends. Then flip the piece and kick the front end up and make another pass on of the retainer.

AUXILIARY FENCE

GUIDE STICKS

An auxiliary fence on your table saw makes cutting the spline groove simple. Lay out a 45° angle and attach guide sticks as shown. Raise the blade to cut as much as possible without penetrating the interior of the door and make the cuts.

After the glue on the splines has dried, trim the keys to the piece with a flush-cutting hand saw, then sand to a smooth finish.

After defining the face shoulders for the tenon for the front door panel, offset the edge shoulder to create a haunch on the tenon. That offset is ⅜", or the depth of the groove that will hold the raised panels.

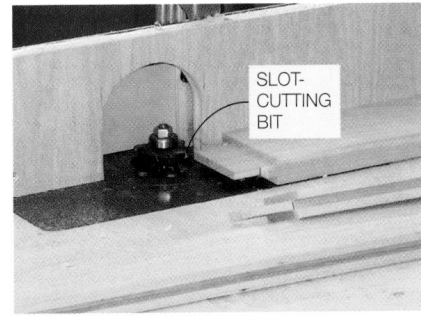

To cut the panel groove, set up an auxiliary fence on your router table. Align the cutter with the tenon, and cut the groove on the interior edge of the door rails and stiles and on both muntin edges.

without glue and make any necessary adjustments to the pieces. While the frame is together, check the measurements of the panel spaces. Add ⅝" to the opening to arrive at the final sizes of the panels.

Next, mill the panels to size and raise their edges. You can use a router bit, the shaper or a table saw to raise the panels. Once complete, assemble the entire front and allow the glue to dry.

When the front is ready, check the fit of the panel to the door frame. Glue the panel to the frame leaving an even

overhang on all sides. Clamp the front in place and set it aside to dry. Then use a straight router bit with a bottom-mounted bearing to trim the panel to the frame, then sand flush.

Front Door Storage

Next up is the shelves and retainer dowels for the front door. I chose pocket screws here because I wanted to remove the shelves to make finishing easier.

The dowel retainers are the last step before fitting the front door to the case. Locate and drill a ⁵⁄₁₆" hole that is 2" above each shelf and the door bottom, and ⅜" from the back edge of the door. Then simply bow the dowels and spring them into the holes.

Glue the door panel to the door frame, allowing an even overhang on all sides. Check the door for square after glue-up.

Using pocket hole screws to attach the shelves allows you to remove the shelves to make finishing easier.

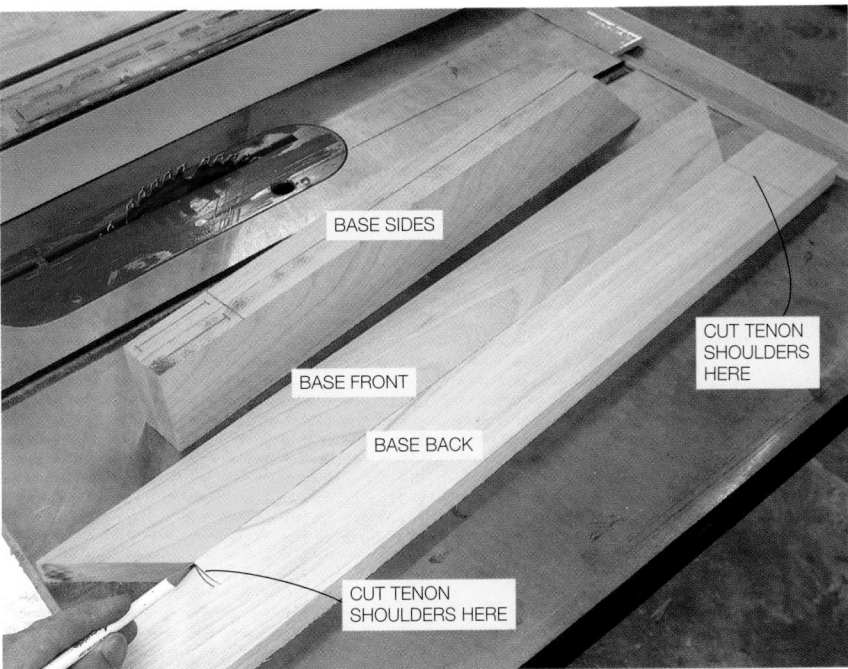

Transfer the tenon width to the end of the back. Then position that line at the rear edge of the angle cut in the base frame front and mark the opposite end also at the rear of the angle cut. Cut the back to the mark.

Remember when making the 45° cut for the splines that you need to adjust the blade height as well. Then make the splines that will fit into the slots and glue the front feet together.

Home Base With Feet

The base frame is mitered at the front, but not at the rear. To make the base frame, mill the pieces to size, miter the front corner pieces, then lay out and cut the mortises in the base frame sides. To get an accurate length for the base frame back piece, lay out the location of two tenons on the base back using the base front as a guide.

Cut biscuit slots in the mitered ends of the front and sides and make tenons to match the mortises in the ends of the back. To assemble the unit, apply glue to the mortises, then slip them together. Glue the biscuits and apply the remaining clamps. You will be able to apply the necessary pressure to each clamp to align the mitered ends and close up any gaps.

To give your cabinet legs (or in this case, feet), select and mill the material for your front and side feet, then use the pattern to cut the profile of the pieces (shown at right) at the band saw.

The front feet pieces are joined together at a miter, so the next step is to miter those mating edges. Because the blade on a table saw tilts only one way, and you want as large a surface as possible to support the foot during the cut, you'll have to do some shifting to miter the mating feet.

Two feet are cut using the miter gauge in the normal method. To miter the mating feet you need to reverse the miter gauge (still in the same slot) with the auxiliary fence at the outfeed end of the table saw.

Set the A foot to the blade in order to determine where to set a stop block to keep the foot from moving away from the blade while cutting. Position the B foot with the face up and the top edge against the fence. Push the foot through the blade while holding it flat to the table and tight to the fence. The miters need to be cut in only the four pieces selected to be the front feet of your piece.

With the feet cut to matching angles, leave the blade at 45° and move your fence to the blade to make the first cut for a spline. Geometry is your friend here. With the blade set to cut at a 45° angle, making a cut into the mitered corner of the foot results in a cut that will

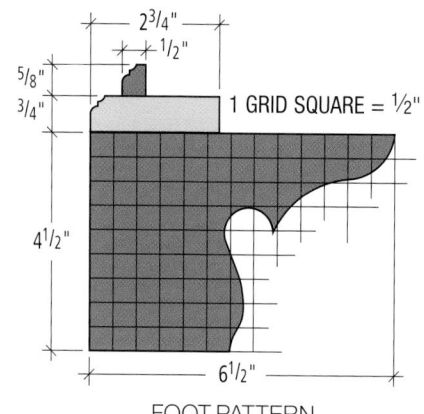

FOOT PATTERN

The screws at front and middle of the base hold the two assemblies tight at the front and force any wood movement to the back where the nails will allow slight movement.

In order to avoid any cross-grain construction problems, the grain in the front-to-back pieces runs the same direction as the grain in my top.

line up with the groove in its mate. Raise the cut to just over $\frac{3}{8}$" and make a pass on the saw. Reposition the fence so that a second pass over the blade will produce a $\frac{1}{4}$" groove. The side and back feet are joined with screws. Place the back foot into a $\frac{3}{4}$" x $\frac{5}{8}$" rabbet made in each side foot, add glue and attach.

The completed foot assemblies are then attached to the base frame. After the glue is set, add glue blocks to all corners of each assembly.

Sand the base to 180 grit, profile the edge with your favorite router bit, and attach it to the case with $1\frac{1}{4}$" screws at the front and halfway down each side. Finish the process with $1\frac{1}{4}$" nails along the balance of each side and the back

Tri-fold Storage Cabinet

	NO.	ITEM	DIMENSIONS (INCHES)			DIMENSIONS (MILLIMETERS)			MATERIAL	COMMENTS
			T	W	L	T	W	L		
CARCASE										
❏	1	Left side	$\frac{3}{4}$	$12\frac{3}{4}$	46	19	324	1168	Cherry	
❏	1	Right side	$\frac{3}{4}$	$5\frac{7}{8}$	46	19	150	1168	Cherry	
❏	1	Right side	$\frac{3}{4}$	$6\frac{7}{8}$	15	19	174	381	Cherry	
❏	2	Bottom & sub-top	$\frac{3}{4}$	$19\frac{5}{8}$	24	19	499	610	Cherry	
❏	1	Lower shelf	$\frac{3}{4}$	$12\frac{3}{4}$	23	19	324	584	Cherry	
❏	1	Case back	$\frac{1}{4}$	$23\frac{1}{2}$	$45\frac{1}{2}$	6	572	1156	Plywood	
❏	2	Shelves	$\frac{3}{4}$	$5\frac{5}{8}$	23	19	143	584	Cherry	
FRONT DOOR										
❏	2	Door stiles	$\frac{3}{4}$	$2\frac{1}{2}$	$44\frac{5}{16}$	19	64	1126	Cherry	
❏	1	Top rail	$\frac{3}{4}$	$2\frac{1}{2}$	$21\frac{1}{2}$	19	64	546	Cherry	$1\frac{1}{4}$" TBE
❏	1	Bottom rail	$\frac{3}{4}$	$3\frac{1}{4}$	$21\frac{1}{2}$	19	82	546	Cherry	$1\frac{1}{4}$" TBE
❏	1	Muntin	$\frac{3}{4}$	$2\frac{1}{2}$	$41\frac{1}{16}$	19	64	1043	Cherry	$1\frac{1}{4}$" TBE
❏	2	Panels	$\frac{5}{8}$	$8\frac{7}{8}$	$39\frac{3}{16}$	16	225	996	Cherry	$\frac{5}{16}$" RAS
❏	2	Stile returns	$\frac{3}{4}$	$6\frac{1}{8}$	$44\frac{5}{16}$	19	155	1126	Cherry	
❏	2	Rail returns	$\frac{3}{4}$	$6\frac{1}{8}$	24	19	155	610	Cherry	
❏	3	Front door shelves	$\frac{3}{4}$	$5\frac{5}{8}$	$22\frac{1}{2}$	19	397	573	Cherry	
❏	4	Dowels	$\frac{5}{16}$	–	23	8	–	584	Cherry	
SECOND DOOR										
❏	2	Door sides	$\frac{3}{4}$	$6\frac{7}{8}$	$30\frac{1}{16}$	19	174	764	Cherry	
❏	2	Door top & bottom	$\frac{3}{4}$	$6\frac{7}{8}$	23	19	174	584	Cherry	
❏	2	Inner door shelves	$\frac{3}{4}$	$5\frac{5}{8}$	$21\frac{1}{2}$	19	143	546	Cherry	
❏	2	Retainers	$\frac{3}{4}$	$1\frac{1}{4}$	$21\frac{1}{2}$	19	32	546	Cherry	
❏	40	Spline keys	$\frac{1}{8}$	$1\frac{1}{4}$	$2\frac{1}{2}$	3	32	64	Cherry	
❏	1	Door back	$\frac{1}{4}$	22	$29\frac{1}{16}$	6	559	739	Plywood	
BASE										
❏	1	Base front	$\frac{3}{4}$	$2\frac{3}{4}$	$26\frac{1}{4}$	19	70	666	Cherry	MBE
❏	2	Base sides	$\frac{3}{4}$	$2\frac{3}{4}$	$20\frac{3}{4}$	19	70	527	Cherry	MOE
❏	1	Base back	$\frac{3}{4}$	$2\frac{3}{4}$	$23\frac{1}{4}$	19	70	590	Poplar	$1\frac{1}{4}$" TBE
❏	6	Base feet	$\frac{3}{4}$	$4\frac{1}{2}$	$6\frac{1}{2}$	19	115	165	Cherry	
❏	2	Rear feet	$\frac{3}{4}$	$4\frac{1}{2}$	$6\frac{1}{2}$	19	115	165	Poplar	
❏	4	Foot blocks	$\frac{3}{4}$	$\frac{3}{4}$	$4\frac{1}{2}$	19	19	115	Poplar	
❏	8	Foot blocks	$\frac{3}{4}$	$\frac{3}{4}$	3	19	19	76	Poplar	
❏	3	Mouldings	$\frac{1}{2}$	$\frac{5}{8}$	26	13	16	660	Cherry	Miter to fit
TOP										
❏	1	Case top	$\frac{3}{4}$	$21\frac{3}{4}$	$28\frac{1}{4}$	19	552	717	Cherry	
❏	1	Torsion block	$\frac{3}{4}$	$1\frac{1}{4}$	24	19	32	610	Cherry	
❏	3	Torsion blocks	$\frac{3}{4}$	$18\frac{7}{8}$	$1\frac{1}{4}$	19	479	32	Poplar	
❏	3	Cove	$\frac{3}{4}$	$2\frac{1}{4}$	28	19	57	711	Cherry	Miter to fit
DRAWER										
❏	2	Drawer front & back	$\frac{3}{4}$	$6\frac{3}{4}$	22	19	171	559	Cherry	
❏	2	Drawer sides	$\frac{3}{4}$	$6\frac{3}{4}$	$11\frac{1}{2}$	19	171	292	Cherry	
❏	1	Drawer bottom	$\frac{1}{4}$	$12\frac{1}{4}$	$22\frac{7}{8}$	6	311	583	Plywood	
❏	20	Drawer splines	$\frac{1}{8}$	$1\frac{1}{8}$	$2\frac{1}{2}$	3	29	64	Cherry	

Key: TBE= tenons both ends; RAS=rabbets all sides; MBE= miters both ends; MOE=miter one end

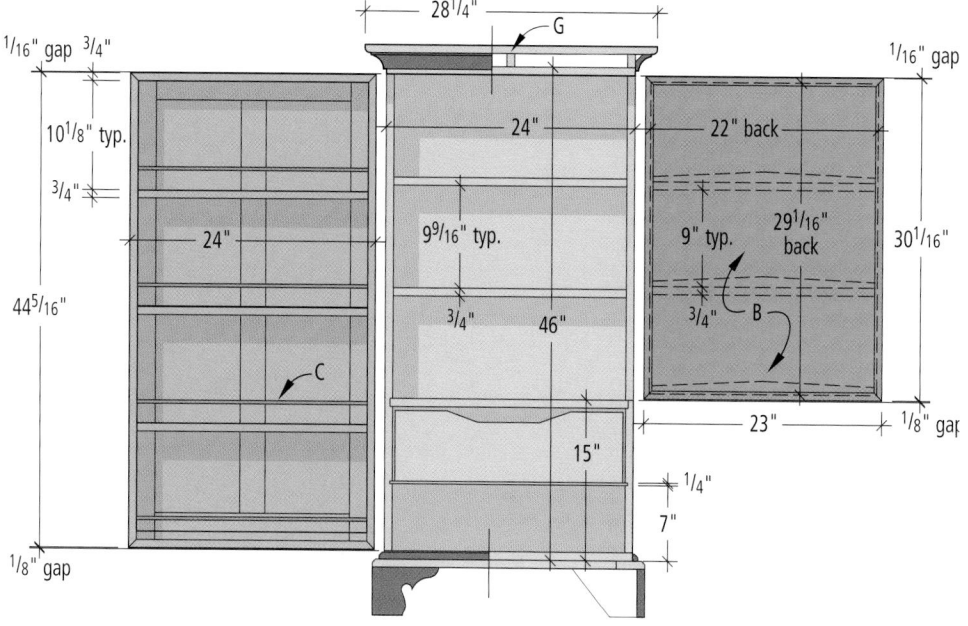

ELEVATION – DOORS OPEN
TRIM IN PLACE/TRIM REMOVED

Supplies

Rockler
800-279-4441 or rockler.com

1 • 1¹/16" x 36" piano hinge
#19241, $8.99

1 • 1¹/16" x 48" piano hinge
#19259, $9.99

Woodcraft
800-225-1153 or woodcraft.com

1 • draw catch w/eye
#85H98, $2.99

Prices correct at time of publication.

edge. Next, add the transition moulding that also has a routed edge.

Hanging the Doors

The doors for this project are built to fit exactly, as in no additional room for hinge gap. Therefore, before each door is hung you need to create a rabbet in the edge of the hinge side of each door to compensate for the hinge spacing.

When attaching the hinge, use the hinge as a template to locate the screws in both the door and the case. Set the two side by side, reposition the hinge, and attach the door to the case. The hinge for both doors will need to be cut to length.

A bi-metal blade at the band saw or a hacksaw would work equally well.

Torsion Top

I wanted to add support to the top unit of this project because of the amount of overhang that was needed to swing the second door. I decided to use a torsion box design, building a stable box structure by adding ribs between the top and sub-top.

Mill the material for your top to size, then rout a ¹/2" roundover profile on the front and sides. Set the top in place on the cabinet and draw a line around the case top, defining its location on the top.

I chose to use 1¹/4" pieces that are countersunk and screwed to the top along those lines made in the previous step. Next, invert the case onto the top unit and attach the two assemblies with screws.

To complete the furniture look of the piece I added a shop-made cove moulding below the top, covering the torsion pieces. The cove moulding is made at the table saw (See *Popular Woodworking* issue #117 for further information), though you could use a piece of stock moulding if you prefer.

A Drawer and a Finish

The drawer box for this project is made in the same way as are the door frames. The corners are mitered and then spline keys are added for support. The entire box is set onto a piece of ¹/4" plywood where it will slide into the grooves that were dadoed into both sides of the cabinet.

Finally, the front door is attached to the case. Remember to create the rabbet in the hinge side of the door frame that will compensate for the hinge gap. Hang the front door to the case, then make any necessary adjustments.

Before starting to finish the project you will need to cut and fit the plywood for the case back. Do not attach this until after the finishing of the project because

The cove moulding is attached to the torsion buildup, below the top. I used a shop-made cove for this piece.

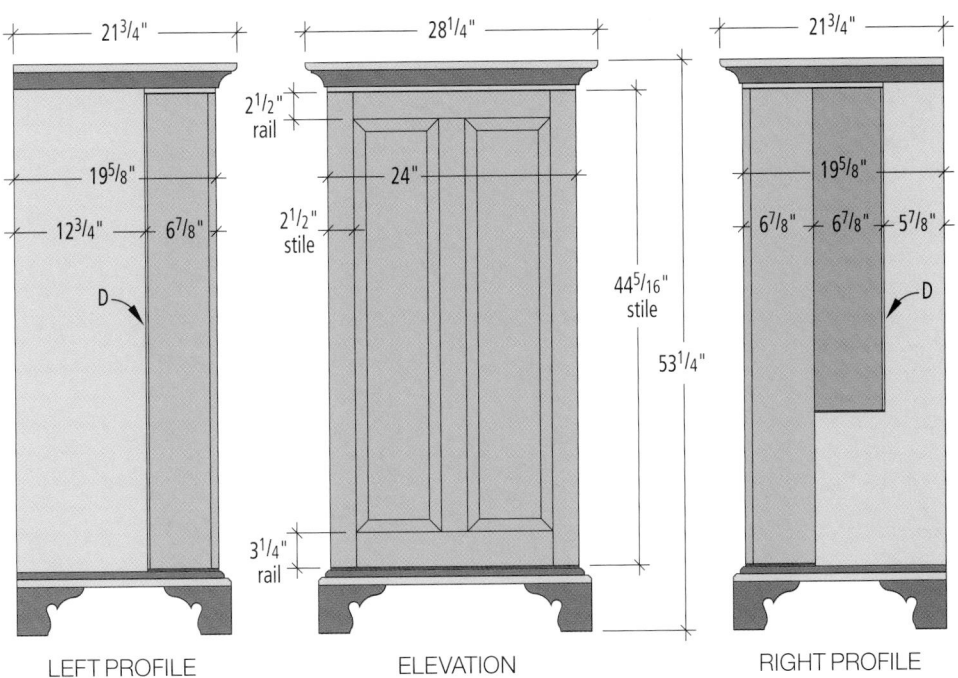

21³/₄" — LEFT PROFILE

28¹/₄" — ELEVATION

21³/₄" — RIGHT PROFILE

Left Profile: 21³/₄", 19⁵/₈", 12³/₄", 6⁷/₈", D

Elevation: 28¹/₄", 2¹/₂" rail, 24", 2¹/₂" stile, 44⁵/₁₆" stile, 53¹/₄", 3¹/₄" rail

Right Profile: 21³/₄", 19⁵/₈", 6⁷/₈", 6⁷/₈", 5⁷/₈", D

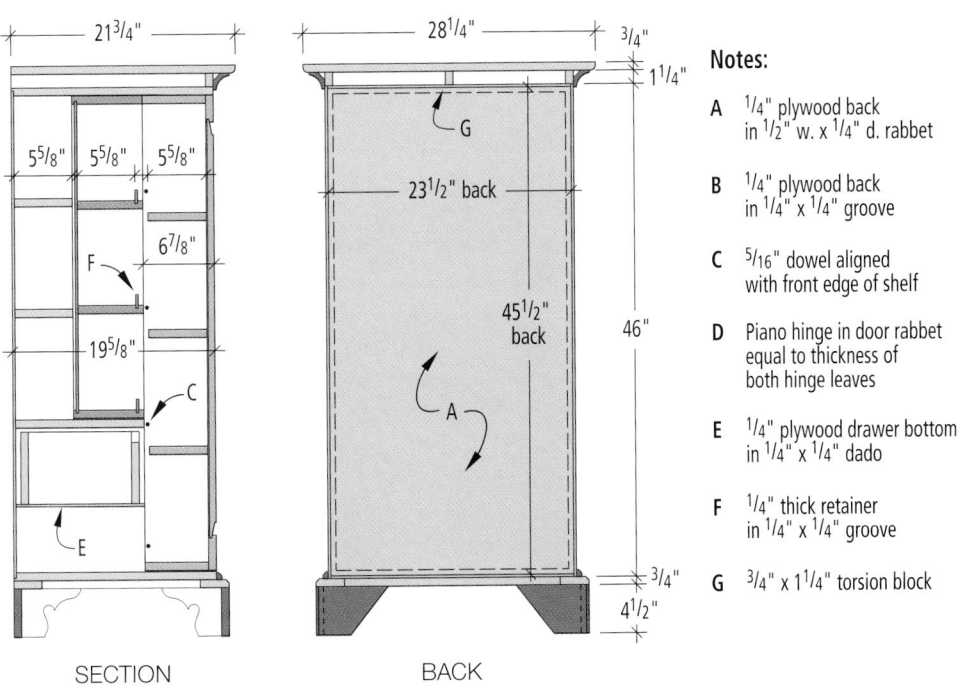

SECTION   BACK

Section: 21³/₄", 5⁵/₈", 5⁵/₈", 5⁵/₈", 6⁷/₈", F, 19⁵/₈", C, E

Back: 28¹/₄", 3/₄", 1¹/₄", G, 23¹/₂" back, 45¹/₂" back, 46", A, 3/₄", 4¹/₂"

Notes:

A ¹/₄" plywood back in ¹/₂" w. x ¹/₄" d. rabbet

B ¹/₄" plywood back in ¹/₄" x ¹/₄" groove

C ⁵/₁₆" dowel aligned with front edge of shelf

D Piano hinge in door rabbet equal to thickness of both hinge leaves

E ¹/₄" plywood drawer bottom in ¹/₄" x ¹/₄" dado

F ¹/₄" thick retainer in ¹/₄" x ¹/₄" groove

G ³/₄" x 1¹/₄" torsion block

you'll want to access the piece from all angles while applying your finish.

I elected to apply a shellac and prec-atlyzed lacquer finish to this piece – the shellac (GarnetLac) for a mellow shading and the lacquer for protection. This also would have been a great piece for an oil/varnish finish. From there, just add the continuous hinges and the exterior door latch.

My finished piece is a nice combination of traditional furniture styling with high-tech entertainment storage. I just hope the next electronic "medium" is of a similar size to today's.

Byrdcliffe Linen Press

BY ROBERT W. LANG

The history of most pieces of furniture can be traced back to one individual – usually the designer, the maker or the client. The roots of this linen press spread to include a fascinating group of people at an early 20th-century art colony known as Byrdcliffe, located near Woodstock, N.Y.

With its carved door panels and distinctive colors, this unusual cabinet is one of the finest examples of the Arts & Crafts period. The basic form can be traced back to English designs of the period, but the stylized carving and overall proportions make it unique. The original is part of the collection of the Metropolitan Museum of Art in New York.

Fewer than 50 pieces of furniture were made at Byrdcliffe between 1903 and 1905. Fewer than half of those found buyers; the remaining pieces were found in various buildings at the colony after the 1976 death of the founder's son. Many of these had been left unfinished, the idea being that the buyer could choose a color when purchasing.

The Cast of Characters

Byrdcliffe was founded and financed by Englishman Ralph Radcliffe Whitehead. He inherited the family's felt fortune at age 32, and was a follower of John Ruskin. Although not an artistic man himself, he married a painter, and enjoyed the company of many prominent artists and intellectuals.

In the early 1890s, he wrote about an idealized community of artists, but didn't act on these plans until the birth of his two sons gave him a desire to do

something useful with his fortune. He purchased 1,300 acres of land, built about 30 buildings, including a well-equipped woodshop and surrounded himself with a talented group of artists and writers.

Although Whitehead held artists in high esteem, he had a rather low opinion of craftsmen. In his written plan for his community he stated: "Now, in order to have anything good made in stuff, or in hard material, we must seek out the artist to provide us with a design, and then a workman to carry it out as mechanically as possible, because we know that if he puts any of his coarser self into it he will spoil it."

Who actually made and carved the furniture produced at Byrdcliffe is not known. Apparently there were several different cabinetmakers, as the quality of construction varies from piece to piece. Although Byrdcliffe was intended to be self-supporting, Whitehead was wealthy enough to abandon the furniture-making part of his plan after a little more than a year of dealing with the "coarser" workmen.

Many of the artists in residence created furniture designs. Apparently Whitehead selected a general form, and drawings were made by individual artists. Decorative panels were a common feature, although most were painted, not carved. Among the most talented designers at Byrdcliffe were Edna Walker and Zulma Steele. This piece was designed by Walker.

The designs by Walker and Steele are the most beautifully proportioned and distinctive pieces of Byrdcliffe furniture.

This cabinet in particular is a refreshing break from the mass and machismo of many Arts & Crafts pieces.

100 Years Later

Usually when I make a reproduction of an existing piece I try to stay as close as possible to the original. In building this cabinet, however, I had to make some guesses, and I made a few changes to suit my own taste. I had only a photograph of the front of the cabinet and overall dimensions to work with, so the layout of the side panels and the details of construction are my best guesses.

In the original, the carvings are very flat. They are simply outlines of leaves and branches with the edges rounded over. I originally carved the panels this way, but just wasn't happy with the effect. I thought they seemed rather lifeless and static, so I recarved the panels and added more relief.

Additionally, the crown moulding on the original comes flush to the bottom edge of the top, apparently attached to the edges. The closest router bit I could find (Freud 99-406) had a small fillet at the top. I thought this looked nicer, and rather than wrap the crown around the perimeter of the top, I set it below, letting the top overhang by $\frac{1}{8}$". This added one more shadow line, and if the top expands or contracts, then the joint between the moulding and the top won't show.

The third change was to the color. The oranges and reds on the panels are the same as the original, but the green stain is darker and deeper in color. The finish on the original varies

Byrdcliffe Linen Press

	NO.	ITEM	DIMENSIONS (INCHES)			DIMENSIONS (MILLIMETERS)			MATERIAL	COMMENTS
			T	W	L	T	W	L		
CARCASE										
❑	8	Leg front & back	1	2½	54¼	25	64	1378	Quartersawn white oak	Miter long edges
❑	8	Leg sides	1⅛	2½	54¼	29	64	1378	Quartersawn white oak	Miter & rabbet long edges
❑	4	Side panel stiles	¾	3½	44½	19	89	1131	Quartersawn white oak	
❑	2	Side panel top rails	¾	6½	8⅜	19	165	213	Quartersawn white oak	1¼" TBE
❑	2	Side panel middle rails	¾	5⅛	8⅜	19	130	213	Quartersawn white oak	1¼" TBE
❑	2	Side panel bottom rails	¾	3⅝	8⅜	19	92	213	Quartersawn white oak	1¼" TBE
❑	2	Lower arched rails	⅞	5⅛	8⅜	22	130	213	Quartersawn white oak	1¼" TBE
❑	2	Top side panels	⅝	6⅞	13	16	174	330	Quartersawn white oak	½" TAS
❑	2	Bottom side panels	⅝	6⅞	18¼	16	174	463	Quartersawn white oak	½" TAS
❑	1	Top	¾	18¾	41	19	476	1041	Quartersawn white oak	
❑	1	Front top rail	⅞	2⅝	34¾	22	67	883	Quartersawn white oak	1" TBE
❑	2	Drawer rails	⅞	1¼	34¾	22	32	883	Quartersawn white oak	1" TBE
❑	1	Bottom front rail	⅞	1⅜	34¾	22	35	883	Quartersawn white oak	1" TBE
❑	1	Bottom apron	¾	6¾	34¾	19	171	883	Quartersawn white oak	1" TBE
❑	2	Stiles @ doors	¾	2³⁄₁₆	19¾	19	59	502	Quartersawn white oak	
❑	2	Stiles @ top drawer	¾	2³⁄₁₆	7½	19	59	191	Quartersawn white oak	
❑	2	Stiles @ bottom drawer	¾	2³⁄₁₆	8½	19	59	216	Quartersawn white oak	
❑	1	Drawer rail support	¾	1⅜	32¾	19	35	832	Quartersawn white oak	
❑	2	Fill behind crown	⅜	1⁵⁄₁₆	12⅛	10	33	308	Quartersawn white oak	
❑	1	Fill behind crown	¼	1⁵⁄₁₆	32¾	6	xx	832	Quartersawn white oak	
❑	6	Web frame stiles	¾	2½	35½	19	64	902	Poplar	
❑	9	Web frame rails	¾	2½	10⅞	19	64	276	Poplar	¾" TBE
❑	4	Web frame panels	¾	10⅜	14¾	19	264	349	Plywood	
❑	2	Crown moulding	1	2	48	25	51	1219	Quartersawn white oak	
DOORS										
❑	2	Door hinge stiles	¾	3⅞	19¾	19	98	502	Quartersawn white oak	
❑	1	Left lock stile	¾	3⅞	19¾	19	98	502	Quartersawn white oak	
❑	1	Right lock stile	¾	4⅛	19¾	19	105	502	Quartersawn white oak	
❑	2	Door top rails	¾	3⅞	9¾	19	98	248	Quartersawn white oak	1" TBE
❑	2	Door bottom rails	¾	3⅞	9¾	19	98	248	Quartersawn white oak	1" TBE
❑	2	Door panels	⅝	8¾	13	16	222	330	Basswood	½" TAS
DRAWERS										
❑	1	Top drawer front	¾	7½	31¼	19	191	793	Quartersawn white oak	Opening size trim to fit
❑	1	Bottom drawer front	¾	8½	31¼	19	216	793	Quartersawn white oak	Opening size trim to fit
❑	2	Drawer sides	¾	7½	14¼	19	191	362	Maple	Dovetailed to front
❑	2	Drawer sides	¾	8½	14¼	19	216	362	Maple	Dovetailed to front
❑	1	Drawer back	¾	7½	32¾	19	191	832	Maple	In dado in sides
❑	1	Drawer back	¾	8½	32¾	19	216	832	Maple	In dado in sides
❑	2	Drawer bottoms	¼	14½	30⅜	6	369	772	Plywood	
❑	4	Drawer runners	1	1½	14¼	25	38	362	Quartersawn white oak	¾" TOE
BACK										
❑	3	Back frame rails	¾	2½	30	19	64	762	Poplar	¾" TBE
❑	3	Back frame stiles	¾	2½	43⅜	19	64	1102	Poplar	
❑	2	Back planks	½	4⅞	43⅜	13	124	1102	Poplar	¼" rabbet one edge
❑	4	Back planks	½	4⅞	43⅜	13	124	1102	Poplar	¼" rabbet both edges

TBE = Tenon Both Ends; TAS= Tenon All Sides; TOE= Tenon One End

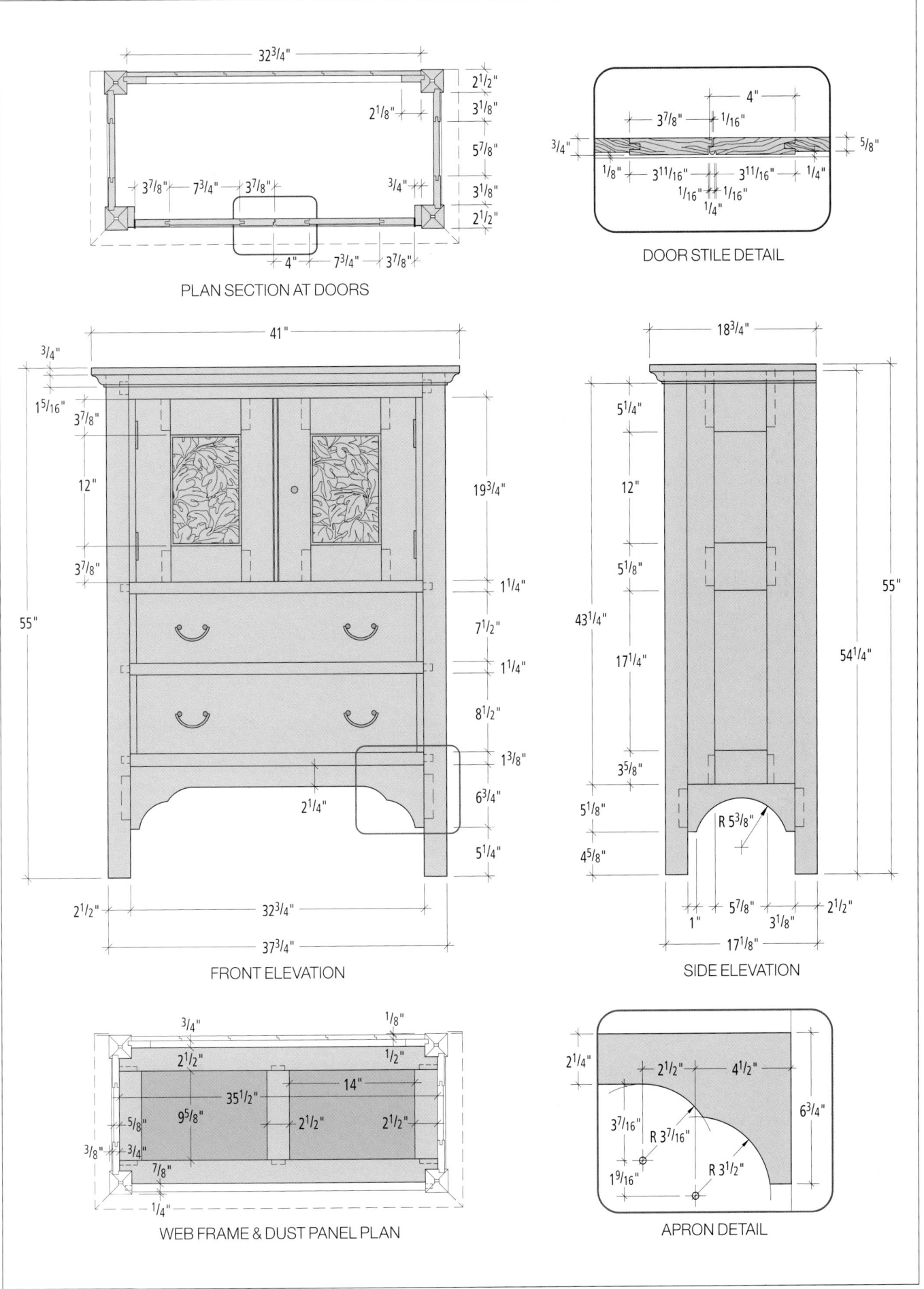

PLAN SECTION AT DOORS

DOOR STILE DETAIL

FRONT ELEVATION

SIDE ELEVATION

WEB FRAME & DUST PANEL PLAN

APRON DETAIL

in color, and I suspect that it may have faded or been refinished at some point. I decided to use a richer forest green, similar to a color that can be seen in another Byrdcliffe piece, a fall-front desk designed by Steele.

Oak and (not) Sassafras

Like the original, the visible parts of this cabinet are made of quartersawn white oak. The carved panels are often described as being made from sassafras, but they are obviously not. The carving depicts the leaves of a sassafras tree and in the original the panels are either poplar or basswood. I used basswood for the carvings, soft maple for the drawer boxes, and poplar for the interior web frames and back of the cabinet. The dust panels are birch plywood.

I brought the rough white oak into the shop and let it acclimate while I worked on carving the panels (below). I'm a decent carver, but not a fast one, so the oak had plenty of time to adjust. *Popular Woodworking* will be running some articles in the coming months on basic carving techniques, and full-size patterns for the panels are available in

pdf format from our web site using this address: popularwoodworking.com/magazineextras.

I gave the completed panels a thin coat of blonde shellac before coloring them with watercolor pencils, available from any artist's supply store. The colors are applied dry, then blended with an artist's brush dipped in water. I let the panels dry for several days, then gave them two coats of amber shellac to seal in the color and warm up the background.

The Real Work Begins

I milled all of the oak parts slightly oversized, and let them sit for a few days before planing them to finished dimensions. Absolutely straight stock is essential for a project like this. The side panels are all joined with mortises and tenons. Once these were assembled, I cut a rabbet on the long edge of each panel so that the faces of the stiles fit in a stopped groove cut in the legs as seen at right (next page). This makes the sides of the case very strong, and if the stiles shrink in width over time, the joints won't open up.

The web frames and dust panels are

A group of stiles for the web frame is clamped together to lay out the joints. Leaving the stack clamped together provides a stable base for the router used to cut the mortises.

also mortise-and-tenon construction. I clamped the stiles together to lay out the mortises and then realized that leaving them clamped together would provide a stable base for the small plunge router I used to cut the mortises (above).

Doors Carved, Then Colored

After tracing the pattern on the basswood panels, the design of sassafras leaves is carved.

The completed carving is given a wash coat of shellac, then colors are applied with watercolor pencils.

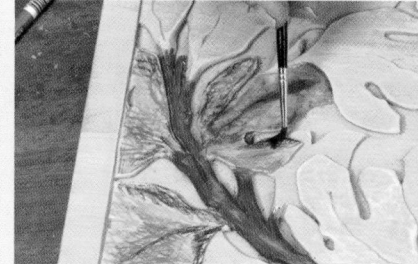

The colors are blended with an artist's brush dipped in water.

After the coloring is complete, the panels are allowed to dry several days before being finished with amber shellac.

Impossible Legs

Like a lot of Arts & Crafts furniture, the legs are an important element. The problem with quartersawn oak in this situation is two-fold: Thick stock usually isn't available, and the edge grain is ugly compared to the face grain. There are several ways to work around this, and the method I developed shows quartersawn figure on all four faces of the legs, and is relatively simple to mill and assemble.

I could have laminated the legs from thinner stock and then veneered the edges, but I have seen too many old pieces constructed this way that have cracks in the veneer. Quartersawn wood moves more in thickness than in width, so there's a good chance that this method will eventually fail.

Mitering four pieces together is a logical alternative, but without some way to keep the pieces from sliding during glue-up, assembly can be very difficult. In the early 1900s, Leopold Stickley developed a method that used rabbeted miters to form what he called a quadralinear leg. It's a good method, but without the custom-made shaper cutters he used it is difficult to mill.

Looking for a simpler method, I realized that by making the front and

The side panels are assembled as a unit, then fit in a groove in the leg, and butted at the bottom to the thicker arched rail.

back pieces of the legs a different thickness than the sides, I could make two of the pieces with simple miters, and use a small rabbet on the thicker pieces to keep the parts from sliding during assembly. The photos on pages 40-41 show the steps I took.

When I had the legs assembled, I used a plunge router with a fence to cut the stopped grooves for the side and

The web frames are notched around the legs and attached to the side rails with pocket screws. The front and back edges will be glued to the rails as they are assembled.

Several joints must be fit at one time as the second panel and leg assembly is put in place. Get some help so both sides can be fit and clamped at the same time.

Making the Legs

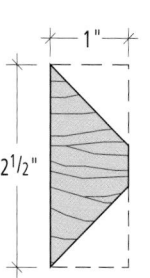

First, bevel the edges of the thinner piece without reducing the width. (See photos 1 and 2 below.)

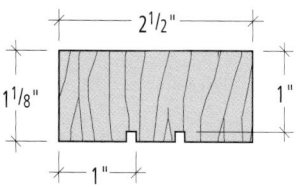

Second, cut grooves in the bottom of the thicker piece. (See photos 3-7 below.)

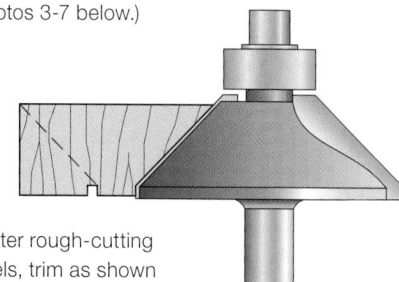

Third, after rough-cutting the bevels, trim as shown with bevel-cutting bit on the router table. (See photos 8-10 below.)

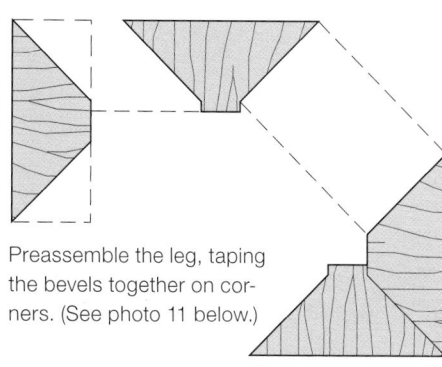

Preassemble the leg, taping the bevels together on corners. (See photo 11 below.)

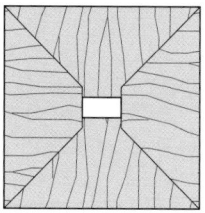

The assembled leg shows quartersawn figure on all four faces. (See photo 12 below.)

1. After ripping all the parts to finished width, cut a 45° bevel on both long edges of the thinner parts. Cutting the second bevel brings the part to its finished width.

2. Be careful ripping the second bevel. After the leading edge clears the blade, use a push stick centered in the stock's width to move the material past the saw blade without tilting it.

3. Set up to cut the grooves in the bottom of the thick pieces. With a thin piece of scrap against a thicker one, draw a line to indicate the difference in thickness. Flip the thicker piece over and use the pencil line to set the height of the saw blade.

7. With the blade height and fence settings adjusted, cut two grooves in the back of the thicker leg parts.

8. After the grooves are cut, the saw is again tilted to 45° and the waste is removed. Leave about ¼" of flat on the edge to ride against the router table fence.

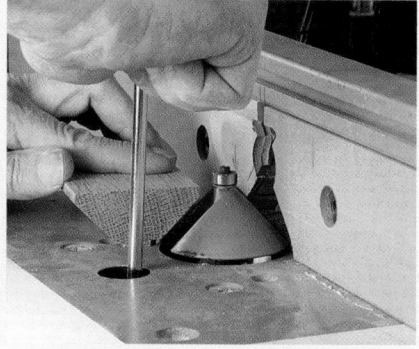

9. The 45° bevel bit is set to intersect the corner of the groove and the edge of the workpiece. The goal is to create the bevel without reducing the width on the face of the piece.

back panels, then laid out and cut the mortises in the front legs for the rails at the front of the carcase.

The side panel assembly is placed in the groove in the leg, and the arched bottom rail is placed in its mortise. The two pieces are then glued and butted together where they meet before the second leg is put in place. With the left and right leg and panel sides together, the entire carcase can be assembled.

With one side panel and leg assembly face down on some horses, I notched the corners of the web frames around the legs, and held them in place with pocket screws. The back frame was then put in the groove in the rear leg, followed by the front rails in their mortises. The butt joints between the rails and the front edge of the frames were glued and clamped at this time, as were the joints between the web frames and the back frame.

Putting the second leg and panel assembly on is straightforward, but there are a lot of parts that need to come precisely together. I made a dry run, and then got some help to fit it all together and apply the clamps.

Not Done Yet

Usually, getting the carcase assembled means that the end is in sight, but this cabinet contains several details that require additional work. Much of the interest of this design comes from the varying setbacks of the faces of the parts, particularly those on the front elevation.

The side panels are set back $3/8$" from the face of the legs, and the arched rail below it is $1/8$" thicker. On the front of the cabinet, the rails are back $1/4$" from

The drawers and drawer fronts are fit before finishing the cabinet. After hanging the doors, I mark where the right door overlaps the left before cutting the rabbet.

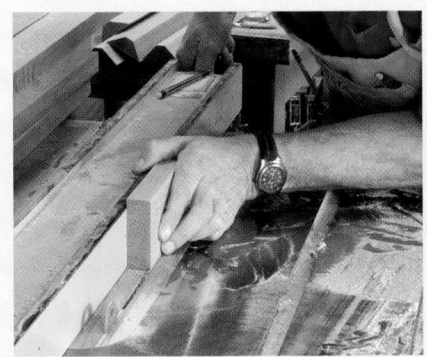

4. Set the distance from the blade to the fence by lining up the edge of a thin piece of stock to the left side of the blade. I use the saw cut in the table saw's zero-clearance insert as a guide.

5. Make some test cuts in scrap. Check the width of the groove by placing the edge of the scrap against the fence, and a thin piece of scrap on top. When the corner of the thin piece meets the far edge of the groove, the fence is set correctly.

6. Check the depth of the groove by placing a thin piece on the saw table, and butt the thicker piece against it. The face of the thin piece should meet the bottom of the groove.

10. After making some test cuts and fine tuning the router table setup, the edges are beveled. The block behind the featherboard holds it away from the fence, so it is pushing down on the narrow flat left between the two bevels.

11. After all the parts are milled, I assemble the corners and hold them together with packing tape. All but the last corner is taped before gluing. I then flip the taped parts over, put glue on the edges, then fold the parts back together, taping the last corner.

12. The completed legs have a small rectangular hollow in the center, and show quartersawn figure on all four sides. This is a stable assembly, relatively quick to make and easy to assemble.

The drawer runners have a tenon on the front end that fits in a mortise in the stile. These are placed in position before the stile is glued in place.

The back of the drawer runner is screwed to the back leg after being squared to the front of the cabinet. A groove in the side of the drawer box lets the drawers slide nicely.

the legs. At the top of the cabinet, filler strips were glued on so the back of the crown moulding would be flush with the outside edges of the legs.

The lower front rail and the stiles for the door hinges are $1/16$" back from the rails, as are the vertical pieces beside the drawers.

The hinge stiles allow the doors to swing clear of the legs, and this detail is seen in many pieces of Arts & Crafts furniture. The doors and drawer fronts are $1/16$" back from the front edge of the stiles. On the doors this offset is accomplished when locating the hinges. The placement of the stopped groove in the side of the drawer boxes locates the face of the drawer fronts.

The stiles for the hinges were cut and put in place, and the doors were assembled without glue so that all of the cutting for the hinge mortises could be done conveniently. Once I was satisfied with the fit of the doors, I marked where the right door overlaps the left, took everything apart and then glued the hinge stiles in place.

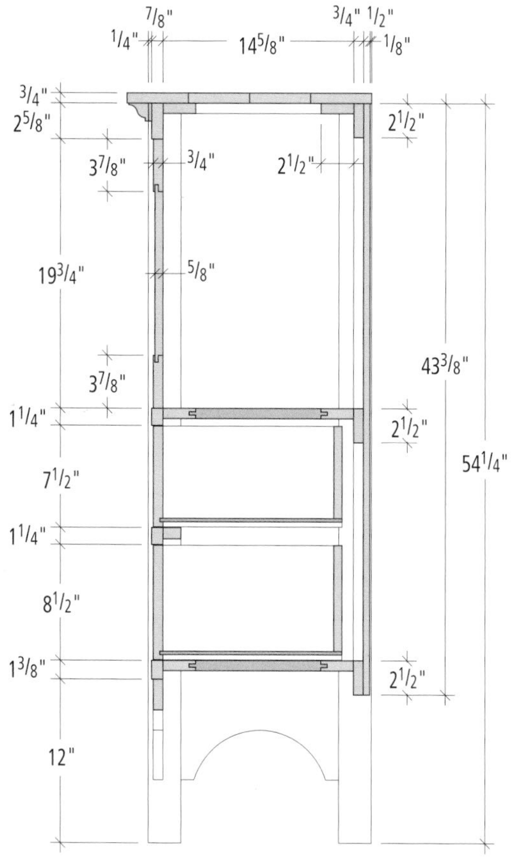

CABINET SECTION

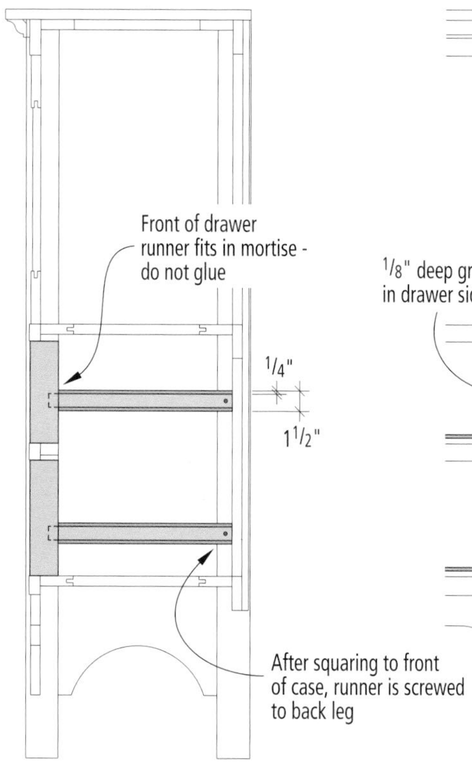

DRAWER RUNNER DETAIL

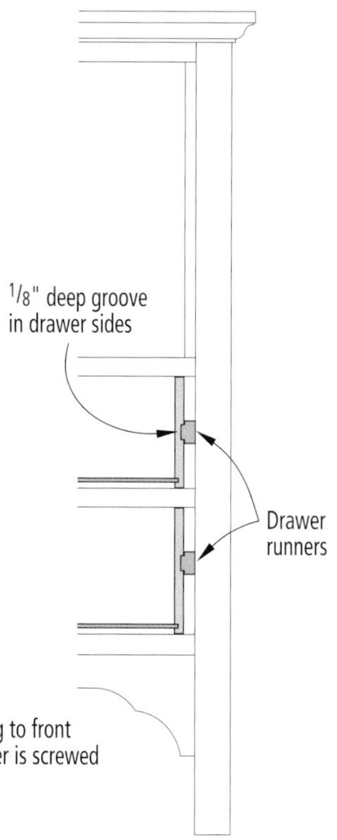

Front of drawer runner fits in mortise - do not glue

After squaring to front of case, runner is screwed to back leg

DRAWER RUNNER DETAIL

$1/8$" deep groove in drawer sides

Drawer runners

Drawer Runners

The drawers are rather wide, so I decided to use wood runners to guide them in and out without the bottoms of the drawer box sides rubbing on the web frames or the front rails of the cabinet. At the front of the cabinet, the runners fit loosely in mortises in the stiles beside the drawers. At the back, the runner is held to the back leg with a screw. This method allows minor adjustments to be sure that the runner is square to the face of the cabinet.

After securing the runners, I used a plunge router with a fence attached to cut the grooves in the sides of the drawer boxes. Squaring the ends of the grooves with a chisel and some test fitting allowed me to fit the drawer fronts precisely. I rubbed a pencil on the edges of the runners and moved the drawers in and out several times. This marked any high spots on the runners and the grooves. I used a shoulder plane to fine-tune the fit of the drawers and runners. I then rubbed a block of paraffin on the runners to let the drawers move effortlessly.

I fit and mitered the three pieces of crown moulding together, and attached them as a unit to the cabinet. I glued the front edge in place, and attached the returns to the sides of the cabinet with a few 23-gauge pins. The top is attached

to the cabinet with pan head screws through the web frame in oversized holes from below. With everything complete and fitted, I hand sanded the entire cabinet to #150 grit before staining.

It's Not Easy Being Green

At the art supply store, I picked up two 1.25 oz. tubes of artist's oil color; one phthalo blue and one chrome yellow. To make the green stain, I mixed half of each tube together with a pallet knife on a scrap of wood and added this to a pint of natural Watco Danish Oil, an oil/varnish blend. While stirring the mixture I added one-third of a pint of mineral spirits. This turned out to be twice as much liquid as I needed, but it's better to have too much than to run out halfway through.

I applied this stain to the cabinet, saturating the surface. After letting it sit for 15 minutes, I wiped off the excess with a clean rag and allowed the stain to dry overnight. I dissasembled the doors and stained the stiles and rails separately before gluing them together so that I wouldn't get any stain on the finished panel.

The stain dries to a rich deep color and leaves some pigment in the open pores of the oak. The stain was followed with a coat of natural Watco. This coat was rubbed on sparingly with a rag. This tends to float the color off the harder, smoother areas, changing the color to more of an olive tone and highlighting the flakes and rays of the quartersawn oak. This coat was allowed to dry on the

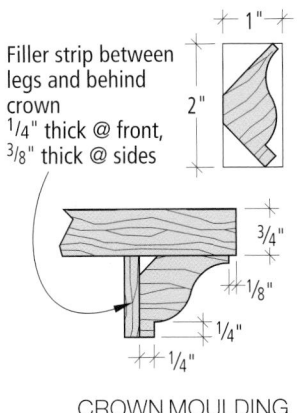

Filler strip between legs and behind crown
1/4" thick @ front,
3/8" thick @ sides

1"

2"

3/4"

1/8"

1/4"

1/4"

CROWN MOULDING

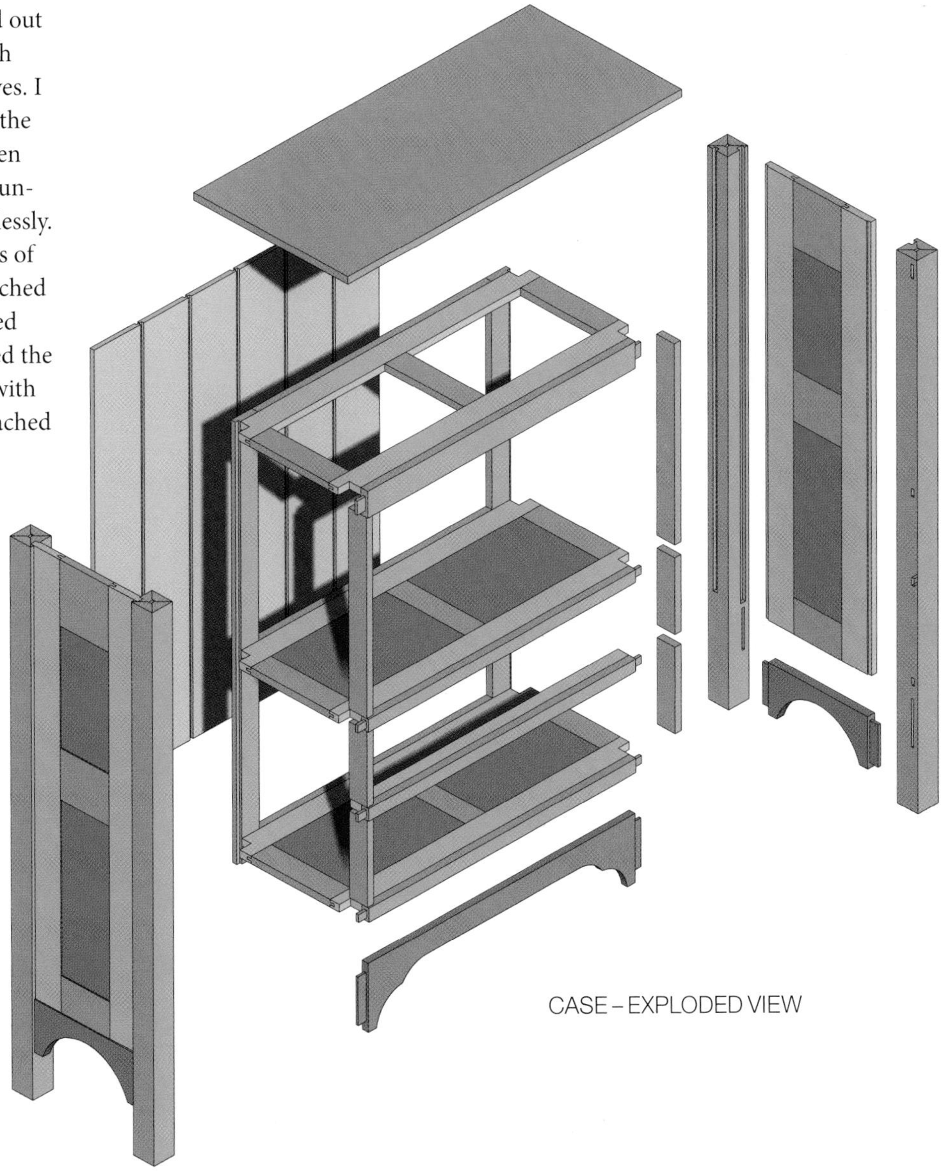

CASE – EXPLODED VIEW

The stain, a mixture of artist's oil colors and Watco Danish Oil is liberally applied. After letting it soak into the surface for 15 minutes the surface is wiped dry.

After staining, the wood is a rich green color and the open pores of the wood are filled with pigment.

surface for 48 hours, and then the cabinet was scuffed with a Scotch-brite pad.

Some areas were a little too green, so I used some medium walnut Watco in those areas, carefully blending the color. This was allowed to dry on the surface overnight, and once dry these areas were scuffed with the abrasive pad. The entire cabinet was then given two additional coats of natural Watco, followed by a coat of paste wax.

I finished the inside of the cabinet with shellac, then installed the shiplapped back planks, screwing them at top and bottom to the cross rails of the back frame.

I wanted the hardware to look old, so I soaked it in lacquer thinner and scrubbed the finish off with a nylon abrasive pad. I then put the parts in a plastic container along with a smaller container. I poured some ammonia into the smaller container, and put the lid on the larger one. Fumes from the ammonia oxidized the hardware in a few hours, giving me the patina I wanted.

I hung the doors on the cabinet, used a pair of ball catches at the top to keep them closed, and installed the pulls and knob.

The stain is followed by a coat of natural color Watco, which lightens the color and highlights the figure of the quartersawn wood.

Post Script

As a commercial enterprise, the furniture made at Byrdcliffe was a dismal failure. As examples of fine design, however, they were a tremendous success. In making this piece, I wanted to add the finest craftsmanship I could to this wonderful design, paying some respect to the anonymous craftsmen that Ralph Whitehead assumed would spoil the work if left unattended.

I knew I had succeeded when I showed my wife the finished cabinet. She looked at it for a while and then said, "It's like looking through pine trees on the edge of a forest on a perfect day in the fall." When craftsmanship evokes poetry, it's been a pretty good day.

Supplies

Whitechapel Ltd.
800-468-534 or
whitechapel-ltd.com

4 • 3" x 1⅝" butt hinges
   #205H1, $5.28 ea.

4 • polished rosette pulls
   #5PR14, $12.11 ea.

1 • hollow brass knob
   #98KSB9, $5.48

Lee Valley
800-871-8158 or
leevalley.com

2 • ball catches
   #00W12.01, $1.80 ea.

Cornell University
museum.cornell.edu/byrdcliffe/

• Byrdcliffe: An American
  Arts & Crafts Colony, online exhibition

Prices correct at time of publication.

American Corner Cabinet

BY GLEN HUEY

There is something about corner cabinets that spooks most woodworkers. They look like trouble because they've got a lot of angles and the case isn't square – it's got six sides. Well allow me to let you in on a little woodworking secret. These are easy to build.

If you know how the case goes together, you'll understand what I mean. Essentially, there are three important assemblies: a face frame for the front with a couple extra wings on it, the rear support (which has dados for the shelves), and the shelves themselves. You put these three parts together and everything else – the moulding, doors and back – is easy.

I've made this project even easier for you by providing the exact layouts for the shelves. Even the angled work is easy. You'll only need to adjust your saw blade's bevel to 22½° and 45° during this project, two common settings.

Pick your wood carefully for this project because what shows in the front has got to be good. I used curly maple as the primary wood, with poplar as the secondary wood for interior parts. Because so much of this project is behind the face frame, most of this project is made using common poplar.

So not only is this corner cabinet easy to build, it's also pretty inexpensive for such a large case piece.

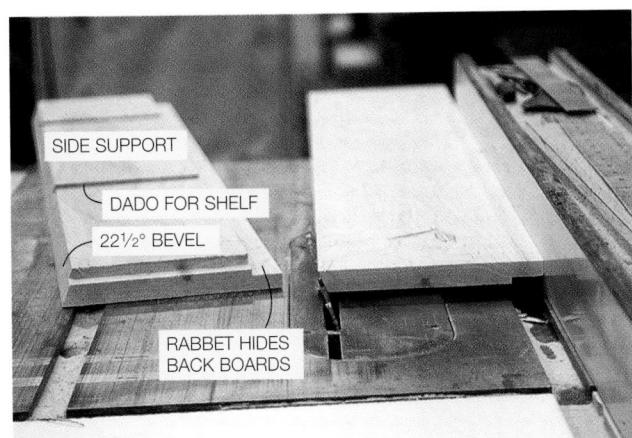

1. Begin by cutting the upper and lower side supports and rear supports to size. Then mark the shelf dado locations using the diagrams and rout ¼"-deep dados in all six pieces for the upper and lower shelves. Now cut a ¾" x ⅜" rabbet on one edge of each side support to hide the backboards, then rip a 22½° bevel on the other edge. On the back supports, cut a 45° bevel on each long edge.

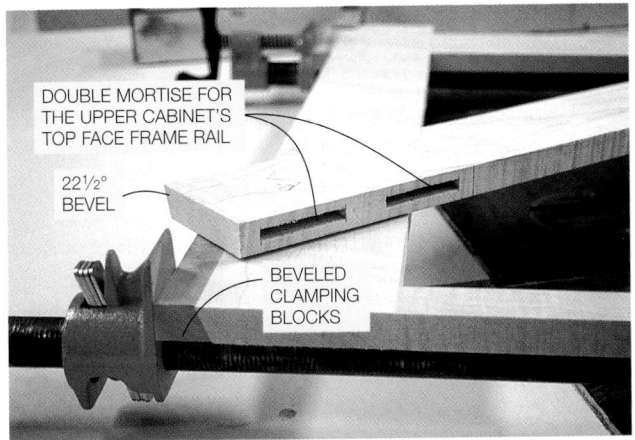

2. Cut the mortise-and-tenon joinery for the upper and lower face frames. Note that the mortise-and-tenon joint for the upper cabinet's top frame rail is a double tenon, and the lower cabinet's bottom rail doesn't extend to the floor. Rip a 22½° bevel on the outside edge of each face frame stile. Assemble the two frames. Use small blocks with a corresponding 22½° angle to make clamping easy.

3. Sand the interior of all pieces and then glue the side supports to the face frames. To make things easier, add a few biscuits to the joint to keep things aligned during glue-up. I use a special clamping jig (see below and right) that I designed for assembling corner cupboards. Make sure you have plenty of clamps.

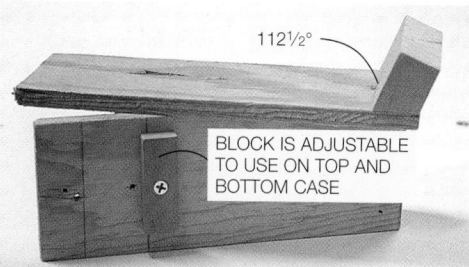

112½°

BLOCK IS ADJUSTABLE TO USE ON TOP AND BOTTOM CASE

CLAMP JIG TO CABINET

CLAMP JIGS TOGETHER

4. The shelves are nearly all the same size, so I milled and glued individual boards to create enough blanks for all eight pieces, using the larger, lower shelf dimension to start. By offsetting the boards, as shown in the photo, you can lay out two interlocking triangular shapes per blank, reducing waste.

5. Next, cut the shelves to size, following the patterns in the diagrams. I generally make one shelf for each section of the cupboard and then use them each as a pattern for the balance of the shelves. Make just three shelves for the top case with the cut as shown. The remainder are straight at the front edge.

REAR SUPPORT

6. Apply glue to the dados in the side supports and slide the shelves into place. Then set the rear support into place and use two #8 x 1¼" screws per shelf to attach everything together.

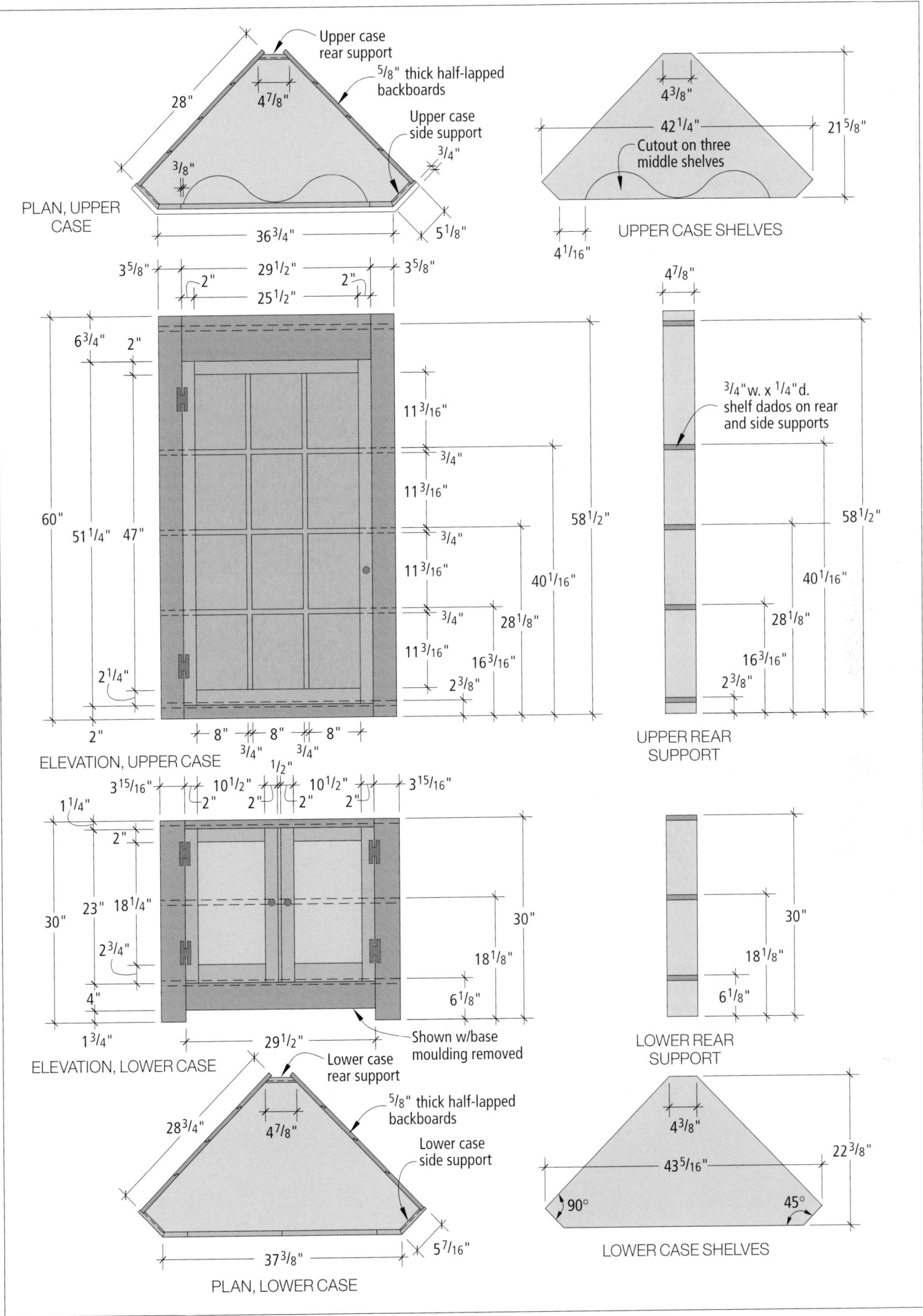

PLAN, UPPER CASE

Upper case rear support
28"
4⁷/₈"
⁵/₈" thick half-lapped backboards
Upper case side support
3/4"
3/8"
36³/₄"
5¹/₈"

UPPER CASE SHELVES

4³/₈"
42¹/₄"
21⁵/₈"
Cutout on three middle shelves
4¹/₁₆"

ELEVATION, UPPER CASE

3⁵/₈" 29¹/₂" 3⁵/₈"
2" 25¹/₂" 2"
6³/₄" 2"
11³/₁₆"
3/4"
11³/₁₆"
3/4"
58¹/₂"
60"
51¹/₄" 47"
11³/₁₆"
3/4"
40¹/₁₆"
28¹/₈"
11³/₁₆"
16³/₁₆"
2¹/₄"
2³/₈"
2"
8" 8" 8"
3/4" 1/2" 3/4"

UPPER REAR SUPPORT

4⁷/₈"
³/₄"w. x ¹/₄"d. shelf dados on rear and side supports
58¹/₂"
40¹/₁₆"
28¹/₈"
16³/₁₆"
2³/₈"

ELEVATION, LOWER CASE

3¹⁵/₁₆" 10¹/₂" 10¹/₂" 3¹⁵/₁₆"
2" 2" 1/2" 2" 2"
1¹/₄"
2"
30" 23" 18¹/₄"
2³/₄"
4"
1³/₄"
29¹/₂"
30"
18¹/₈"
6¹/₈"
Shown w/base moulding removed

LOWER REAR SUPPORT

30"
18¹/₈"
6¹/₈"

PLAN, LOWER CASE

Lower case rear support
28³/₄"
4⁷/₈"
⁵/₈" thick half-lapped backboards
Lower case side support
37³/₈"
5⁷/₁₆"

LOWER CASE SHELVES

4³/₈"
43⁵/₁₆"
22³/₈"
90°
45°

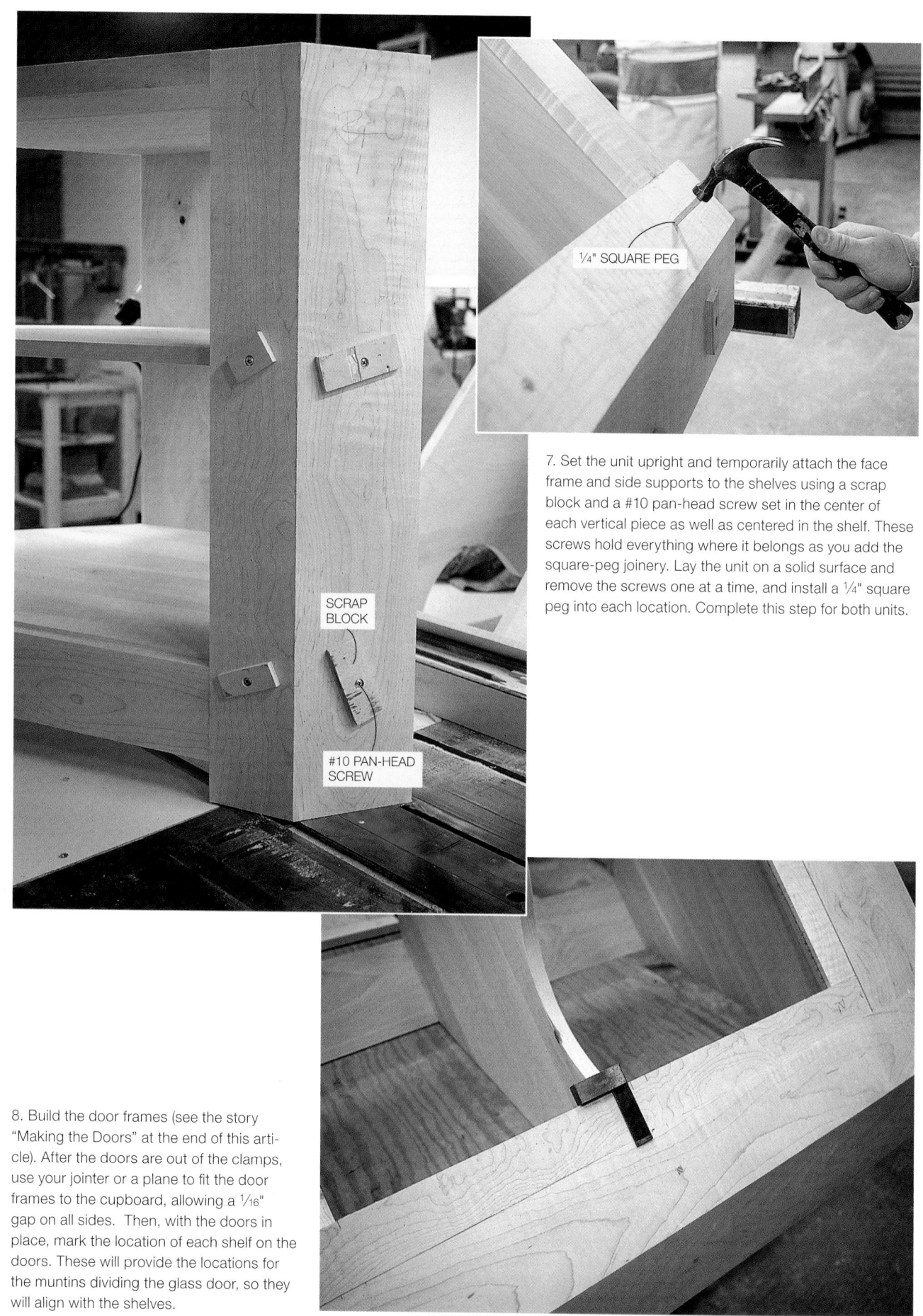

¼" SQUARE PEG

SCRAP BLOCK

#10 PAN-HEAD SCREW

7. Set the unit upright and temporarily attach the face frame and side supports to the shelves using a scrap block and a #10 pan-head screw set in the center of each vertical piece as well as centered in the shelf. These screws hold everything where it belongs as you add the square-peg joinery. Lay the unit on a solid surface and remove the screws one at a time, and install a ¼" square peg into each location. Complete this step for both units.

8. Build the door frames (see the story "Making the Doors" at the end of this article). After the doors are out of the clamps, use your jointer or a plane to fit the door frames to the cupboard, allowing a ¹⁄₁₆" gap on all sides. Then, with the doors in place, mark the location of each shelf on the doors. These will provide the locations for the muntins dividing the glass door, so they will align with the shelves.

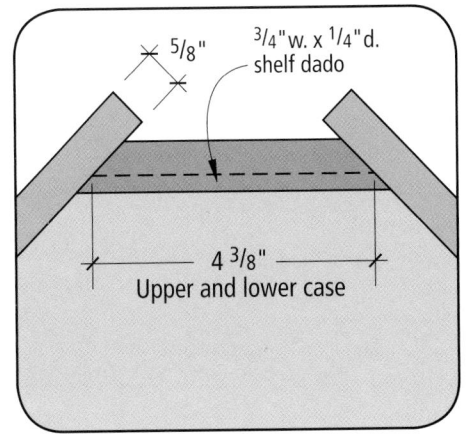

BACK CORNER DETAIL

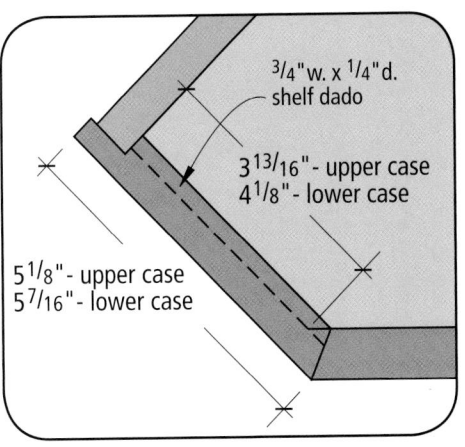

LEFT AND RIGHT CORNER DETAIL

Supplies

Hardware from Horton

Brasses, horton-brasses.com, 800-754-9127

Door hinges:
3 pair of #HH-2 3"hinges
$16.50 per pair

Upper door knob:
1 • H-97L - $6.50

Lower door knobs:
1 • K-12 (1") - $3.75 each

1 • H97 - $6.00

Interior finish:
Brierwood Green acrylic latex (#2024) from Olde Century Colors, oldecenturycolors. com, 800-222-3092

American Corner Cabinet

	NO.	ITEM	DIMENSIONS (INCHES)			DIMENSIONS (MILLIMETERS)			MATERIAL	COMMENTS
			T	W	L	T	W	L		
CASE										
☐	1	Upper rear support	3/4	4 7/8	60	19	124	1524	Poplar	
☐	1	Lower rear support	3/4	4 7/8	30	19	124	762	Poplar	
☐	4	Eight shelves	3/4	22 3/8	66	19	569	1676	Poplar	Glued offset to create two shelves
☐	2	Upper side supports	3/4	5 1/8	60	19	130	1524	Maple	
☐	2	Upper face frame stiles	3/4	3 5/8	60	19	92	1524	Maple	
☐	1	Upper top FF rail	3/4	6 3/4	32	19	171	813	Maple	1 1/4" TBE
☐	1	Upper bottom FF rail	3/4	2	32	19	51	813	Maple	1 1/4" TBE
☐	2	Lower side supports	3/4	5 7/16	30	19	138	762	Maple	
☐	2	Lower FF stiles	3/4	3 15/16	30	19	100	762	Maple	
☐	1	Lower top FF rail	3/4	1 1/4	32	19	32	813	Maple	1 1/4" TBE
☐	1	Lower bottom FF rail	3/4	4	32	19	102	813	Maple	1 1/4" TBE
LOWER DOORS										
☐	2	Outside stiles	3/4	2	23	19	51	584	Maple	
☐	2	Inside stiles	3/4	2 7/16	23	19	62	584	Maple	
☐	2	Top rails	3/4	2	13	19	51	330	Maple	1 1/4" TBE
☐	2	Bottom rails	3/4	2 3/4	13	19	70	330	Maple	1 1/4" TBE
☐	2	Door panels	5/8	11 3/8	19 1/8	16	289	486	Maple	
UPPER DOOR										
☐	2	Stiles	3/4	2	51 1/4	19	51	1301	Maple	
☐	1	Top rail	3/4	2	27 1/2	19	51	699	Maple	1" TBE
☐	1	Bottom rail	3/4	2 1/4	27 1/2	19	57	699	Maple	1" TBE
☐	8	Grid pieces (approx.)	1/4	1/2	26 1/2	6	13	673	Maple	
☐	2	Grid pieces (approx.)	1/4	3/4	50	6	19	1270	Maple	
☐	3	Grid pieces (approx.)	1/4	3/4	26 1/2	6	19	673	Maple	
MOULDING										
☐	1	Base	5/8	4 1/2	5lf	16	115	1524	Maple	
☐	1	Waist	13/16	1	5lf	21	25	1524	Maple	
☐	1	Crown	3/4	4 5/8	5.5lf	19	118	1676	Maple	
BACKBOARDS										
☐	2	Upper	5/8	27	57 1/2	16	686	1461	Poplar	Multiple half-lapped pieces
☐	2	Bottom	5/8	28	26 1/2	16	711	673	Poplar	Multiple half-lapped pieces

KEY: TBE = tenon on both ends

9. To begin the muntin section of the doors, cut three horizontal $\frac{1}{4}$" x $\frac{1}{2}$" backer strips to divide the glass area into four horizontal rectangles. The fit should be snug, but not so tight as to bow the frame. Glue the backer piece into the rabbet area and clamp until dry. Flip the door over. Then install the two vertical $\frac{3}{4}$"-wide x $\frac{1}{4}$" face pieces that divide the glass into three vertical rectangular sections. These are glued to the first three backer strips at the intersections, but left loose at the edges of the frame for now. This technique is covered in more detail in the August 2002 issue of *Popular Woodworking*.

$\frac{1}{4}$" X $\frac{1}{2}$" BACKER STRIPS

$\frac{3}{4}$" X $\frac{1}{4}$" FACE STRIPS

BACKER STRIPS

FENCE SCREWED OR CLAMPED TO SAW TABLE

10. When your spring clamps are available again, flip the door to the back side and install the eight remaining vertical $\frac{1}{4}$" x $\frac{1}{2}$" backer strips to the back of the two vertical face pieces. When dry, all that is left are the nine $\frac{3}{4}$"-wide x $\frac{1}{4}$" facing strips on the front side of the door.

11. I used my table saw to mill the one-piece, bold crown moulding (as shown at right), then created a molded edge on both the top and bottom edges before final sanding. If this is a new technique to you, it is detailed in issue #117 of *Popular Woodworking*, or you can simply purchase a suitable pre-made crown moulding.

12. Next, cut the crown to length, fitting it to the upper case, and attach it using square-head reproduction nails. When finished, cut reinforcement blocks and install them between the face frame and the crown.

REINFORCEMENT BLOCKS

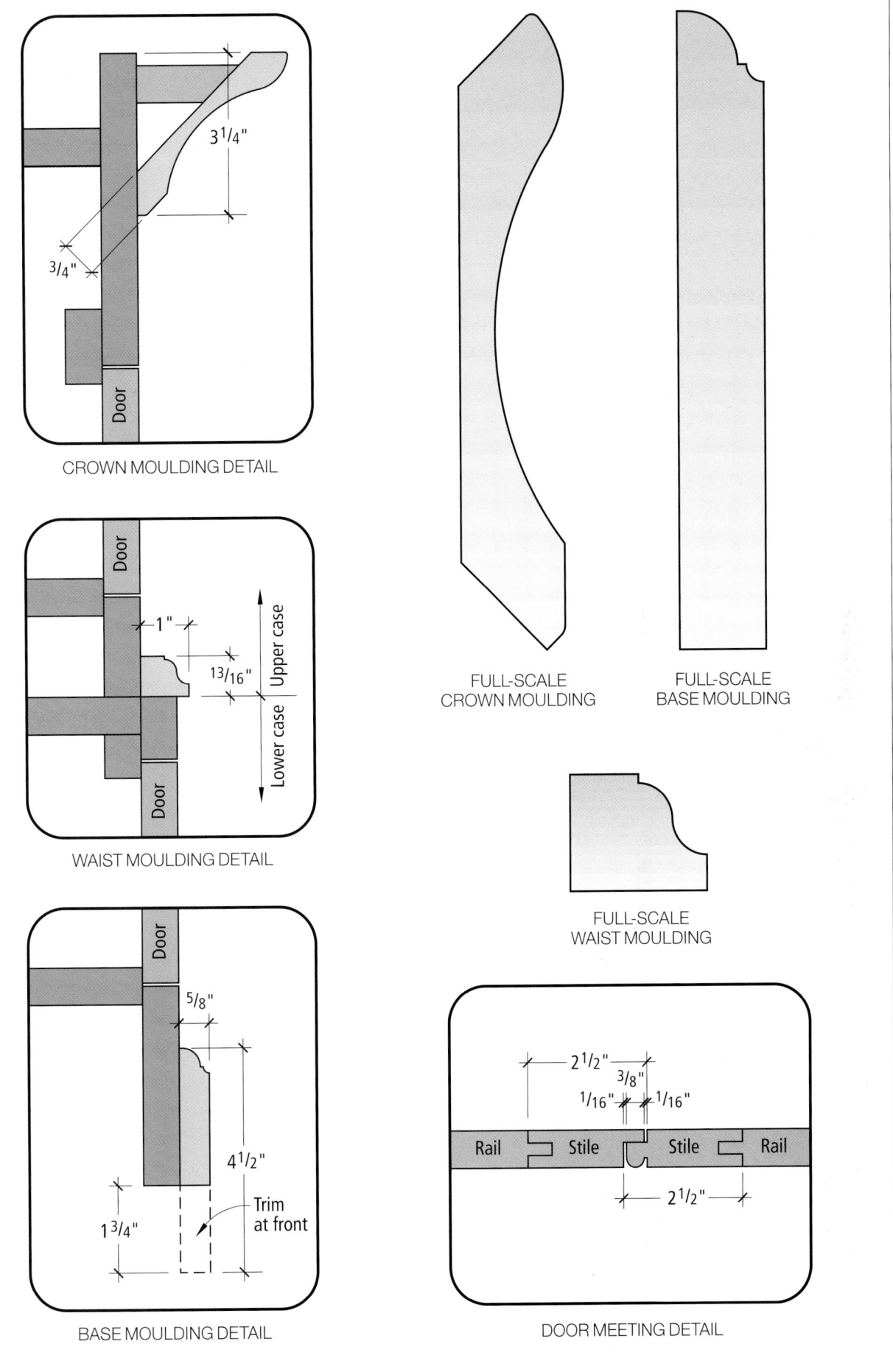

CROWN MOULDING DETAIL

3 1/4"

3/4"

Door

WAIST MOULDING DETAIL

Door

1"

13/16"

Upper case

Lower case

Door

BASE MOULDING DETAIL

Door

5/8"

4 1/2"

1 3/4"

Trim at front

FULL-SCALE CROWN MOULDING

FULL-SCALE BASE MOULDING

FULL-SCALE WAIST MOULDING

DOOR MEETING DETAIL

2 1/2"

3/8"

1/16"   1/16"

Rail   Stile   Stile   Rail

2 1/2"

13. Mill the base moulding for the lower cabinet and rout the top edge profile. Fit and cut the base to the cabinet; but before attaching it, create the cut-away area on the front base. The curve is a 2" radius that starts 5½" from the corner. Then glue and nail the base in place.

14. The waist moulding is next. Set the upper unit onto the lower unit, aligning the rear supports and sides. Fit the waist moulding to overlap the two sections, tacking the moulding in place on the lower unit, but not the upper unit. Separate the two sections, then finish nailing the waist moulding to the top edge of the lower unit.

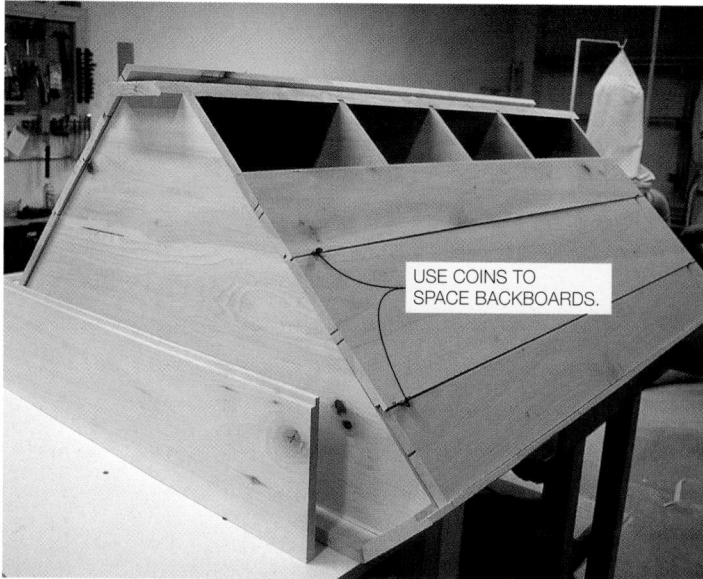

USE COINS TO SPACE BACKBOARDS.

15. Before attaching the back pieces, use a ½" core box or roundnose bit to rout a plate groove into the top side of the three cut-out shelves and bottom shelf of the top section. Set the center of the cut at 1½" from the wall sides of the shelves.

16. Create the backboards using half-lap joints, but leave the pieces loose at this time. Finish sand all the pieces, and you're ready to add the finish. After the piece is stained and complete, paint the interior with two coats of a simulated milk paint, including the backboards. When dry, install the backboards using nails or screws, allowing a bit of a gap for expansion.

17. To complete the project, fit the glass into the upper door and install the hardware. The glass is held in place using Durham's water putty. For the hardware on this cupboard I used surface-mounted H-hinges and brass door catches.

I dyed this project using J.E. Moser's golden amber maple water-based aniline dye (available from Woodworker's Supply (800-645-9292 or woodworker.com).

Making the Doors

The lower doors are simply a raised-panel style door with a half-lap center and a bead detail at the lap. A ¼"-wide x ½"-deep groove in the stiles and rails hold the raised panel.

Begin the upper glass door by milling the lumber according to the cut list and cutting the mortises in the stiles, leaving a minimum ⅜" interior shoulder. Next, cut a ⁵⁄₁₆" x ½" rabbet on the interior, inside edge of all four door pieces.

Make the face shoulder cut so that the blade just clears into the rabbet.

Next, change the fence location by ⁵⁄₁₆" by moving it closer to the blade. Then make the second shoulder cut, creating an offset of the cuts.

With the fence at the same location, cut to create the edge shoulder. Remove the cheeks and the shoulder, remembering that there are two different cheek heights to cut.

With the joints finished, you are ready to assemble this door frame. As you can see, the rabbet for the glass is created, and the joinery is professional.

Greene & Greene Medicine Cabinet

BY ROBERT W. LANG

This cabinet caught my eye on my first visit to the Gamble house. I had an hour to kill before the tour began, and spent that time in the bookstore, which is housed in the original garage. Charles and Henry Greene added nice details to every facet of their work, even places the owners would rarely, if ever, see. The Gamble garage is a very nice garage.

At the back of the building is a small restroom provided for the chauffeur. That is where the original version of this cabinet has lived for almost 100 years. A picture of the original cabinet is on page 68 of the November 2008 issue of *Popular Woodworking* (#172).

I was taken with the form and proportions. The case is very simple, with curved forms on the top and bottom of the sides, and a wonderfully proportioned door. I promised myself to someday build a version.

I had a small amount of bird's-eye cherry that I had been hoarding for several years. There wasn't enough of it to build a large piece of furniture, but there was too much for a small project, so it sat in my garage. The day after completing the drawings for this project I tripped over the precious pile of cherry and decided it was time to use it. Some quick measurements revealed that I had just enough to build this cabinet.

Details Make Simple Into Sublime

My widest piece of cherry had enough material for the two carcase sides and the door panels. I took the piece intended for the panels, resawed it at the band

saw, and set it aside while I worked on the case.

I sketched, then printed full-size paper patterns of the top and bottom side profiles, using the dimensions from the illustrations on page 160, and adhered them to the sides with spray adhesive.

I held the two sides together with double-stick tape, cut the profiles at the band saw, and cleaned up the cuts with a rasp followed by a scraper. Working on both sides at the same time ensured a good match, and cut the time for making the sides in half.

The top and bottom of the case fit in stopped dados. I made a jig to guide my router for cutting the dados by clamping two pieces of scrap to each side of the top. I then screwed a third piece at a right angle to the other two to register the router on the front of the case side.

Using a $\frac{5}{8}$"-diameter mortising bit with a bearing mounted above the cutter, I made a test cut in some scrap, then clamped the jig to the side and routed a $\frac{1}{4}$"-deep dado, stopping $\frac{1}{2}$" short of the width of the finished top and bottom.

STOP ACTION. A pencil mark indicates the end of the dado, and because the router will leave rounded ends, I stop just short of the mark.

The top overhangs the door, and the bottom sits behind the door, so I laid out the exact dimensions before cutting the dados.

I squared off the ends of the dados with a chisel, and cut a notch in the front edge of the two horizontal pieces. The only other joinery on the case is a

VINTAGE CABINET, SPECIAL WOOD. Originally designed for the Gamble house a century ago by Charles and Henry Greene, this small cabinet is worthy of a prominent place in any home.

½"-wide by ½"-deep rabbet for the back panels. I used a rabbeting bit in a hand-held router, cutting the rabbet along the entire length of the top and bottom. The rabbets in the sides stop where the rabbets meet the dados.

Before assembling the case, I drilled ³⁄₁₆"-diameter holes for the two adjustable shelves. I brushed the end grain of the top and bottom with yellow glue, and also coated the end grain inside the dados. After waiting 10 minutes, I brushed a second coat of glue inside the dados, and clamped the case together. Sizing the end grain like this makes for a stronger glue joint.

A Well-made Door

The door is rather wide, and the components of it are rather thin, so I paid careful attention to the joinery. The first step was to cut a ¼"-wide by ⁵⁄₁₆"-deep groove on one edge of the outer stiles and the top and bottom rails. The narrow intermediate stiles were grooved on both edges.

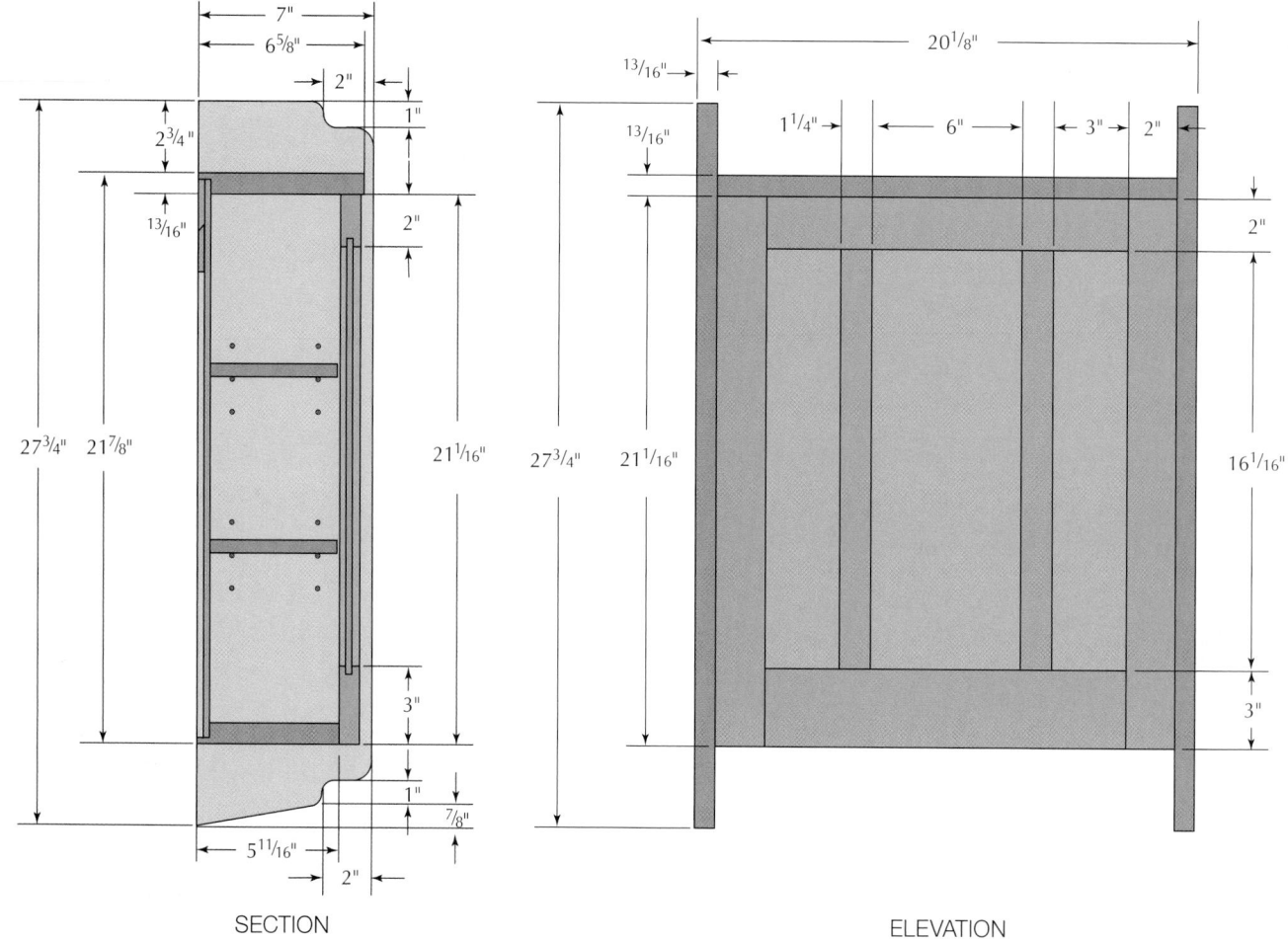

SECTION   ELEVATION

Greene & Greene Medicine Cabinet

	NO.	ITEM	DIMENSIONS (INCHES)			DIMENSIONS (MILLIMETERS)			MATERIAL	COMMENTS
			T	W	L	T	W	L		
❏	2	Sides	¹³⁄₁₆	7	27¾	21	178	705	Cherry	
❏	1	Cabinet top	¹³⁄₁₆	6⅝	19	21	168	483	Cherry	
❏	1	Cabinet bottom	¹³⁄₁₆	5¹¹⁄₁₆	19	21	144	183	Cherry	
❏	2	Shelves	⅝	5⅛	18⁷⁄₁₆	16	130	468	Cherry	
❏	4	Back boards	¼	5	21⅜	6	127	543	Cherry	Shiplapped
❏	2	French cleats	¼	2	18½	6	51	470	Poplar	
❏	2	Outer door stiles	¹³⁄₁₆	2	21¹⁄₁₆	21	51	535	Cherry	
❏	2	Inner door stiles	¹³⁄₁₆	1¼	18⁹⁄₁₆	21	32	471	Cherry	1¼" tenon both ends
❏	1	Top door rail	¹³⁄₁₆	2	17	21	51	432	Cherry	1¼" tenon both ends
❏	1	Bottom door rail	¹³⁄₁₆	3	17	21	76	432	Cherry	1¼" tenon both ends
❏	1	Center door panel	¼	6½	16⁹⁄₁₆	6	168	420	Cherry	
❏	2	Outer door panels	¼	3½	16⁹⁄₁₆	6	90	420	Cherry	

I made the grooves by passing the edges of the pieces over a stack dado set at the table saw, running the grooves all the way along the edges of the stock. The groove is located $\frac{1}{4}$" in from the back of the door making it offset by $\frac{1}{16}$" in the $\frac{13}{16}$" material.

This meant all the grooving had to be done with the face against the saw fence, but from that point on there was no confusion regarding which was the front and which was the back on the door parts; the fat side was out and the skinny side was in.

I set up the hollow-chisel mortiser with a $\frac{1}{4}$" chisel and with the face of one of the stiles against the machine fence, I adjusted the fence so the chisel was aligned with the groove. I set the depth of the chisel to cut $1\frac{5}{16}$" deep from the edge of the stiles and cut the four mortises in the outer stiles. I wasn't sure how my material would behave, so I kept the ends of the mortises 1" away from the ends of the stiles to keep the ends from blowing out.

The top rail is the same width as the outer stiles, so the same machine settings could be used to make the mortises for the intermediate stiles. The lower rail is wider, so I had to readjust the depth of cut before cutting the last two mortises.

I used a wheel cutting gauge to define and mark the shoulders of the tenons. The fine cut left by the gauge is actually the finished edge of the shoulder. I made the cheek cuts for the tenons on the table saw using a tenoning jig that rides the

saw's fence, and used the sliding crosscut table to cut the shoulders.

To avoid over-cutting the tenon shoulders, I left a little bit of material on the inside corner. I used the cutting gauge to remove this and refined the fit of the tenons with a paring chisel and a rasp.

The groove for the panels continues beyond the tenons, so I needed to cut a

haunch on the sides opposite the groove in the top and bottom rail tenons. Using my adjustable square, I set the stock on the edge of a rail, and dropped the blade into the groove.

This provided the exact dimension for the haunch without measuring. I then placed the end of the square against the shoulder and marked the cut line.

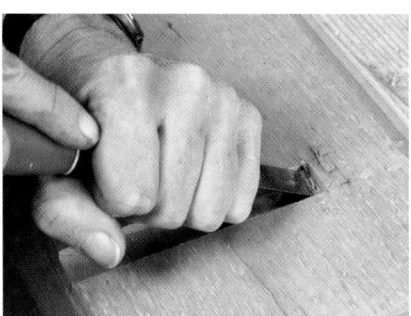

FINISH BY HAND. A few cuts with a chisel complete the end of the dado for the top and bottom shelves. The front edge of the shelf is notched and ends $\frac{1}{2}$" past the end of the dado. The notch is cut by hand with a dovetail saw.

DUAL-PURPOSE TOOL. The cutter on the gauge removes the remaining material where the tenon cheek and shoulder meet. After scoring it with the gauge, pare with a chisel.

DROP-IN MEASUREMENT. With the adjustable square sitting on top of the groove in the stile, the blade is bottomed out to obtain the exact measurement for the depth of the groove.

EASY TRANSFER. Setting the end of the square's blade against the shoulder, and marking with a pencil at the bottom of the stock, transfers the depth of the groove to the haunch in the tenon.

FASTER BY HAND. Cutting the haunch by hand is faster than setting up to make these cuts by machine. Only the end of the haunch will be seen in the finished door, so this is a good place to practice making cuts by hand.

After marking the width of the haunch, I made the cuts with a dovetail saw. In addition to filling in the groove, the haunch serves to keep the faces of the rails and stiles aligned.

The Focus of Attention

The panels of the door presented an aesthetic problem. I started with one piece of material, $13/16$" thick and 7" wide. I resawed it down the middle and planed the two pieces to a finished thickness of $1/4$". My original plan was to use one piece

DOUBLE DUTY. The haunch fills the panel groove on the outer edges of the door. It also will keep the stile and rail faces aligned if the wood warps.

for the center panel, and rip the other in half for the two outer panels.

The grain pattern was straight on one half of the panel, but the other half contained a cathedral arch at the bottom. The three panels together wouldn't have looked right with an arch on the left, an arch and straight grain in the center, and straight grain only on the right-hand side.

My solution was to bookmatch the panels, so I flipped one piece over, and glued the straight-grain portions together in the center. After the glue dried, I made two rip cuts in the panel, leaving a wide, straight-grained section and two narrow pieces with mirror-image arches in the lower corners.

I assembled the door in two stages. First I put the center panel in place ,and glued and clamped the two intermediate stiles between the top and bottom rails. I let this sit in the clamps over a long lunch, and then inserted the outer panels, brushed glue in the mortises of the stiles and completed the assembly.

I did this to help keep the door square. The glue on the interior joints

had set, and held the top and bottom rails in position as I glued on the outer stiles. I only had to keep an eye on a few joints rather than wrestling with several clamped in opposing directions.

The Search for the Right Hardware

One of the distinctive features of this cabinet is the position of the door, set back from the front of the case $1/2$". This looks cool, but it presents a problem: There isn't any room for the barrel of standard butt hinges. The original solution was to use hinges known as "parliament hinges" commonly found on casement windows of the period.

This isn't the type of hinge likely to be found at the local hardware store, and a search of the Internet led to one source that had the correct size and configuration. The only finish available was polished brass, so when the hinges arrived, I soaked them overnight in lacquer thinner, then scrubbed them with an abrasive pad.

With the finish removed, I put the hinges inside a plastic storage container with an air-tight lid. Putting on my respirator, goggles and rubber gloves, I poured a couple ounces of strong ammonia into a small cup, put that in the container along with the hinges then sealed the lid. In about two hours, the brass had the patina I was looking for.

I set a hinge on the cabinet side with the barrel even with the edge and marked a line at the bottom of the leaf. This gave a reference for the edge of the hinge mortise on the edge of the door.

I set up a small plunge router with a $1/2$"-diameter straight bit, and set the fence so that the edge of the bit was just inside the line of the leaf edge. To set the depth of cut to the thickness of the hinge leaf, I first leveled the bottom of the bit with the base of the router. Then I placed the hinge leaf between the depth stop and the adjustment rod. Lowering the rod set the cut depth to the exact thickness.

I placed the door in my bench vise with the edge flush with a small box. This prevented the router base from tipping as I cleared the waste from the hinge mortise. A little work with a chisel

TWO STEP GLUE-UP. The center panel is put in place and the intermediate stiles glued between the top and bottom rails. After letting the glue cure, the outer panels are inserted, and the stiles are glued to the rail ends.

BETTER THAN MEASURING. Use a leaf of the hinge to set the depth stop on the plunge router. Set the bottom of the bit flush with the router base, then set the depth stop to the hinge. Plunge the router to the stop and you're set.

SUPPORT GROUP. I clamp the door in my vise with the top edge of the door even with the top of a wood block. The fence on the router sets the distance for the hinge mortise, and the base of the router can't tip.

cleaned out the rounded corners left by the router.

Because the barrels of the hinges are in front of the door, the door swings in a different arc than it would if hung on standard butt hinges. This allowed a narrow gap on the stile opposite the hinges, and I only needed to plane a slight back bevel to fit the door. The hinges are simply screwed to the side of the cabinet; no mortise is needed.

Getting a Handle on Things

I had hoped to use a casement window latch to hold the door closed, as had been used on the original. A second look at the photo of the original revealed the latch actually came past the edge of the case side, with the strike plate extending about ¼" beyond the cabinet. I wasn't happy

---

Supplies

Hardware Source
877-944-6437 or
hardwaresource.com

2 • solid brass parliament hinges,
2¼" x 3", #817000, $12.97 each

Lee Valley
800-871-8158 or
leevalley.com

1 • double ball catch, 38mm x 7mm
#00W12.00, $1.40

8 • steel shelf supports,
#00S10.01, $3.70 pkg. of 50

Prices correct at time of publication.

---

with that detail, and searched in vain for a casement latch that looked like the original without the plate sticking out.

In a moment of Krenovian inspiration, I took a scrap of cherry, $^{13}/_{16}$" x 1" x 1¾", and sketched a profile on the side. I carefully made some rough arced cuts at the band saw, then smoothed the profiles with the round side of a rasp. I attached the handle to the door with a screw from behind, slightly below the center of the stile.

To keep the door closed, I used a small double-ball catch placed near the upper corner of the door. The bottom of the door stops on the bottom shelf. The shelves sit on 5mm-diameter pins and to keep the pins out of sight, I used a ⅜"-diameter core box bit to rout two grooves in the bottom edge of each shelf.

The back consists of four ¼"-thick x 5"-wide pieces, with a rabbet on adjoining edges. These shiplapped pieces are held to the top and bottom of the cabinet with #6 x ⅝" screws. After attaching the back, I screwed a ¼"-thick French cleat across the top of the back to hold the cabinet to the wall.

My favorite finish for cherry is several coats of Danish oil, applied with a rag and wet-sanded with a nylon abrasive pad. I planed and scraped all of the cabinet parts before assembly, to keep sanding to a minimum. Before finishing, I hand-sanded with #240-grit Abranet, then sanded again with #320-grit, leaving a smooth surface.

FINAL CUTS. The router leaves a flat bottom and a straight back edge to the hinge mortise. The rounded corners, however, need to be removed with a chisel. Knifed-in layout lines provide a reference for the chisel.

I wanted to warm and darken the color so I used Watco "Medium Walnut" for the first three coats of finish. I flooded the surface for the first coat, and kept the surface wet for 45 minutes, adding oil to any areas that dried out. Then with a clean rag, I wiped the surface dry, and left things alone for a couple hours.

The second coat can be applied the same day as the first, but I only left it wet for 15 or 20 minutes before wiping it dry. This and subsequent coats were left to dry overnight. Three coats of "Natural" Watco followed the first three coats, and after 48 hours of drying, I applied a coat of paste wax. The completed cabinet is destined for a nicer home than the back of the garage.

Shaker Shelves

BY MEGAN FITZPATRICK & GLEN D. HUEY

Basic skills with portable power tools and hidden screws are all it takes to create this graceful set of shelves. With this project we'll teach you a few clever tricks to draw arcs without a compass, and to straighten twisted boards – which is often a problem when working with wider pieces of wood.

This modified Shaker design, downsized from a set of creamery shelves, is adapted from a Shaker Workshops catalog. To ensure our ¾"-stock would not bow under the weight of even the heaviest items, we decided to make these shelf pieces a bit shorter than those you'll find on the company's web site (shakerworkshops.com).

Many home centers carry only pine, poplar and oak (you may also find maple or aspen, depending on your region). We decided on oak because we think it has the best natural appearance.

One of the biggest challenges you'll have with this project is finding wide boards that are straight and flat ... and that remain straight and flat after you cut them to size. Take time to look through the racks for the best boards – and if at all possible, avoid shrink-wrapped boards, no matter how pretty. You'll need two 6' and one 4' 1 x 12s (or one 10' and one 8' length). You'll also need a 6' length of 1 x 4 for the supports.

Once you're back in the shop, your first step is to cut the sides to length on your miter saw. If you have a 10" miter saw, your crosscuts on the sides (and shelves) will be a two-step process because the diameter of the saw blade limits the width of the cut. You'll need to

Pocket screws and two back supports make this handsome Shaker-inspired shelf simple to build.

first cut on one side of your board, then flip it over and carefully line up the kerf with the saw blade before completing the cut (see picture at right).

Now, you're ready to lay out the arched top and cutout at the bottom. Align the top edges of the sides and stick the faces together with double-stick tape to keep them from slipping, then clamp both pieces together flat to your workbench. Now, measure across the width to find the center of your board, and make a mark. That measurement is the same distance you'll measure down from the top edge to mark the intersec-

Because the wood for the sides and shelves is 11¼"-wide and your miter saw is likely a 10" model, you'll have to cut the pieces in two steps. Measure and make the first cut. Then flip the board over and line up the saw blade to the kerf you've already cut, and make the second cut.

A thin piece of scrap, a nail and a drill are all it takes to make this simple compass jig.

You can pull a cup out of a board by clamping the piece to a straightedge and pulling it tight with clamps before screwing it down.

Make sure your drill is at a 90° angle to the most narrow stock through which you're drilling – in this case, the ¾" edge of the side beneath the support.

tion of the two points (5⅝"unless you've resized the plan, or used different-sized stock). This point is where you'll place your compass point to draw the half-circle arch across the top.

And if you don't have a compass, it's no problem. It's easy to make a compass jig. Simply grab a thin piece of scrap and drive a nail through the middle near one end. Now, using the same measurement you already established to find the compass point (again, it's 5⅝" on our plan), mark and drill a hole that distance from

the nail, and stick a pencil point through it. Voilà – a compass jig.

You can use that same jig for the bottom arched cutout. Simply drill another hole 3⅛" away from your nail. Set the nail as close to the center of the bottom edge as possible and mark the cutout arch. Or, mark the arch with a traditional compass.

Now use your jigsaw to cut as close to the lines as possible, and use a rasp and sandpaper to clean up the cuts. If you keep the pieces clamped together during this process, you should end up with nearly identical arches. If you're not confident in your jigsaw skills, practice making curved cuts on some scrap pieces before moving on to the real thing.

Now cut the shelves to length.

Set up your pocket-hole jig for ¾"-thick material. Mark the placement for three pocket holes on each end of each shelf, two of them ¾" from each long edge, and one in the center of the end. Drill the holes. Cut the back supports to length, and sand all pieces to #150-grit before assembly (#120 if you're planning to paint).

Now you're ready for assembly, and the second trick we promised. Lay one

side flat on your bench and mark the location of the top shelf at either side. You may not be able to line up the shelf with your marks because of cupping in the wide board; that's where the trick comes in. Position the back support (or any straight piece of scrap) along the bowed side of the shelf, if there is one, and use clamps to bring the edges of the shelf flat to the support or straight scrap. Slide the clamped unit to the layout lines, hold or clamp it in place then use screws to attach. This trick will work to pull the bow from any of the shelves.

Attach all three shelves to both sides, straightening the pieces where necessary.

Now lay the assembly face down, line up the support with the top of your top shelf. Drill countersunk holes at the top shelf, at the bottom shelf, and at the inside edge where the support meets the middle shelf. Be sure to hold your drill at 90° to the sides; because you're drilling into ¾" stock, you could easily drill through the side if you're not careful.

Attach the uprights with #8 x 1¼" screws (rubbing the threads on some wax will help them seat more easily). Pay particular attention at the top and bottom as the stock can easily split. If it does crack, stop your drill immediately – but don't panic. Just back the screw out a tiny bit, and the split will close up.

Finish the shelves with two coats of wiping varnish.

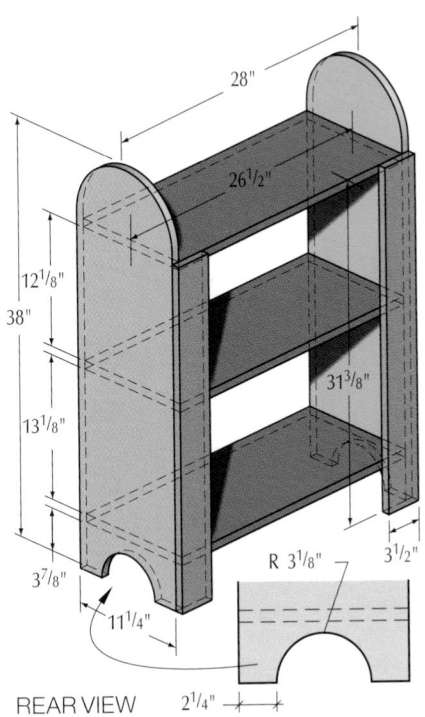

28"
26½"
12⅛"
38"
31⅜"
13⅛"
3⅞"
R 3⅛"
3½"
11¼"
REAR VIEW 2¼"

Shaker Shelves

| NO. | ITEM | DIMENSIONS (INCHES) | | | DIMENSIONS (MILLIMETERS) | | | MATERIAL |
		T	W	L	T	W	L	
❏ 2	Sides	¾	11¼	38	19	285	965	Oak
❏ 3	Shelves	¾	11¼	26½	19	285	673	Oak
❏ 2	Supports	¾	3½	31⅜	19	89	797	Oak

Shaker Stepback

BY MEGAN FITZPATRICK

I have a love-hate relationship with my television. I love (too much, perhaps) to watch shows, but I hate having the TV out in the open as the focal point of my living room. But I also dislike most commercial entertainment centers, as I've a penchant for antique and antique-style furniture.

So, I flipped through a pile of books on Shaker furniture and auction-house catalogs to cull design ideas for a stepback cupboard that could be repurposed as a modern entertainment center that would not only allow me to hide a 32" flat-panel TV behind doors, but also house the cable box, DVD player and various stereo components. (Of course, if you want to use it in your dining room, just omit all the holes in the backboards for air flow and cord management.)

A Plethora of Panels

While this project is quite large, it's suprisingly easy to build – though it's an exercise in organization to keep all the parts straight. The upper face frame, lower carcase and all four doors are simple mortise-and-tenon joints, with panels floating in grooves in the doors and carcase sides.

The first step is to mill and glue up all the panels. Use your best stock for the door panels, as they'll show the most. And here's a tip I didn't know until after it was too late: Keep all your cathedrals facing in the same direction and your panels will be more pleasing to the eye.

For the four doors, you'll need six ⅝"-thick panels, two each of three sizes.

You'll also need two ⅝"-thick panels for the lower carcase sides.

Unless you have access to a lot of wide stock, you'll also need to glue up ¾"-thick panels for the upper carcase sides, top, bottom and shelves, and the lower carcase bottom, shelf and top.

I glued up all my panels oversized. After the glue was dry, I took them out of the clamps, stickered them and set them aside. I cut each to its final dimension as it was needed, after calculating its exact measurement from the dry-fit frames and carcase sides. I don't trust cut lists; no matter how religiously I stick to the plan, measurements change in execution.

Mortises and Tenons Galore

With the panels set aside, I moved on to all the pieces that would be joined with mortise-and-tenon joints. Initially, I'd planned to concentrate on one carcase at a time to more easily keep things organized. I quickly realized that's an inefficient work method, as the mortise-and-tenon setups are the same on both the top and bottom pieces of the project. Rather than create each setup twice on the machines, I prepared all my stock and cut the joints at the same time.

First, chuck a ¼" chisel and bit in the mortiser, and take the time to make sure the chisel is dead parallel to the machine's fence. I began with the leg mortises – the only pieces on which the mortises aren't centered. After choosing the best faces for the show sides of each, mark which leg is which. Mark out your mortises. On the inside back of the rear legs, they're set in 1" so the rail can

accommodate the ⅝"-thick backboards. On the front and sides, they're ¼" back from the show faces, so that the rails end up flush with the front of the leg faces. The top rails are flush with the top of the legs, so lay out 1½" mortises on the inside front of the two front legs, and 2½" mortises on the side, ¼" down from the top. The bottom rails are all 3", so your mortises will be 2½", 1¼" up from the bottom of the leg.

Cut the mortises for the back rail first with 1" distance between the chisel and the fence, then change the setup to ¼" spacing, and cut the remaining mortises in the legs. To make clean mortise cuts, most of the *Popular Woodworking* editors

HIDDEN ENTERTAINMENT. This traditional cupboard hides a flat-screen television and all the accompanying audio and video accoutrements.

SHAKER STEPBACK ■ 167

use the "leap-frog method." That is, skip a space with every hole, then clean up between the holes. Some woodworkers prefer to overlap each hole to get a clean cut. Try both methods on scrap pieces, and use whichever you prefer.

Assuming your stile stock is exactly ³⁄₄" thick, the setup should remain the same for the face frame and door mortises, but double check that the chisel is centered in your stock before making that first frame cut. And, make sure you always work with the same side against the fence – if you are off a little bit, you'll be equally off on every joint, and cleanup will be easier.

Lay out all the mortises on your face frame and door frames and make the cuts. (A sturdy 6" rule is my preferred tool for cleaning the detritus out of the bottom of each mortise.)

Now it's on to the tenons. I prefer to set up the full ¹³⁄₁₆"-wide dado stack at the table saw, and raise it to just shy of ¹⁄₄". That way, I can make two passes on each end of my tenoned workpieces, and simply roll around each face to create the tenons, without having to change the setup at all for any of my 1¹⁄₄"-long tenons.

With the tenons cut just a hair oversized in thickness, I test-fit each one individually in its mortise and used a shoulder plane to reach the final fit. Planing a slight chamfer at the end of the tenon will help it seat. (The fit should be a tight press fit. The tenon shouldn't move around in the mortise – nor should you need a mallet to get things together.)

Grooves for Floating Panels

With the mortise-and-tenon joints all dry-fit, it's time to cut the grooves that will accept the floating panels. Chuck a ¹⁄₄" three-wing cutter into your router table, and raise it ¹⁄₄" (you can use your already cut mortises to set the height – no measuring necessary). Set the fence to make a ³⁄₈"-deep cut.

Start with the legs – and double check to make sure you have the faces marked correctly. The floating panels are on each side of the carcase, so a groove is needed from mortise to mortise on the front face of both back legs, and on the back face of both front legs. Unless your ear protection blocks out all noise, you should be able to hear the difference in sound as the router cutters move from the hollow of the mortise into the groove cut (mark the starting and stopping point if you're worried about recognizing the sound differential). With the leg flat to the table and the mortise toward the bottom, push

A SEA OF PANELS. I wanted to glue up all the panels at the same time – but I ran out of clamps and space. Above are the six door panels and two lower side panels.

MANY MORTISES. The majority of joints in this project are mortise and tenon. Take the time to set the hollow-chisel mortiser to cut dead-on centered mortises, 1¹⁄₄" deep – it will save you a lot of frustration and time later.

TABLE-SAW TENONS. The full dado stack on our table saw is ¹³⁄₁₆" and the tenons are 1¹⁄₄" long, so I made the first cut on each face with the workpiece tight to the fence, then slid it to the left for a second pass. The blades are raised just shy of ¹⁄₄" so I was able to simply roll the end of each ³⁄₄" workpiece to cut the tenons with one setup.

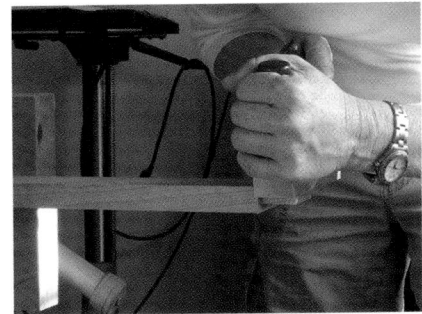

FINAL FIT. I purposely cut the tenons just a hair oversized. I reached the final fit by testing each tenon in its mortise, then shaving each cheek as needed with a shoulder plane. And, I planed a slight chamfer on the tenon ends to make them easier to fit.

A HOME FOR FLOATING PANELS. To cut ³⁄₈"-deep grooves for the floating panels, set up a ¼" three-wing cutter (also known as a slot cutter), using your mortises to set the cutter height. The groove will run from mortise to mortise.

RAISED PANELS. Set up a fence-extension jig on the table saw, set the blade at a 12° angle, set the distance between the fence and blade at ³⁄₁₆" and raise the blade until it just clears the workpiece as the cut is made. This jig, built by Senior Editor Glen D. Huey, slides along the rail, so the workpiece can be clamped in place.

the leg against the fence so that the router bit is spinning in the empty mortise hole, then move the leg across the table, cutting a groove that stops in the other mortise, then pull the leg away. Repeat until all four leg grooves are cut, and set the legs aside.

Test the bit height on your ¾" stock before proceeding. It shouldn't need adjustment … but it never hurts to be sure. Grooves are needed on all frame pieces that will house a panel – that's the inside edges of all the door rails and stiles, and on both long edges of the medial rails for the upper doors. On the stiles, the groove goes from mortise to mortise. On the rails, in order to cut a full ³⁄₈" deep across the rail, you'll be nipping the inside edge of the tenon. That's OK – but be careful to cut away as little as possible so that the joint retains maximum strength.

Raised Panels

Now dry-fit the sides and doors and take the final measurements for all the panels. Add ⁵⁄₈" to both the height and width of each; with ³⁄₈" hidden in the groove on all sides, you build in an ⅛" on either side for your panel. Retrieve the door and side panels from your stickered stack; cut them to final size at the table saw.

Now, set up a fence-extension jig on your saw – a stable flat panel attached to your rip fence will work, but that jig will be stationary and you'll have to carefully move your workpiece across the spinning blade. It's safer to make a jig that fits over the fence and slides along it.

That way, you can clamp the workpiece to the jig and move the unit instead.

For any stock thickness, set the blade angle to 12°, and set the fence so there's ³⁄₁₆" between the fence and the inside saw tooth as the tooth clears the bottom of the throat plate. Raise the blade enough so that the stock fits between the blade and the fence (approximately 2¾"). This ensures the blade will clear the stock completely as the cut is made. Make sure you use a zero-clearance throat plate; otherwise, the thin offcuts will get caught and kick back.

Cut across the grain first, at the top and bottom edges. Any tear-out will be cut away on your second two cuts, which are with the grain. Clamp your workpiece firmly to the fence extension and slide it smoothly across the blade. Now repeat until all six panels are raised, and sand away the mill marks. These panels will fit snug in the ³⁄₈"-deep grooves, and allow for seasonal expansion and contraction. And if you prefer a more country look to a Shaker style? Face the raised panels to the outside of the piece and you're there.

Shapely Feet

At some point before you do any glue up, you'll want to turn your feet at the

lathe and create a tenon at the end to join to the leg. (Of course, you could also add 6" to your leg length, and turn the foot on the leg stock. However, I decided I'd rather muck up a 6" length of wood than a 34" piece, so I made the feet as separate pieces.) I first milled each foot blank square, then turned them round and shaped each foot, following the pattern at right.

Even if each foot is slightly different (you can't tell unless they're right next to one another), be careful to turn the tenoned ends as close in size as possible. To achieve this, I set my calipers to ¾" and held them against the tenon as I cut the waste away with a wide parting tool. As soon as I reached a ¾" diameter, the calipers slid over the piece. I then turned the rest of the tenon to match.

Why make those tenons the same? Well, you have to fit the tenons into drilled holes that are centered in the bottom of each leg, and I wanted to use but one drill bit and achieve a tight fit.

I clamped each leg perpendicular to the floor, and drilled ¾"-diameter x 1¼"-deep holes centered in the bottom of each leg. Be careful to keep your drill straight (or set up a drill press for greater accuracy). With the holes drilled, I set the feet aside until the rest of the bottom carcase was done.

Time for Glue Up

Dry-fit all your panels to the grooves inside the door frames and the bottom case sides, and make any necessary adjustments. Once everything fits snug, get your clamps ready and work with one glue-up at a time (I started with the lower doors and side panels, as they involved fewer pieces).

Use an acid brush to apply a thin layer of yellow glue on the walls of your mortises and the tenon faces, slip the rails in place, then slide the panel in place and cap it off with the opposite stile (keep a damp rag handy to wipe away any squeeze-out). Clamp until the glue is dry. (Again, add glue only to the mortise-and-tenon joints; the panels should float.) The upper doors are a bit tricky to glue up, with two panels plus the medial rail in each. I'm sure my contortions were amusing to watch. I recommend getting a friend to help wrangle things in place.

While you're waiting for the lower sides to dry, glue up the upper face frame, check it for square, clamp and set it aside. Once the lower side panels are set, complete the lower carcase's mortise-and-tenon joints by gluing the lower back rail, the front rails and the center stile in place. (The upper back rail is notched around the legs at both ends, so it's easier to use pocket screws for that joint, though you can cut a mortise-and-tenon joint if you prefer.)

Now it's on to the upper section. Cut your sides, top, bottom and shelves to final size. The ¾"-thick top, bottom and shelves are housed in ¼"-deep grooves cut into the side pieces. So set up the dado stack again at the table saw but use only enough blades and chippers to create a ¾"-wide cut (and be sure to run a few test pieces first). Raise the stack to ¼". Mark the cuts on one of the case sides and set the fence off that piece, making the cuts in both sides before moving the fence for the next location. Make sure your cuts are on the inside faces of your sides. Note in the illustration that the top and bottom pieces are not at the ends;

they're set in to add rigidity, and the bottom protrudes ¼" above the face-frame bottom and thus functions as a door stop.

Before you take off the dado stack, run a ¾"-deep x ⁷⁄₁₆"-wide rabbet up the back of each side; these will house the backboards.

Now lay one side piece flat on your workbench (groove-side up) and fit the top, bottom and shelves into place. Set the other side piece on top, and use a dead-blow mallet to fully seat the pieces in the grooves. (This is a big workpiece – you might want to grab a helper.) If the

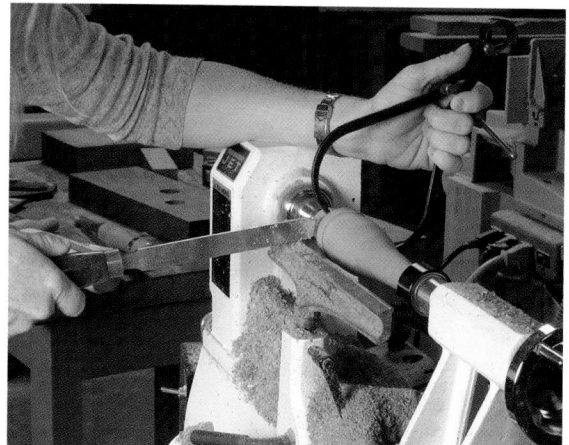

CUSTOM FEET. I shaped my 6" feet on the lathe and turned a ¾" x 1¼" tenon at the top of each. While the feet needn't be identical, the tenons should be close in size. I held calipers set to ¾" against the piece as I used a parting tool to make the cut. When I reached ¾", the calipers slipped over the tenon and I was done.

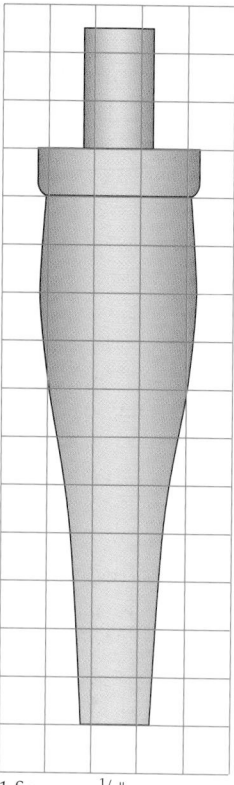

1 Square = ½"

FOOT LAYOUT

FOOT HOLES. Before the bottom carcase is glued up, drill holes to receive the tenons on the turned feet. I used a ¾" Forstner bit to drill 1¼"-deep. Match your bit and depth to the size of the tenons on your feet.

Supplies

Lee Valley
800-267-8735 or leevalley.com

4 pr. • 3" x 1¹¹⁄₁₆" narrow extruded brass fixed-pin butt hinges #00D02.04, $19.60 per pair

Rockler
800-279-4441 or rockler.com

4 • 1⅛" cherry Shaker pegs #78469, $5.99 per pair

Prices correct at time of publication.

pieces fit together snug, you could pull them back out, add a little glue and refit them. But after struggling to get them in place once, I didn't want to go through that exercise again (and it was a lot of exercise). Instead, I chose to toenail the shelves in place from the bottom face at both the front and back edges.

At this point, I also pegged all the mortise-and-tenon joints, and pegged the shelves in the upper carase into the sides, using ¼" white oak pegs.

Now fit your doors to the face frame, and mark then cut the hinge mortises. Keep the door fit tight – you'll do the final fitting once the entire carcase is together (things could move when you add the backboards later – trust me). You might as well fit the lower doors and hinges at the same time.

Now, flip the upper carcase on its back and glue the face frame in place, adding enough clamps to pull it tight along each side. If things work out correctly, you'll have a slight overhang on both sides, which, after the glue dries, you can flush to the face frame with a trim router or handplane.

Backboards

Is that dado stack still in your table saw? Good. Mill enough ⅝"-thick stock for your backboards for both the top and bottom, and run ⁵⁄₁₆" x ⅜" rabbets on opposing edges for shiplaps (and don't forget to calculate the rabbets as you're measuring the width of your rough stock). The outside pieces get only one rabbet each.

I used random-width boards pulled from an old stash of sappy cherry. Because the backboards will be on view with the doors open as I watch TV, I didn't want to use a less attractive secondary wood. So I used less-attractive pieces of primary wood. With the rabbets cut, change the table saw set-up back to a rip blade, and rip the outside backboards to final width (the humidity was low here when I built this, so I used dimes as spacers).

Screw the backboards in place, with one screw at the top and bottom of every board set just off the overlapping edge. (That screw holds the joint tight, but allows for slight movement of the under-

lapped piece. Your last board needs two screws at the top and bottom to keep it secure.) Now do the final fit on your doors, taking passes with a handplane or on the jointer (take a 1" cut on the trailing end first, then reverse the piece to avoid tear-out). I aimed for a ¹⁄₁₆" gap all around (on some sides, I even hit it). After marking locations for any necessary wire and air-circulation holes in the backboards, take the doors and backboards off, drill any needed holes at the drill press, then set the doors and backboards aside for finishing. Drill any cord/air holes at the drill press with a Forstner bit.

Complete the Bottom

Flip the lower carcase and choose your foot position. Line up the grain of the foot with its matching leg so the look is pleasing. One of my holes was a bit off straight, so I used a rasp to take down one side of my tenon until I could adjust the angle accordingly. Once everything fits to your satisfaction, drip a little yellow glue in the holes and seat the feet. You don't need clamps here (unless you're using them to pull something in line). If the fits are good, simply flip the piece upright and the weight will keep the feet in place as the glue dries.

With the backboards and doors off, now's the time to fit the cleats that support the bottom and shelf in the lower section, and cut button slots in the top rail to attach the top. The bottom is notched around the legs and the back edge is rabbeted to fit neatly over the back

BUTTONED DOWN. The top of the bottom section is attached to the side and front rails with buttons. I used a biscuit joiner to cut two ½"-deep x 1¼"-wide slots on each side, and three along the front. I simply screwed through the back rail into the top's bottom to secure it at the back.

rail. But because I need airflow in the bottom section for A/V equipment, I fit the shelf to the inside corner of each leg and to the front center stile where it serves as a door stop. I left a gap at the back and sides to run wires and for air circulation.

To complete the bottom section, use a biscuit cutter to cut slots in the front and side rails for buttons, and notch the upper back rail around the rear legs and use pocket screws to hold it in place. For added strength, countersink a screw through the front edge at each end into the leg, too. Cut the top to final size, and attach it with buttons at the front and sides. Countersink screws underneath through the back rail into the bottom of the lower section.

The Crowning Touches

Set up your table saw to cut crown moulding, and sand it smooth before fitting. (If you're not familiar with this method of creating crown moulding, you can purchase a piece of crown from your woodworking supply store as an option.)

Often, the crown is connected with a flat piece to the top edge of the sides and face frame. But my face frame and sides weren't high enough, so instead, I cut blocks with 45° angles (on two faces for the corner pieces), glued those to the inside of the crown and added brads to the top of the carcase for a bit of additional strength.

The Finish

I sanded each piece to #180 as I went along, so once the construction was complete, I was ready for the finish. Because I didn't have two decades to wait for a nice warm patina to develop (we shot the opening picture just 20 minutes after the handles were in place), I added warmth with two sprayed coats of amber shellac and a top coat of dull-rubbed-effect, pre-catalyzed lacquer.

Because I couldn't afford five sets of hand-forged iron hinges but wanted an aged look to the hardware, I de-lacquered then added patina to brass hinges with gun bluing.

Oh yes – the handles. I tried to turn them, but ran out of time and talent.

Thank goodness for our local woodworking store and its Shaker pull supply. The handles were sprayed separately, set in a scrap of plywood. You see, I didn't know where I wanted to place them until the entire piece was assembled and the A/V components were in place. A friend helped me hoist the upper piece atop the lower cabinet, where it's held in place simply by gravity. I then marked my pull locations, drilled ⅜" holes with a Forstner bit and glued the pulls in place.

CUTTING CROWN. The crown is cut by running ⅞" x 4" stock at an angle over the table saw. Raise the blade to ⁷⁄₁₆" then center your stock to the blade. Clamp a long straightedge to the table to guide the stock, then lower the blade and make a series of passes as you gradually raise the blade until you reach ⁷⁄₁₆" (or your desired depth).

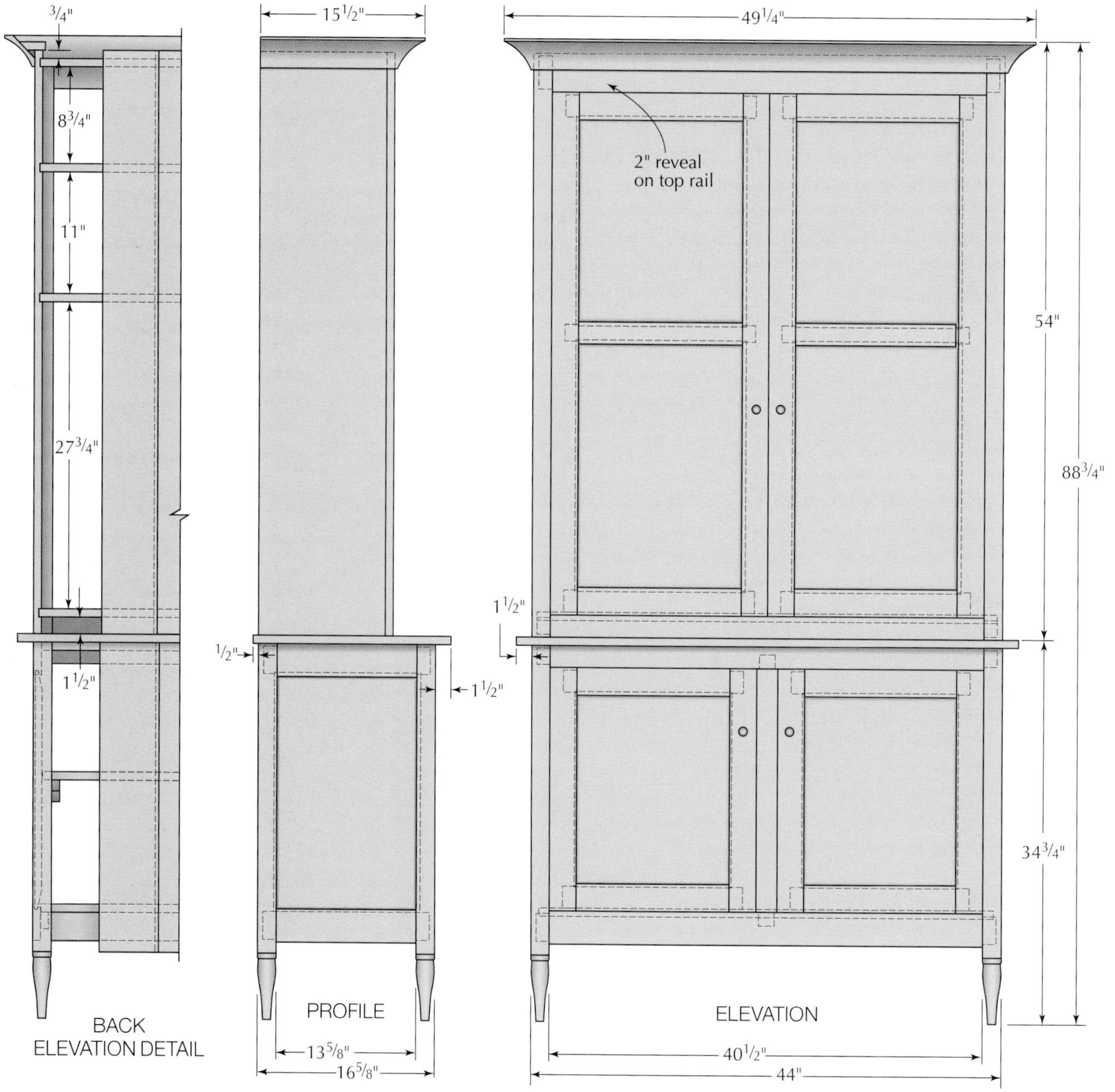

BACK ELEVATION DETAIL

PROFILE

ELEVATION

2" reveal on top rail

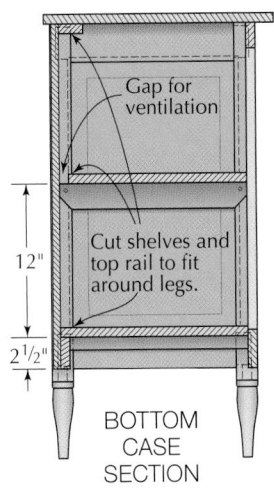

BOTTOM CASE SECTION

Gap for ventilation

Cut shelves and top rail to fit around legs.

12"

2½"

BLOCKED IN PLACE. I intended for the top of the carcase to match the top of the crown, so I could attach the crown with a piece that tied into both. That didn't happen. So instead, I cut blocks with a 45° angle on the front, and glued them to the top of the carcase and the inside face of the crown — one at each front and back corner and three more along the front. You can also see the shiplapped back in this picture. Each piece is secured top and bottom at the corner by a screw.

Shaker Stepback

NO.	ITEM	DIMENSIONS (INCHES) T	W	L	DIMENSIONS (MILLIMETERS) T	W	L	MATERIAL	COMMENTS
UPPER SECTION									
2	Face frame stiles	¾	1¾	52¾	19	45	1339	Cherry	
1	Upper face frame rail	¾	3½	43	19	89	1092	Cherry	TBE*
1	Lower face frame rail	¾	2	43	19	51	1092	Cherry	TBE*
2	Side panels	¾	12	52¾	19	305	1339	Cherry	
1	Top	¾	11⅜	43	19	289	1092	Cherry	
1	Bottom	¾	11⅜	43	19	289	1092	Cherry	
2	Shelves	¾	11⅜	43	19	289	1092	Cherry	
4	Door stiles	¾	2½	47¼	19	64	1200	Cherry	
2	Door top rails	¾	2½	17¾	19	64	451	Cherry	TBE*
2	Door center rails	¾	2	17¾	19	51	451	Cherry	TBE*
2	Door bottom rails	¾	2½	17¾	19	64	451	Cherry	TBE*
2	Upper door panels	⅝	15⅞	17¾	16	403	451	Cherry	
2	Lower door panels	⅝	15⅞	22¾	16	403	578	Cherry	
1	Front crown	⅞	4	49½	22	102	1258	Cherry	Trim to fit
2	Side crown	⅞	4	15¾	22	102	400	Cherry	Trim to fit
Varies	Backboards	⅝	varies	52¾	16	varies	1339	Cherry	
LOWER SECTION									
4	Feet	1¾	1¾	7¼	45	45	184	Cherry	1¼" dowel at top
4	Legs	1¾	1¾	28	45	45	711	Cherry	
2	Side panels	⅝	13⅞	21⅝	16	352	549	Cherry	
4	Side rails	¾	3	15¾	19	76	400	Cherry	TBE*
1	Upper front rail	¾	2	43	19	51	1092	Cherry	TBE*
1	Lower front rail	¾	3	43	19	76	1092	Cherry	TBE*
1	Upper back rail	¾	2	42½	19	51	1080	Poplar	
1	Lower back rail	¾	2½	43	19	64	1092	Poplar	TBE*
1	Center stile	¾	2	24½	19	51	623	Cherry	TBE*
2	Door panels	⅝	14⅞	17⅝	16	378	448	Cherry	
4	Door stiles	¾	2½	22	19	64	559	Cherry	
4	Door rails	¾	2½	16¾	19	64	422	Cherry	TBE*
2	Middle shelf cleats	¾	15½	2	19	394	51	Cherry	
2	Bottom shelf cleats	¾	14½	1	19	369	25	Cherry	
1	Top	¾	18¾	47	19	476	1194	Cherry	
1	Shelf	¾	14½	42½	19	369	1092	Cherry	
1	Bottom	¾	15¼	42½	19	1080	1092	Cherry	
Varies	Backboards	⅝	random	27	16	random	686	Cherry	

* TBE=Tenon both ends, 1¼"

Traditional Hanging Shelves

BY TROY SEXTON

These shelves are quite popular with my two best customers: my wife and my daughter. We have them hanging in several rooms of our farmhouse where they hold plates and knickknacks.

Not surprisingly, these shelves are also popular with my paying customers. While many of them may dream of buying a custom corner cupboard, sometimes what they can best afford are the hanging shelves. So these small projects make everyone happy.

For the home woodworker, these shelves are a home run. These two traditional designs look great in most homes, and the woodworking part is so simple that almost anyone should be able to build these in a weekend.

Patterns and Dados

Both of these shelves are built using the same techniques and joints. The only significant difference is that the Shaker-style unit has three shelves and the 18th century "Whale Tail" project has four shelves and a more ornate profile that looks vaguely like a whale's tail. To me, it looks more like a goose.

Begin your project by selecting your lumber and planing it down to ½" thick. Using the supplied patterns and the construction drawings, draw the profile on your side pieces and mark where the dados should go.

Now set up your dado stack in your table saw so it makes a ½"-wide cut that's ³⁄₁₆" deep. As you can see in the photo, I made this cut using only the fence. I feel real comfortable with this cut; but if you're not, I recommend you

use your miter gauge and a stop block attached to your fence to guide the work instead.

Cut the dados and then head for the band saw.

Cutting the Details

I use a band saw to shape the sides. Begin by making several "relief" cuts along the profile of your side. These allow you to remove the waste in chunks so your blade and workpiece are easier to maneuver through the cut.

Once you've completed both sides, sand the edges using a drum sander that's chucked into your drill press. I recommend you tape the two sides together using double-sided tape and sand them simultaneously. It's faster and the sides end up identical.

Once that's complete, fit the shelves and sides together for a dry fit. Notice anything? The square edges of the shelves don't match the sides exactly.

Mark the shape of the sides onto the end of the shelves. Now, using a jointer with the fence beveled (or a hand plane), shape the front edge to match the side. You just want to get in the ballpark; sanding can take care of the rest of the contouring job.

Now cut the plate rail groove in the shelves. I used a router bit with a core box profile and a router table. The plate rail is $\frac{1}{8}$" deep and $1\frac{5}{8}$" in from the back edge.

Before you assemble the unit, finish sand all the surfaces except the outside of the sides. Begin with 100-grit sandpaper and work your way up to 120, 150 and finish with 180.

Assembly and Finishing

Put a small bead of glue in each dado and put the shelves in place. Clamp the shelves between the sides and check your project to make sure it's square by measuring diagonally from corner to corner. If the measurements are equal, nail the sides to the shelves using a few 18-gauge brads.

If your measurements aren't equal, clamp the project diagonally from one corner to another. Clamp across the two corners that produced the longest mea-

surement. Apply a little pressure to those corners and keep checking your diagonal measurements. When they are equal, nail the project together.

After an hour, take the project out of the clamps and sand the outside of the side pieces and putty your nail holes. Ease all the sharp edges of the project using 120-grit sandpaper. I dyed my project using a water-based aniline dye that I mixed myself from several custom colors. I recommend you use

J. E. Moser's Golden Amber Maple dye for a similar effect. It's available from Woodworker's Supply at 800-645-9292 or woodworker.com.

Finally, add a couple coats of your favorite top-coat finish and sand between coats. Hang your shelf using some common picture hooks, available at any home center or from the source listed in the box below.

Cut the dados in the sides using a dado stack in your table saw. If you're a beginning woodworker, I recommend you perform this operation with a miter gauge to guide the work instead of the fence. I've made a lot of these shelves and am quite comfortable with this method.

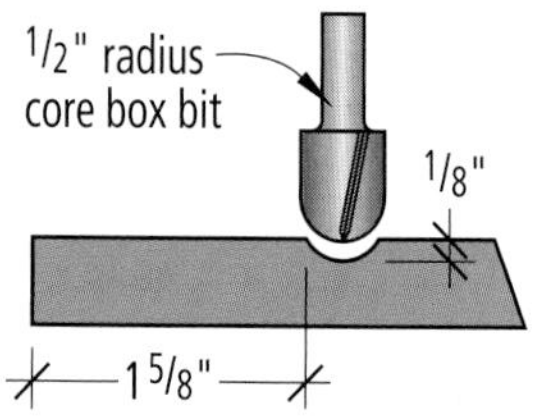

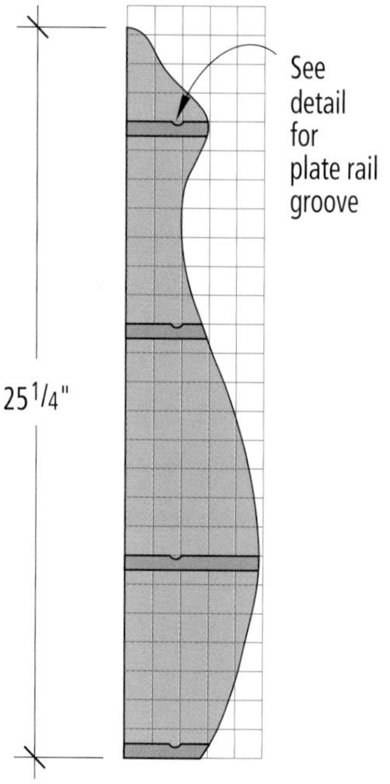

See detail for plate rail groove

$25^{1/4}$"

SECTION
1" GRID

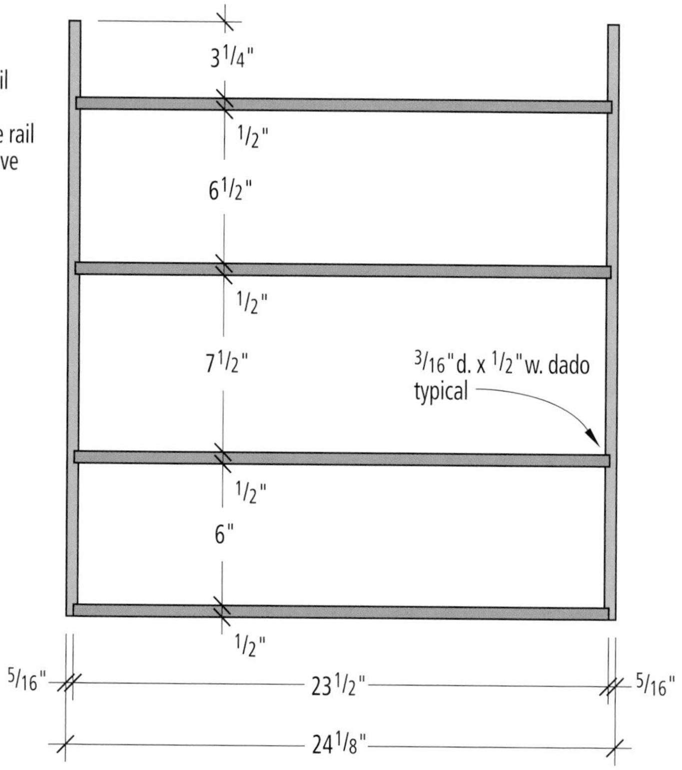

$3^{1/4}$"

$1/2$"

$6^{1/2}$"

$1/2$"

$7^{1/2}$"

$3/16$"d. x $1/2$"w. dado typical

$1/2$"

6"

$1/2$"

$5/16$" — $23^{1/2}$" — $5/16$"

$24^{1/8}$"

ELEVATION

$1/2$" radius core box bit

$1/8$"

$1^{5/8}$"

PLATE RAIL GROOVE
DETAIL

Whale Tail Shelf

	NO.	ITEM	DIMENSIONS (INCHES)			DIMENSIONS (MILLIMETERS)			MATERIAL	COMMENTS
			T	W	L	T	W	L		
❏	2	Sides	$1/2$	$4^{7/8}$	$25^{1/4}$	13	124	641	Maple	
❏	1	Bottom shelf	$1/2$	$3^{1/8}$	$23^{1/2}$	13	79	597	Maple	in $3/16$" x $1/2$" dado
❏	1	Middle shelf	$1/2$	$4^{7/8}$	$23^{1/2}$	13	124	597	Maple	in $3/16$" x $1/2$" dado
❏	1	Middle shelf	$1/2$	3	$23^{1/2}$	13	76	597	Maple	in $3/16$" x $1/2$" dado
❏	1	Top shelf	$1/2$	3	$23^{1/2}$	13	76	597	Maple	in $3/16$" x $1/2$" dado

Notice the relief cut I made in the sides. By removing the waste in smaller hunks (instead of all at once), the blade is more maneuverable.

RELIEF CUT

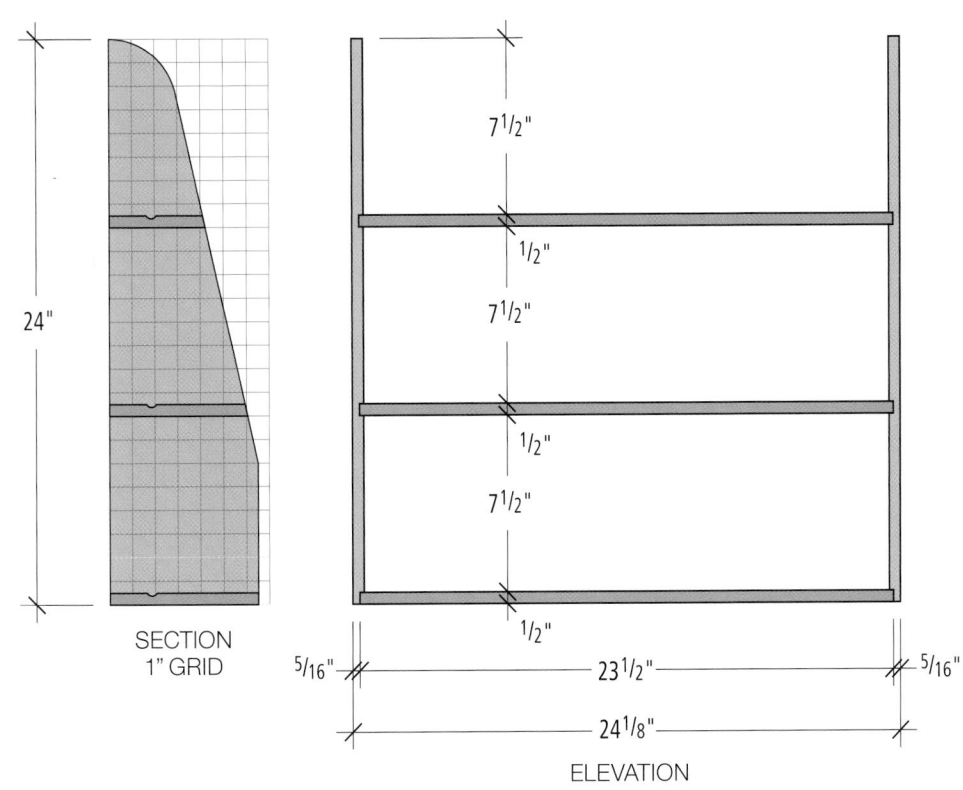

24"

SECTION
1" GRID

7¹/₂"

¹/₂"

7¹/₂"

¹/₂"

7¹/₂"

¹/₂"

⁵/₁₆" 23¹/₂" ⁵/₁₆"

24¹/₈"

ELEVATION

Supplies

Picture Hooks available from home-center stores or from Lee Valley Tools, 800-871-8158 or leevalley.com

Item # 00D78.02, 50 picture hooks, $3.90 plus shipping

Shaker Hanging Shelf

	NO.	ITEM	DIMENSIONS (INCHES)			DIMENSIONS (MILLIMETERS)			MATERIAL	COMMENTS
			T	W	L	T	W	L		
❏	2	Sides	¹/₂	6¹/₂	24	13	165	610	Cherry	
❏	1	Bottom shelf	¹/₂	6¹/₂	23¹/₂	13	165	597	Cherry	in ³/₁₆" x ¹/₂" dado
❏	1	Middle shelf	¹/₂	6	23¹/₂	13	152	597	Cherry	in ³/₁₆" x ¹/₂" dado
❏	1	Top shelf	¹/₂	4¹/₄	23¹/₂	13	108	597	Cherry	in ³/₁₆" x ¹/₂" dado

Stickley Music Cabinet

BY ROBERT W. LANG

One hundred years ago, when people wanted to listen to music at home, they cracked their knuckles and headed for the piano. This small cabinet was originally intended to store sheet music, and although times have changed, it is a nice, small-scale piece of furniture.

The overall form is appealing, and much of the charm is in the details. The exposed through-tenons in the cabinet often are seen in Gustav Stickley furniture, but the joinery in the door is unusual. The mitered intersections on the door are authentic to early Stickley pieces, but within a few years these joints disappeared from production.

I found three variations of the joinery at the outer stiles: full miters, partial miters and butt joints. I chose partial miters to maximize the holding power of the joints while retaining at least some of the look. I couldn't find an original example of this cabinet with that detail, but I included it in this project because it adds to the charm and presence of this piece. It was also an interesting and challenging exercise in joinery.

Making a Mitered Mullion Door

The obvious solution, mitering individual pieces, would have little strength and no built-in way to keep the parts aligned. The miters are for show; unseen joints provide strength and alignment. Mortises and tenons are used behind the miters at the intersections at the outer stiles.

In the middle, there isn't enough room in the 1¼"-wide stile to include a practical mortise-and-tenon joint. My solution was a modified lap joint; the miters are cut down to where the rabbet for the glass begins, and the back part of the short pieces simply butt against the center stile.

The matching cutouts in the center stile prevent the ends of the muntins from moving out of place and provide some face-grain-to-face-grain glue surface. It's stronger than you might think. The tricky part is getting the four points of each joint to meet neatly in the middle.

Careful layout is essential, and I began by clamping the three stiles together so I could mark them all at once. I set the vertical distance between the muntins on my combination square, and used the square to step off the spaces. After marking each space, I use a scrap of muntin stock held against the square to mark the width of those parts.

Before working on the miters, I cut a rabbet for the glass, leaving ¼" of material at the face. I used the back of a chisel

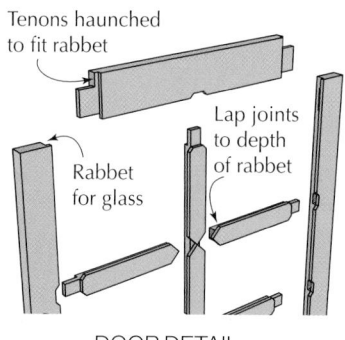

Tenons haunched to fit rabbet

Lap joints to depth of rabbet

Rabbet for glass

DOOR DETAIL

BETTER THAN NUMBERS. A combination square does an excellent job of laying out repeating spaces, in this case the openings in the door.

THE REAL THING. A scrap of muntin stock is held against the square to mark the stiles. This speeds the process and ensures accuracy.

RUN IN REVERSE. The back of a chisel makes a great scraper, just the ticket for cleaning out the corner of rabbets.

to clean the corners of the rabbets, then I made ¼"-wide by 1¼"-deep mortises aligned with the rabbet at the muntin location on the outer stiles, and upper and lower rails.

The Fussy Part

I marked off the miters with my combination square on the vertical mullion, by drawing two pencil lines to form an "X." For the joints to look good, the end of the miters need to meet at a single point. To preserve the points, I used my knife to mark just inside the pencil lines on each side of the mullion.

My first plan was to make a template and form the mitered cutouts with a router. After a couple test joints, I decided that the router alone would be too risky. Quartersawn white oak is tenacious stuff and tends to break off in big chunks when it's routed. In addition, the router would leave a rounded surface at the very point that would need to be chiseled to a sharp point.

I used a fine toothed dovetail saw to establish straight, clean lines at the edges of the joints. I added a couple thicknesses of veneer to the fence of the template to move it out from the cut lines. The router, equipped with a bearing above the ⁹⁄₁₆"-diameter straight cutter, left a flat surface at each joint; a chisel was used to trim back to the finished joint lines made by the saw.

The mating pieces were made by first cutting a square shoulder on the back, with a ⅝"-long lap. I marked the miters from the intersection of the shoulder and lap, using my knife and combination

SIMPLE SETUP. Set the fence on the mortiser by lining up the chisel with the back of the rabbet.

X MARKS THE SPOT. The joints in the central mullion meet in the exact center. A knife cut along the lines will help to guide the saw.

ON THE RIGHT SIDE. For the points of the miters to meet, the saw cuts must be on opposite sides of the lines on each side of the mullion.

CUTTING CORNERS. The router will leave material in the corner, which can be removed with a chisel. The finished edges of the joint have been established with the knife and saw.

STEP BACK AND CONSIDER. The router jig is mainly to provide a flat bottom for the lap joint. Set the fence to keep the bit on the waste side of the saw cuts.

DOUBLE DUTY. This jig guides the bearing on a flush-trim router bit, then is used to guide a chisel to pare into the mitered corners.

square. I sawed outside the lines with a dovetail saw, then used a shooting board with my block plane to fit each joint.

This isn't as tedious as it sounds. It comes down to marking clean lines, cutting as close as possible to them, then testing the fit. Two pieces of wood against each other will tell you where to take another swipe or two on the shooting board. And with the number of joints in this door, there are plenty of opportunities to practice. By the time you get to the last joint, you'll know how to work these joints efficiently.

The Other End

At the other end of the cross pieces, the mitered corners go back only to the edge of the rabbet, and a tenon is added. After marking the cuts in the stiles with a marking gauge and knife, I put together another simple router jig. I made the jig to fall inside the layout lines, and nibbled away at the thin part of the stile with a flush trim bit.

This jig served double duty. After routing, I reclamped the jig directly on the cut lines and used it to guide my chisel in paring the openings. The other half of the joint was made on the face of the muntin by first cutting the square shoulder by hand. Then I used the bandsaw to cut the tenon cheeks.

I carefully made a 45° cut in the fence of my bench hook, and used that to guide my saw for the short miter cuts. I left the mortises a bit wide so that I could move the muntins laterally if needed while fitting. After getting the cheeks to fit by filing them with a joinery float, I trimmed the mitered edges with my shoulder plane until they matched the joints in the stiles.

After fitting each joint individually, I made a dry-run assembly of the entire door. There were a couple places that needed tweaking, and I gathered clamps and reviewed my strategy. A lot of joints needed to come together at once, and I didn't want to set myself up to panic in the midst of it.

I gathered my clamps, made some battens to hold the joints flat, then got out an acid brush and a bottle of liquid hide glue. I brushed glue on all of the end-grain surfaces, and allowed the slow-setting glue to wick in. Then I went over the parts again, and brushed glue on the tenons.

I placed one of the outer stiles on its edge, and began placing the tenons of the cross pieces. With the four short muntins in place, I assembled the top and bottom rails to the central mullion, then placed the rail tenons in the mortises of the stile. With the door still on edge, the remain-

ing muntins were placed, followed by the second stile.

I laid the assembly flat on some blocks on the bench and began clamping. The major joints, where the top and bottom rails connect were first. Then I clamped a packing-tape covered batten across each of the center miter joints and snugged the clamps. When all the battens were in place, I used bar clamps to bring the ends of the miters together.

I went over the assembly (grateful for the long open time of liquid hide glue) and checked each inside corner for square, and tightened the clamps. I left the door in the clamps overnight, and the following morning, I scraped off the excess glue then leveled the surfaces with my block plane.

There Is a Cabinet, Too

The cabinet assembly is simple, especially when compared to the door; it's just two sides and an identical top and bottom. After assembly, a backsplash is added behind and above the top, and a narrow toe rail is added below the bot-

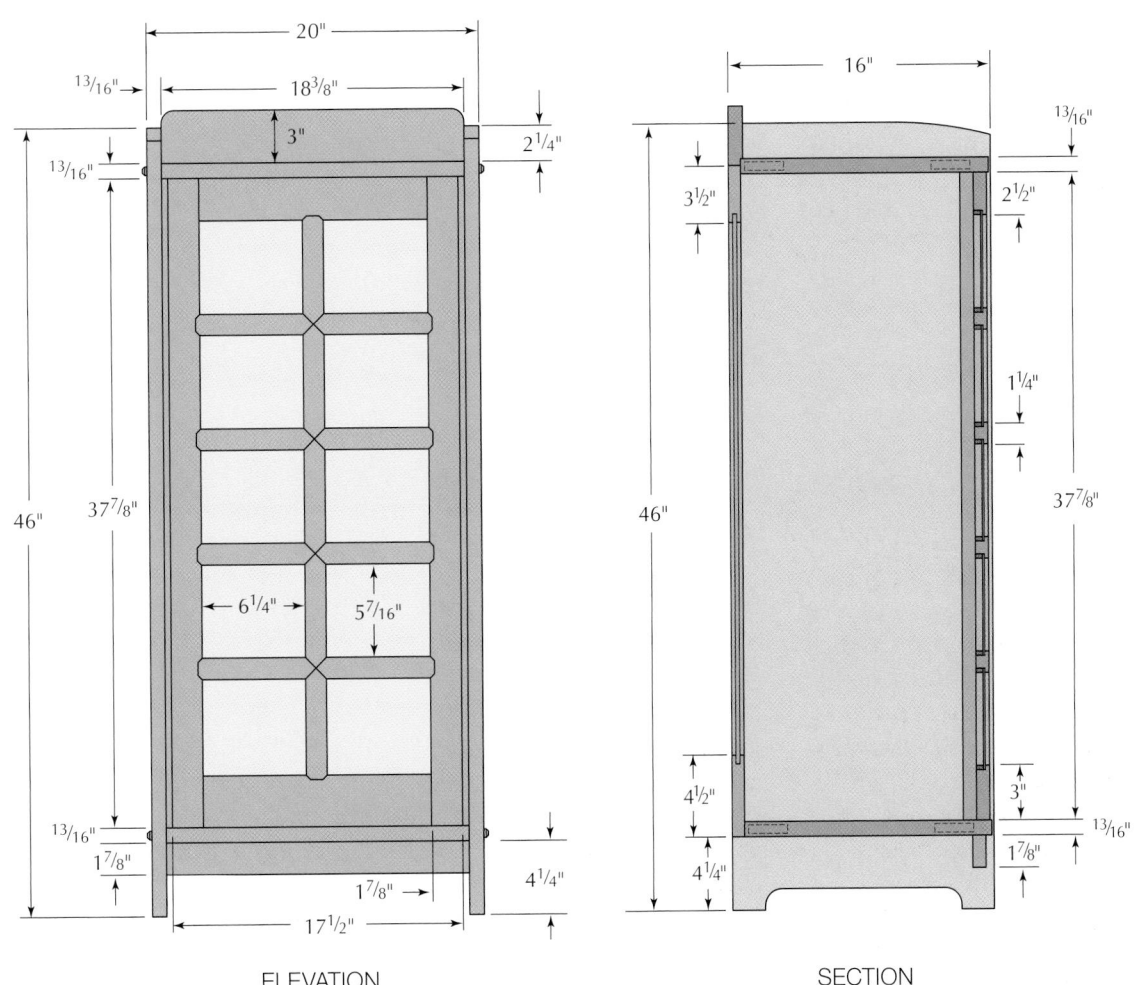

ELEVATION

SECTION

Stickley Music Cabinet

	NO.	ITEM	DIMENSIONS (INCHES)			DIMENSIONS (MILLIMETERS)			MATERIAL	COMMENTS
			T	W	L	T	W	L		
❑	2	Case side	13/16	16	46	21	406	1168	QSWO*	
❑	2	Case top & bottom	13/16	15	20⅝	21	381	524	QSWO	
❑	1	Backsplash	⅞	3⁷/16	18⅜	22	87	467	QSWO	
❑	1	Toe rail	13/16	1⅞	18¼	21	49	463	QSWO	
❑	2	Door stiles	13/16	1⅞	37⅞	21	49	962	QSWO	
❑	1	Door top rail	13/16	2½	16¼	21	64	412	QSWO	1¼" TBE**
❑	1	Door bottom rail	13/16	3	16¼	21	76	412	QSWO	1¼" TBE
❑	1	Door mullion	13/16	1¼	34⅞	21	32	886	QSWO	1" TBE
❑	8	Door muntins	13/16	1¼	7⅞	21	32	200	QSWO	1" TOE***
❑	2	Hinge stiles	13/16	1⅝	37⅞	21	41	962	QSWO	Rabbet long edge
❑	40	Glass stops	¼	⁷/16	7	6	11	178	QSWO	Cut to fit openings
❑	10	Glass	⅛	5⅞	6⅝	3	149	168	Glass	Cut to fit openings
❑	4	Shelves	13/16	14¼	18⅛	21	362	460	QSWO	
❑	2	Back panel stiles	¾	4½	39⅛	19	115	994	QSWO	
❑	1	Back top rail	¾	3½	14⅞	19	89	378	QSWO	1¼" TBE
❑	1	Back bottom rail	¾	4½	14⅞	19	115	378	QSWO	1¼" TBE
❑	1	Back panel	¼	11¼	32⅞	6	285	835	QSWO	

* Quartersawn white oak; **Tenon both ends; ***Tenon one end

USE THE FENCE. Saw cuts in the fence of the bench hook guide the saw to make clean and accurate cuts.

WASTING AWAY. The band saw fence is set to leave just a sliver of material as the tenon cheeks are cut.

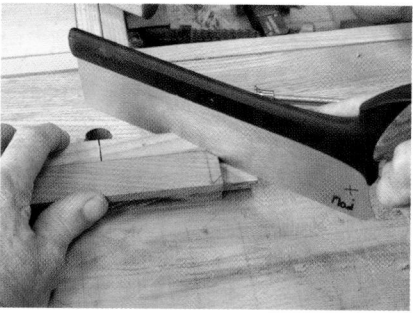
MITERS, TOO. 45° cuts in the fence guide the saw to cut the short miters. Preserve the line at this point, and work down to it while fitting.

COMPLEX GEOMETRY. Test the fit often while fitting the miters. Trimming one edge will lengthen or shorten an adjacent edge as well.

tom. The back is a framed panel that fits in a rabbet at the back of the sides. The back panel is flush with the bottom edge of the cabinet bottom, and ends at the midpoint of the top in thickness.

My first step was to cut the rabbets for the back in the sides. This differentiated the inside from the outside and the top from the bottom. The horizontal cabinet components join the sides with a pair of through-tenons at each intersection. I made a template from ½"-thick birch plywood to keep the mortises consistent in size and location.

The template locates the mortises and defines the shape at the top and bottom of the cabinet sides. I chose a piece as wide as the finished sides, and long enough to contain the mortises. To expedite making the template, I ripped some plywood to ½", the width of the finished mortises. I marked the mortise locations on the template blank, then placed double-sided tape over the layout lines.

I stuck down the thin plywood strips at the end of the mortise locations, then placed wider pieces of plywood tight against the long edges. When all these

pieces were in place, I tapped them with a mallet to set the adhesive on the tape, then drilled a $7/16$"-diameter hole in each mortise location.

These holes are smaller than the mortise, but larger than the flush-trimming router bit I used to cut out the mortises. After routing all four mortises with a flush-trim bit, I popped off the thin plywood pieces, then cut and shaped the top and bottom edges of the template.

I laid out the mortise locations on the outer faces of the cabinet sides, marking the lines with a knife. The knife lines can't be rubbed off and are more precise and easier to see than pencil lines. More important, these lines are the finished edges of the through-mortises; cutting them first helps to keep the router from tearing out the edge and provides a definite point to work to.

I didn't bother to square the corners of the mortises in the template; the

router bit will leave a rounded corner in the cabinet side anyway. I like to drill out as much material as possible before routing, and use the smallest diameter flush-trim bit I can find. Squaring the corners on the real thing looks impossibly difficult, but there are a couple tricks that make it easy.

A Sharp Edge and a Built-in Guide

The first trick is to use a chisel that is as sharp as you can make it. The end grain of quartersawn white oak will mock you if you try to pare it with anything less than a keen edge, and it will wear that edge quickly. Keep your stones handy; you'll need to hone a few times before you're through.

Angle the chisel so that the flat of the chisel rests against the long, flat edge of the mortise. From that position, simply rotate the business end of the chisel into

SEQUENCE IS EVERYTHING. The parts of the door need to be assembled in order. Do yourself a favor by making a dry run, then use a slow-setting glue.

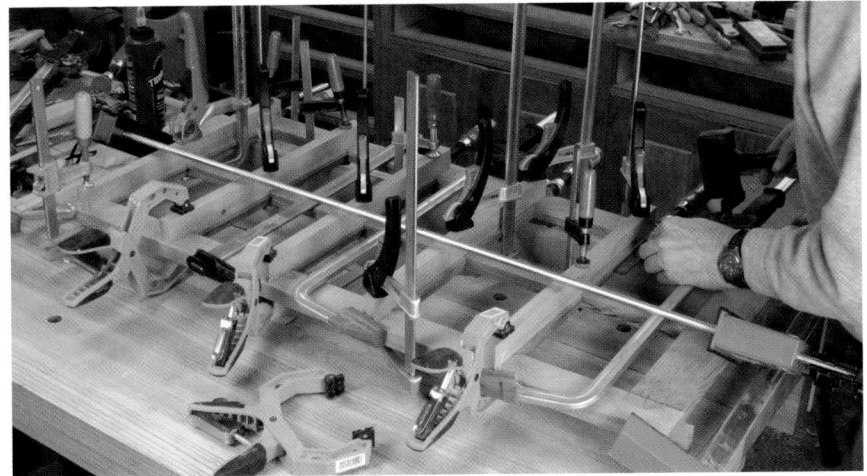

PAYDAY. Flush the surfaces of the completed joints with a sharp block plane, and take a moment to feel proud. Then get back to work; there are a bunch of these.

YOU NEED MORE CLAMPS. The mitered lap joints in the center of the assembly will tend to pop up as clamp pressure is applied to the ends. Battens across the faces hold things together.

BUILD, DON'T CUT. Assemble small pieces around the layout lines, then use a router with a flush-trim bit to make the mortising template.

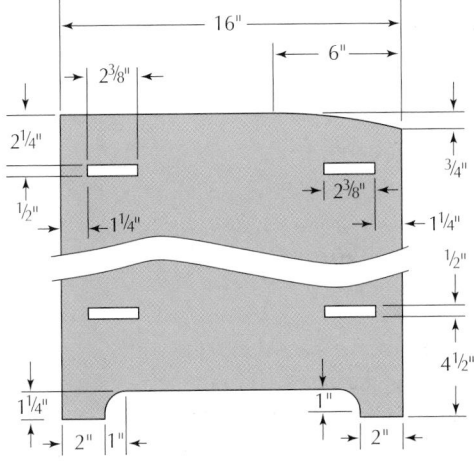

TEMPLATE

the corner while keeping the chisel tight against the mortise edge. Get your shoulder over the chisel, and use your body weight as you bring the chisel to vertical.

After a clean line is established in the corner, back the chisel away from the corner and press down, or give it a good smack with a mallet. The short, long-grain edges are easier to pare. Place the edge of the chisel in the knife line made during layout. A push or a tap will do it.

If your chisel work is less than perfect, a small joinery float can be used to refine the corner. Other than the corners, the mortises should be in good shape, thanks to the router and the template. It is important to leave a clean, square edge on the show side. What goes on behind that can remain a secret, and the joint will be strong.

Tenon Time

To make sure the through-joints look good, I wait until I'm done with the mortises before I start on the tenons. The mortises may grow a little as they are worked, but no one will ever know as long as the tenons fit. I place the board to be tenoned on end, and mark the cuts directly from the mortises.

I cut the shoulder and get a close fit in thickness before worrying about the width of the tenons. I knife in the shoulder line, and clamp a straightedge on the line. With a top-bearing bit in the router, I can sneak up on the right size. I make the first cuts thicker than needed, then measure both the tenon and the mortise with dial calipers.

I then lower the bit by a little less than half the difference of the measurements and check the fit by placing a corner in

AND SWING IT. Keep the back of the chisel pressed against the routed edge of the mortise and carefully rotate the edge into the corner.

the mortise. When the corner can be placed in the mortise I stop. The tenon will be too tight at this point, but it will be close to fitting. The last little bit of thickness will be removed with a float in the next step.

ABOVE IT ALL. Line up your shoulder over your hands so you can use your body weight to increase leverage as you pare the end grain.

MAKE YOUR MARK. Wait until the mortises are completed to lay out the tenons on the cabinet top and bottom. Mark the locations from existing edges.

UNDER CONTROL. Cut the tenon shoulders first, using a straightedge and a bearing-guided router bit. Adjust the depth of cut in small increments to achieve the proper thickness.

The tenons can be cut at the table saw, but that introduces some risk, and it can be awkward to hold the work on end against a miter gauge or crosscut sled. Cutting the tenons by hand is as fast and accurate. After double-checking the layout and marking with a knife, I cut the long edges of the tenons, and the two outside edges by hand.

The waste in between the two tenons is another story. I cut most of it away with a jigsaw, then clamped a straight-edge along the shoulder. With the straightedge in place, I cut a clean edge at the shoulder line with a flush-trim bit in the router.

Before testing the fit, I cut a slight chamfer around the inside edge of the mortise, and around the outermost end of the tenon. This helps to get the tenons started for fitting, and keeps the tenon from chipping out the grain on the outside of the mortise.

Fitting these joints is a bit like detective work. In theory, they should fit at this point, but in reality there will be a bit of wood somewhere that keeps the joint from going home. When the joint sticks, these points need to be found and removed. If you guess and remove mate-

rial in the wrong place, the result will be a gap in the finished joint.

Fit Without a Conniption Fit

I push the tenons in as far as I can, then tap on the end of the board a couple times with a dead-blow mallet. When I was younger and my eyes were better, I could see the shiny spots on the tenon where the joint is too tight. These days, I pull out a pencil and draw cross-hatched lines on the tenon and try the fit again. The graphite smears where the joint rubs, showing the high spots. These can be removed with a shoulder plane, but it's easy to tilt or go too far. A float is almost as fast, and allows more controlled removal.

As the size of the tenon gets closer to the size of the mortise, I slow down and remove material carefully. The difference between a joint that almost goes together and one that is sloppy can be a matter of a stroke or two.

When I'm satisfied with the fit, I run a pencil around the outer edge of the joint, marking where the tenon pokes through the cabinet side. Then I use a rasp to bevel the ends of the tenons, stopping the bevel about $1/16$" from the line. Before assembly, I plane and/or finish-sand the cabinet parts.

It's likely that I will need to refine the surfaces once more after assembly, but the areas around the mortises are difficult to work. This is a point where the

FIRST THINGS FIRST. Test the thickness of the tenon by placing a corner of the shelf in the mortise. Aim for a tight fit at this point.

desire to see an assembled box tries to take over, but it pays to wait. After sanding, I brush glue inside the mortises and on the end of the shelves, and let it wick in for about 10 minutes. Then I put glue on the tenons and assemble the carcase.

After clamping, I remove any excess glue and check for square. I've never liked measuring diagonals, so I place corner clamps or square blocks and check each corner with a reliable square. Then I let the assembly dry overnight.

Details at the End

In most furniture the front is in a single plane, and visual interest comes from applied mouldings. Craftsman furniture does without the trim, and the front of the case is enhanced by setting each element back from its neighbor. The top

BEGIN AT THE END. Cut the ends of the tenons first with a backsaw, then use the same saw to cut away the outside corners.

THIS WILL WORK. Remove the bulk of the waste between the tenons with a jigsaw or coping saw. Then clamp a straightedge between the two tenons and use a router to make a clean, straight cut.

REFINED DETAIL. Make a slight bevel on the ends of the tenons before fitting. After a good dry-fit, mark the outside of the case on the tenon, then increase the bevels to end close to the line.

OVERKILL. The dowel reinforces the through mortise and tenon joint. It isn't needed, but its a nice detail to include.

LAYERED LOOK. Aniline dye stain is coated with tinted Danish oil. This will be followed by a thin coat of amber shellac.

and bottom are $\frac{1}{8}$" back from the sides, the hinges strips are $\frac{1}{16}$" in from the top, and the door is back another $\frac{1}{16}$".

The hinge stiles sit inside the door opening, and are $1\frac{1}{2}$" wide with a $\frac{7}{8}$" deep rabbet, leaving a $\frac{3}{8}$" wide edge beside the door. The rabbet acts as a door stop and keeps dust out of the cabinet. After shaping the strip and fixing the hinges I glued these strips to the cabinet sides.

The back is a simple frame and panel. In original examples of this cabinet, the panel was plywood in a solid-wood frame, but I made a $\frac{1}{4}$"-thick solid-wood panel. I made the stiles and rails wide so that I could use a single panel from the available material. The bottom front rail is glued to the cabinet bottom. The backsplash is $\frac{1}{8}$" thicker than the back panel, with a rabbet on the lower edge to fit over the edge of the cabinet top. This is glued to the edge of the top and at the ends to the sides of the cabinet.

A $\frac{1}{4}$"-diameter dowel is driven into a hole centered on the front edge of the

cabinet side, and the front through tenons. I made the dowels by driving split scraps through a steel dowel plate. The dowels are long enough to reach 1" or so into the edge of the tenons.

This reinforces an overbuilt joint, but it was a feature of the original cabinet, and it looks good after the dowels have been trimmed flush to the front edge. There are four shelves that sit on pins, located so that the shelves fall behind the door muntins.

Our local stained glass shop had textured amber glass for the door, a close match to the original. The glass is held in place with $\frac{1}{4}$" x $\frac{7}{16}$" strips of wood, mitered and pinned to the inside of the rabbets. The door pull is a close copy of the original, and ball-tipped hinges also are typical. A brass ball catch keeps the door closed.

No Fume, No Fuss, No-pop Finish

Don't make the mistake of thinking that the finish should make the quartersawn

oak "pop." If that's what you're after, use a pigment stain and just about any clear topcoat. The flakes won't take the stain evenly and will be quite evident when you're done.

Original finishes were more subdued – the product of fuming the raw wood with ammonia, and coating with shellac followed by a dark wax. In later years, Craftsman pieces were finished with early versions of modern dye stains and lacquers.

Fuming is an interesting process, but it can be unpredictable and time-consuming. Nearly the same look can be achieved with aniline dye. I stained this piece with Lockwood "#94 Fumed Oak" alcohol-soluble aniline dye. You get a good idea of the final color while the dye is wet; when it dries it looks like you made a terrible mistake.

I follow the dye with a coat of Watco Dark Walnut Danish oil. The oil will add some darker color to the open pores of the wood, act as a glaze to even out the tone and seal the surface. After letting the oil soak in for about 15 minutes, I wiped off the excess and let the surface dry overnight.

The oil over the dye creates a nice chocolate brown color, but the finish needs to be warmed up a bit. A thin coat of amber shellac applied with a rag adds that, and provides some surface protection. I follow the shellac with wax after giving it a couple weeks to fully cure. If the color needs to be toned down or evened out, a dark wax can be used instead of clear.

Shaker Cupboard: Rejuvenated

BY GLEN D. HUEY

Shaker stepback cupboards aren't abundant. In fact, there are only a few examples in the many published books on Shaker furniture. Unless you have a sharp eye for Shaker furniture, or are excited about painted furniture with a heavily worn surface, I doubt you would give a second look to the original cupboard on which this project is based. However, the fact that the original is part of the White Water Shaker Village collection propels this piece, in my opinion, toward the top of Shaker cupboards. A reproduction of this cupboard is a must. And in the process, we can turn the clock back to see the cupboard in its earlier days.

Inspiration From the Original

The original Shaker stepback, with its missing crown moulding and other absent features, required detective work before construction began. As we move through the project, we'll examine some missing features and try to reach conclusions that bring this piece back to an earlier day.

The first question is: What about feet? The cupboard at White Water has a three-sided frame that rests on the floor. Was that the original design? Or were the feet worn away or removed?

Also, what happened to the crown moulding? It's obvious there was a moulding, but it is long since gone. What was the profile?

Other features to look at are the unique drawer construction and the use of a half-dovetail sliding joint to secure the shelves to the case sides – even with

SHAKER SERENITY. Inspired by an original cupboard at the White Water Shaker community, our revitalized Shaker stepback blends nicely into the surroundings of the North Family dwelling.

this complex but strong joint, the builder nailed in the shelves.

Face (Frame) Facts

Before we get to the detective work, we need to build the cases and face frames. The frames for both sections use mortise-and-tenon joints. Mill your parts to size according to the materials schedule, but leave an extra ⅛" in width on the stiles. After the frames are fit to the cases you'll use a router and flush-trim bit for a perfect fit.

Locate and mark the mortise locations for ¼"-thick tenons. Wherever possible, each joint should have a 1¼"-long tenon. With the face-frame material at ⅞" in thickness, a ⁵⁄₁₆" face shoulder produces a centered tenon. An edge shoulder of a matching size ensures a stout joint.

There are two frame joints where the matching edge shoulder is not used: on the bottom rail of the lower section where the tenon would end up ⅜" wide, and on the bottom rail of the upper section where the tenon would be ⅝" in width.

As always, cut your mortises first then cut your tenons to fit the mortises. Set up and cut all the mortises on your face-frame parts. It's best to cut the mortise then reverse the position of the workpiece and make a second pass at

WORK METHODICALLY. To assemble the face frames correctly, you'll need to work in a specific order. Plan the steps and have plenty of clamps handy.

each mortise. Yes, the resulting mortise may be wider than ¼", but the joint will be centered on the stock, and that's most important.

Cut your tenons using your favorite method, then test-fit all your joints. When your tenons fit snug and can be slid together with a little muscle, it's time to assemble the face frames. Work methodically through the assembly. Apply glue to both the mortises and the tenons to achieve the most strength. Clamp the frames and allow the glue to dry.

Freaky Dovetail Joints

Dovetails abound in the carcases. Both sections have half-blind dovetailed corners and shelves attached with half-dovetailed sliding joints.

On the upper section the case top is dovetailed to the sides; on the lower section, the case bottom has the dovetails. The pins of the half-blind dovetails are positioned in the sides with the tails in the mating pieces. Also, there is a ¾" difference in widths between the upper case sides and the top, and the lower case sides and the bottom. Those offsets capture the backboards.

The half-dovetail sliding joint is easy with two router setups. You can work with a single router, but you'll need to change the bits multiple times or position the fence in the exact same location each time.

The setups are this: One router has a ¾"-diameter, 14°-dovetail bit coupled with a ⁵¹⁄₆₄" outside-diameter template guide bushing. The second router has a ⅝"-diameter pattern bit with a top-mount bearing.

STRONG JOINERY. The bottom of the lower section is joined to the sides with half-blind dovetails, as is the top of the upper section.

DOUBLE-TEAMED. Two routers, two bits and a guide bushing take the guesswork out of creating the half-dovetailed sliding joints.

Begin by marking lines across the sides at both the top and bottom edges of the dados. Position and clamp a ¾" fence at the top edge of a shelf location. Always work with the fence set to the left of the area to be routed. If these guidelines aren't followed, you can form the half-dovetail on the wrong edge.

Begin with the dovetail router bit setup. Set the bit to cut ½" deep into the case side, then hold the guide bushing tight to your fence as you make a

MISSING FEATURES. The original cupboard, on which our piece is based, has lost its crown moulding. And no one is sure there were ever any feet to lift the cupboard base off the floor.

pass. The cut should be close to, but not beyond, the lower shelf layout line.

Grab your second router, set up with the bit tweaked to cut at the same depth, then make a second pass making sure to hold the bearing tight to your fence. This cut completes the socket. Move to the next shelf location and repeat the process.

Before moving on, cut the grooves in the side pieces for the backboards. The grooves are ⅜" in from the back edge of the case sides; each is ⅜" wide and ½" deep. A dado stack makes this quick work.

Jig Up the Slide

Now it's time to cut the mating shape on the horizontal shelves. To hoist these large panels onto your router table is quite a task. But with a simple shop-made jig, you won't need to. Instead of taking the panel to the router, you'll take the router to the work.

Build a jig to create the sliding half-dovetail with two straight pieces of 2½"-wide and ¾"-thick scrap that are 24" long. Screw the pieces together to form a "T" with one leg of the top piece set at ⅞".

For the jig to work, you'll have to size that top leg according to your router setup. This time use a ¾" outside-diameter template guide bushing with the same dovetail router bit. (The matching diameters allow the router bit to cut where the bushing rubs.) Clamp the jig on a test piece, then make a pass to create the half-dovetail profile as shown below.

Check the test piece in a socket. If the test piece is too wide, take a light table saw cut off the working edge of the jig, make another test cut and check the fit.

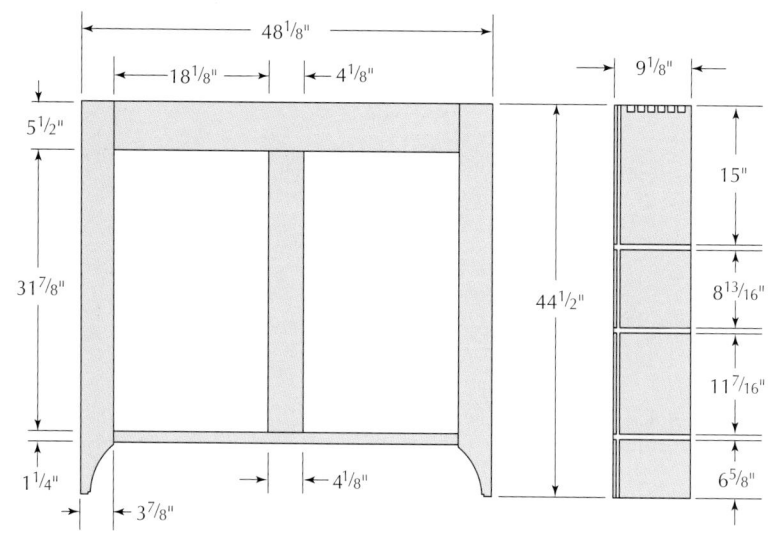

UPPER FACE FRAME & CABINET DETAIL

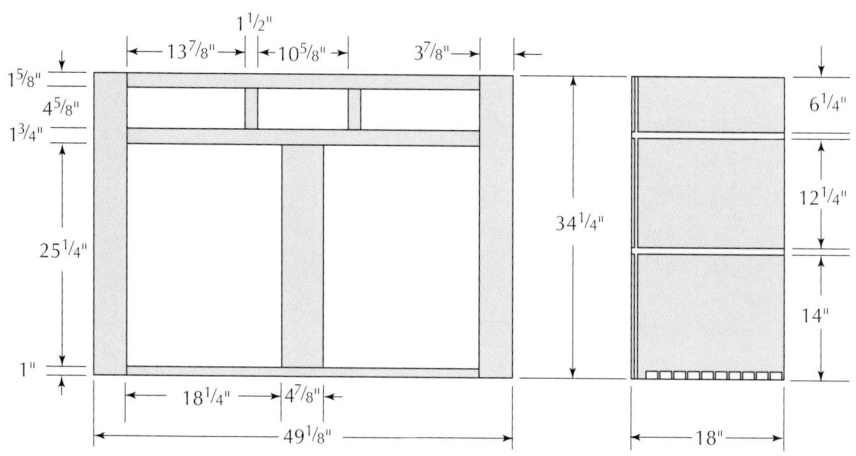

LOWER FACE FRAME & CABINET DETAIL

Continue to take light passes off the jig to sneak up on the correct fit.

If your test piece is too narrow to fill the half-dovetailed slot, you'll have to remove thickness from the bottom piece of the jig, or remove and replace the top

piece at a new location. Once the fit is correct – the workpiece slides into the slot without slop – the jig is ready to go.

Clamp the jig in position, then run the router bit to shape the profile on both ends of each shelf. (Use the jig and clamps to pull out any warp in your shelves.)

Each shelf in the upper case receives two plate grooves on the top face (the lower section's shelf is not grooved). The grooves are 2" and 4¼" from the back edge of the shelf and extend from end to end. Use a router and a core box router bit.

Build the Boxes and Peg the Frames

Assemble the boxes by swabbing glue in the sockets (and a small amount on the shelf ends), then slide the pieces together.

DOUBLE DUTY. This shop-made jig not only dials-in a perfect sliding dovetail, it allows you to pull any warp out of your shelves.

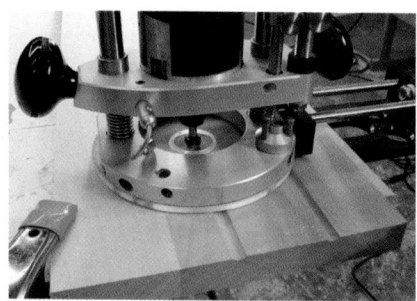

IT'S ODD, BUT TRUE. It's not often you find plate grooves behind blind doors. It's a bigger wonder as to why two different grooves were plowed. Maybe it's for plates and bowls?

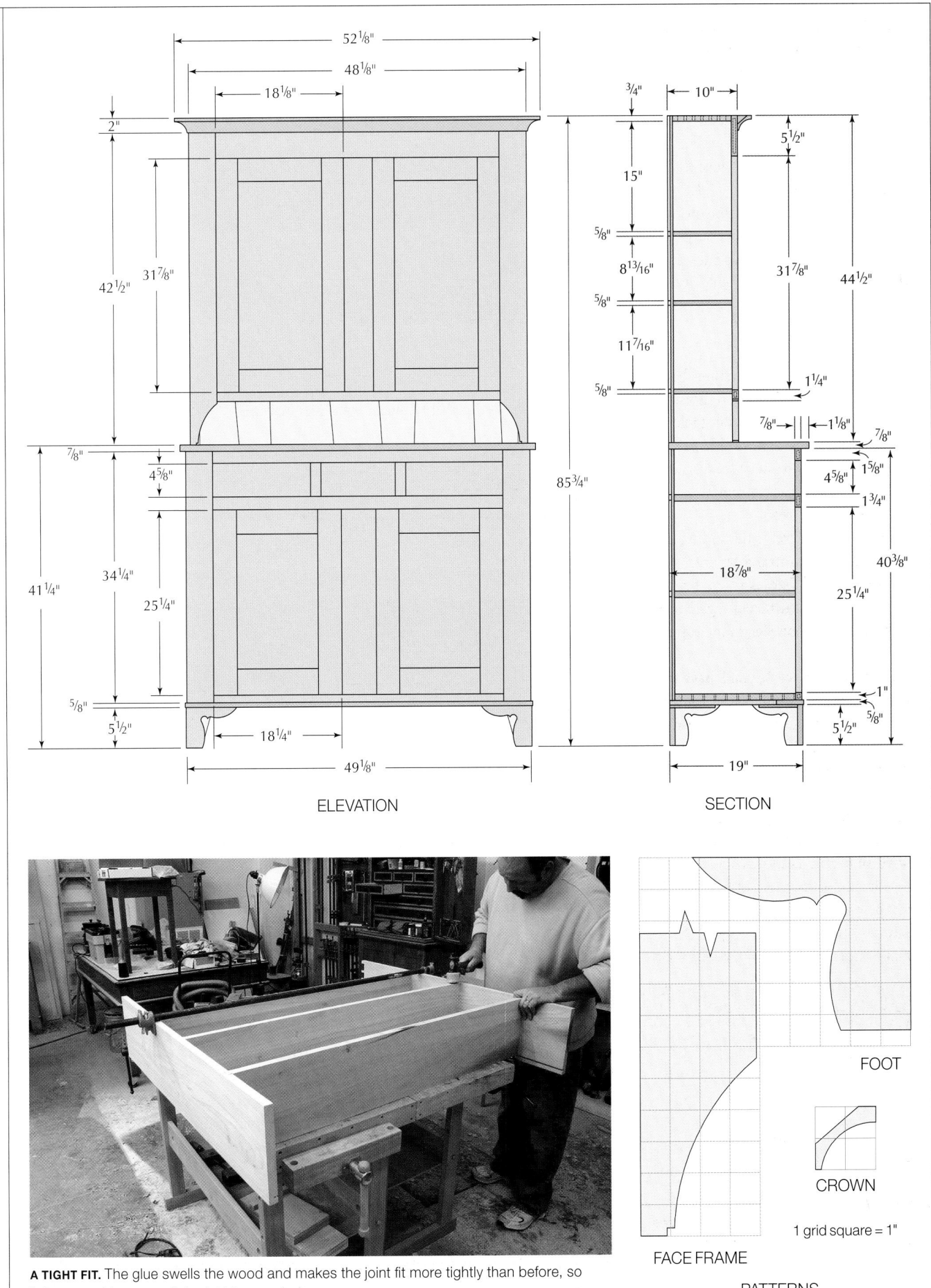

ELEVATION

SECTION

A TIGHT FIT. The glue swells the wood and makes the joint fit more tightly than before, so light taps with your mallet might be needed.

FOOT

CROWN

1 grid square = 1"

FACE FRAME

PATTERNS

After the shelves are installed, butter the dovetail pins with glue, then tap those joints together.

When the glue is dry, fit the face frames to their boxes. It's important to align the middle rail of the lower section with the drawer support. A thin bead of glue secures the frame to the boxes. Position the frames, add clamps then allow the glue to dry.

Drive square pegs into the face frames. Doing this after the glue sets provides additional strength so there is less of a chance to split the frame pieces. To match the original cupboard, evenly space four pegs in each rail and outside stile.

Before adding the pegs, trim the stiles to the case with a flush-trim router bit with a bottom-mount bearing. The uppermost stile's peg is located behind the cove moulding. As is done on the original cupboard, don't forget to drive a couple nails into the shelves.

The detail work on the upper section face-frame stiles is router work. To create the design, make a plywood pattern of the curve – the pattern keeps the look consistent from side to side – then make the cut using a router with a pattern bit. Square the inside corner with a chisel.

Through-tenon Doors

Construction of the four doors is identical, so after you mill the parts to size, gather your stiles and mark them for ¼"-thick tenons with ½" edge shoulders.

With through-mortises, work from both edges of your stile as you mortise so you don't blow out the exit edge. Transfer your layout lines to both edges of the stiles and make sure you work within those confines.

Work past the halfway point of each mortise, then flip the stile edge for edge to clear the mortise.

Most 10" table saws have a maximum 3⅛" depth of cut. The door stiles on this piece are 3¼" in width. Because the through-mortise joinery on the doors exceeds the maximum cut, it's best to install your dado stack and sharpen your shoulder plane or bullnose plane.

Set a dado stack to its widest cut, raise the blade to just less than 5/16", position your fence to create a 3¼"-long tenon, then make the passes needed to clean away the waste.

The door's flat panels fit into a ⅜"-deep x ¼"-wide groove in the rails and stiles. Plow the grooves through the entire length of the stiles. (Doing so requires haunched tenons to fill in the small lengths of groove beyond the edge

WORK AFTER THE FACT. You could complete the face frame stile detail before the frame is attached to the box, but there's added stability afterward. Here, a plywood pattern ensures a perfect match.

SEE RIGHT THROUGH IT. The door mortises are best accomplished by working down from both edges of the stiles. And be sure to keep the slot centered for the best results.

IT'S AN ACCEPTABLE SETUP. Because this dado cut is not a through cut, it's OK to use your fence as a stop when using the miter gauge, too.

TAKE A BREAK, OLD FRIEND. I usually grab my Shinto rasp to fine-tune my tenon fit, but with the amount of work left to do, I found a bullnose plane did the work that much more quickly.

MAKE A PREEMPTIVE STRIKE. With #120-grit sandpaper, knock off the sharp edges around the panel area. This area is difficult to sand after the panels are in place, and the softened edges help age the cupboard's appearance.

JUST FOR LOOKS. Achieving a tight top-to-bottom fit of your tenons takes time and wastes time. The holding power of the joint is the flat-grain connection – and that's not found on the edge shoulders. A small wedge can tighten up the appearance.

IT'S TRADITIONAL WITH A TWIST. Drawer construction for the cupboard is in typical 18th-century fashion, but the drawer backs are below the sides by a ¼". Is this a boon or bust?

THE KEEPER OF GUIDES. Small profiled pieces of wood hold the drawer guides from side-to-side movement while glue at the guide fronts and a few brads keep things tight to the dust board.

of the mortise. The haunches are formed with the dado stack as well.)

Fit each joint so the tenon fit is snug, but doesn't require a mallet to assemble.

Dry-assemble the frames, then measure the openings for the panels. Measure across the opening, then add ⅝" (this builds in ⅛" of space for panel movement). Mill the four panels to size. Finish-sand the panels and knock off the sharp inside edges around the panel area before assembling the doors.

When ready, add a thin layer of glue to the tenons and in the mortises, then slip the joints together. Add clamps (keep clear of the through-tenons) and let the glue dry.

Chances are you'll have small top-to-bottom gaps in the tenon fit. If so, cut thin wedges milled to the same width as your mortise to fill them. This cleans up the look.

Fit and hang your doors.

Supplies

Horton Brasses Inc.
horton-brasses.com or 800-754-9127

4 • door catches
  #SL-3

4 • solid brass butt hinge
  #PB-409

Call for pricing.

Woodcraft
woodcraft.com or 800-225-1153

3 • Shaker knobs
  #125433, $7.50 (10 pack)

Prices correct at time of publication.

A Drawer Build – D'oh!

I can't count the number of antique drawers I've studied, or the number of drawers I've built. I don't think I have ever seen drawers built as they are on the original White Water cupboard. The drawers use typical 18th-century construction methods, but the drawer backs are different – the backs are square at the top and bottom and are held a ¼" below the top edge of the drawer sides. At first glance, this looks odd, but there is a nice benefit to it.

The cupboard drawers are flush fitting with minimal gaps between the drawer fronts and the case. If you build with tight reveals, and the wood expands, you have stuck drawers. Drawer sides, stepped down from the fronts, allow the drawers to function, but this says "less-than-perfect craftsmanship" to me.

If you step down the drawer back in relation to the sides, you can fit the drawer front tight to the opening and slightly taper the top edge of the sides from front to back, all without any interference from the drawer back. I like it.

Build and fit your drawers. To keep the drawers traveling straight, you need drawer guides. To locate the guides, hold the drawer in position and mark along its edge.

Installation of the guides is easy. Spread glue on the first 5" of the guides (cross-grain construction precludes fully gluing the guides), place the pieces tight to the back face of the face frame, then tack each in position with brads. Also, add a couple brads near the back

of the guide to keep it tight to the dust panel until the glue dries. (Don't use screws; unlike nails, they won't move with the seasons.)

Restriction of side-to-side movement is another interesting detail found on the original cupboard. The furniture maker added small keepers cut from pieces of ½"-thick stock to both sides of each guide. Create a small bevel on the end of your board, crosscut the length to ¾", then rip pieces to width. (These are small pieces. Use a zero-clearance insert and a push stick, or cut them with a handsaw.) I couldn't tell how the pieces were attached. I used glue and tacked the pieces with a 23-gauge pin.

Swept Off Its Feet

The feet on the original are a mystery. There is no known photo showing any feet. The three-sided frame that today sits on the floor has no noticeable remnants of feet – no glue blocks or nail

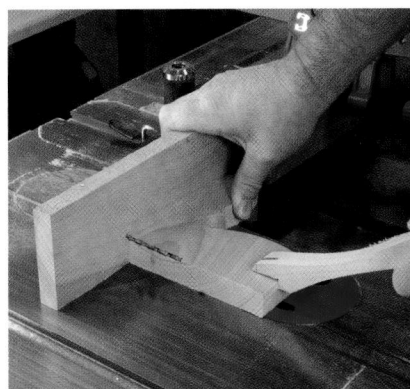

WORKS IN REVERSE. If you flip the position of your miter gauge in the slot, you can guide one half of the foot pairing for its 45°-bevel cut. It's similar to using a panel-cutting sled.

holes. In fact, nothing shows that feet were ever on this stepback. But the piece doesn't look right without something to stand on.

If you're a purist, skip the feet. If you look at the cupboard and think there's something missing, make the feet. Undecided? Make the feet separate and attach them with screws. If you change your mind, remove the feet.

Trace the foot pattern onto your stock, cut the profiles and sand the edges with a spindle sander. Arrange the feet into pairs. At the table saw, cut a 45° miter onto two sets of the pairs. Your miter gauge, with a short wooden fence attached, is the tool to use. Place the top of the foot (the long side) against the fence, then push the foot through the blade to bevel one half of your pair. To cut the opposing foot, reverse your miter gauge in the slot. Again, keep the top edge of the foot tight to the auxiliary fence, then push the piece through the

Shaker Cupboard

	NO.	ITEM	DIMENSIONS (INCHES)			DIMENSIONS (MILLIMETERS)			MATERIAL	COMMENTS
			T	W	L	T	W	L		
BASE										
❑	2	Sides	$7/8$	18	$34^1/4$	22	457	870	Poplar	
❑	1	Bottom	$7/8$	$17^1/4$	$48^3/8$	22	438	1229	Poplar	Dovetailed to sides
❑	2	Shelves	$7/8$	$17^1/4$	$48^3/8$	22	438	1229	Poplar	Sliding dovetail ends
❑	1	Top	$7/8$	20	$50^3/4$	22	508	1289	Poplar	
❑	1	Base frame front	$5/8$	$3^7/8$	$49^5/8$	16	98	1261	Poplar	Miter both ends
❑	2	Base frame ends	$5/8$	$3^7/8$	$19^1/8$	16	98	486	Poplar	Miter one end
❑	6	Drawer guides	$5/8$	$1^1/2$	17	16	38	432	Poplar	
❑	1	Back	$1/2$	$48^3/8$	$34^1/4$	13	1229	870	Poplar	Tongue-and-groove
❑	6	Profiled feet	$3/4$	$5^1/2$	$7^1/4$	19	140	184	Poplar	
❑	2	Rear feet	$3/4$	$5^1/2$	$3^1/2$	19	140	89	Poplar	
❑	4	Foot plates	$3/8$	5	5	10	127	127	Oak	
BASE FACE FRAME										
❑	2	Stiles	$7/8$	$3^7/8$	$34^1/4$	22	98	870	Poplar	
❑	1	Top rail	$7/8$	$1^5/8$	$43^7/8$	22	41	1114	Poplar	$1^1/4$" TBE*
❑	1	Middle rail	$7/8$	$1^3/4$	$43^7/8$	22	45	1114	Poplar	$1^1/4$" TBE
❑	1	Bottom rail	$7/8$	1	$43^7/8$	22	25	1114	Poplar	$1^1/4$" TBE
❑	1	Vertical divider	$7/8$	$4^7/8$	$27^3/8$	22	124	696	Poplar	1" TBE
❑	2	Drawer dividers	$7/8$	$1^1/2$	$7^1/8$	22	38	181	Poplar	$1^1/4$" TBE
BASE DOOR PARTS										
❑	4	Stiles	$7/8$	$3^1/4$	$25^1/4$	22	79	641	Poplar	
❑	2	Top rails	$7/8$	$3^1/4$	$18^1/4$	22	79	463	Poplar	Through-tenons
❑	2	Bottom rails	$7/8$	$3^1/2$	$18^1/4$	22	89	463	Poplar	Through-tenons
❑	2	Panels	$1/4$	$12^3/8$	$19^1/8$	6	315	486	Poplar	
BASE DRAWER BOXES										
❑	2	Outside fronts	$7/8$	$13^3/4$	17	22	349	432	Poplar	
❑	1	Center front	$7/8$	$10^5/8$	17	22	270	432	Poplar	
TOP										
❑	2	Sides	$7/8$	$9^1/8$	$44^1/2$	22	232	1131	Poplar	
❑	1	Top	$7/8$	$8^3/8$	$47^3/8$	22	213	1204	Poplar	Dovetailed to sides
❑	3	Shelves	$7/8$	$8^3/8$	$47^3/8$	22	213	1204	Poplar	Sliding dovetail ends
❑	1	Back	$1/2$	$47^3/8$	$44^1/2$	13	1204	1131	Poplar	Tongue-and-groove
❑	1	Crown front	$3/4$	3	55	19	76	1397	Poplar	
❑	1	Crown end	$3/4$	3	24	19	76	610	Poplar	
TOP FACE FRAME										
❑	2	Stiles	$7/8$	$3^7/8$	$44^1/2$	22	98	1131	Poplar	
❑	1	Top rail	$7/8$	$5^1/2$	$42^7/8$	22	140	1089	Poplar	$1^1/4$" TBE
❑	1	Bottom rail	$7/8$	$1^1/4$	$42^7/8$	22	32	1089	Poplar	$1^1/4$" TBE
❑	1	Vertical divider	$7/8$	$4^1/8$	$33^7/8$	22	108	860	Poplar	1" TBE
TOP DOOR PARTS										
❑	4	Stiles	$7/8$	$3^1/4$	$31^7/8$	22	79	809	Poplar	
❑	4	Rails	$7/8$	$3^1/4$	$18^1/8$	22	79	463	Poplar	Through-tenons
❑	2	Panels	$1/4$	$12^1/4$	26	6	311	660	Poplar	

* TBE = tenon both ends

IT TAKES TWO. Make two passes with your blade set at 45° to form the slots for the splines. Add a fence extension and use a push stick to guide your foot through the blade.

A SIMPLE ALTERNATIVE. One of the easiest ways to join feet to furniture is with a plate added to the top edge of your foot pairs. Screw the plates down then add a single block at the miter for extra support.

blade while using a push stick to hold the stock tight to the tabletop and fence as shown below.

A 45° cut into a 45° angle forms a perfect slot for a spline to hold the pairs as one. Leave your table saw blade set at 45°, add an extension to your saw's fence and slide the fence into position. Make a cut into the bevel of each foot. Reposition the fence to make a second pass to increase the slot width to match a piece of ¼" plywood. Plywood is a great choice for splines because of its strength and stability.

Slip the front feet and splines together with glue. While the glue dries, dovetail the other profiled feet to the rear feet. Place the pins in the shaped feet with the tails in the rear feet.

Each foot unit receives a plate that's set in a ⅜"-deep rabbet at the top edge. Make that cut at a router table using a rabbet bit. The operation leaves a rounded corner. Square the corners or round

the plates to fit. Afterward, glue and nail the plates to the feet.

The base frame's top edge is profiled with a ⅜"-roundover bit set to a ¼" depth of cut. The corners are mitered. I recommend a mitered half-lap. When complete, nail the frame to the case. The feet are then attached to the frame using screws through the top plates.

Tops, Mouldings and Backs

The lower section top is a simple plank of ¾"-thick stock. Cut a stop-rabbet on the underside of the back edge where the backboards attach. Align the top's rabbet with the grooves in both case sides.

The crown moulding is designed from examples found on other Ohio Shaker pieces. The moulding is made using a table saw. Cut the cove while pushing the stock at an angle over the blade. (Raise the blade incrementally with each pass and make multiple passes.) The remaining cuts are made with

the blade angled at 45° and the fence maneuvered to appropriate positions.

Miter the moulding at the corners and fit it in position. Use brads to attach the pieces and make sure to add glue to the short grain of the miters for a better hold.

The backboards on the original cupboard are unusual. Not only is the thickness ½" (rather than the usual ⅝"), the pieces are tongue-and-grooved together. The joint is thin and fragile until installed.

Additionally, the upper section's back is comprised of non-rectangular pieces. It is an interesting assembly, but one that is difficult to copy without increasing the workload.

An Updated Finish

The finish schedule for the cupboard is involved, but easy to replicate. Sand the piece to #180-grit. Dye the piece with a water-based cherry aniline dye. A couple coats of 1½-pound shellac, sanded between coats with #400-grit sandpaper, allow the top coat of acrylic latex paint to be manipulated. Apply the paint, then rub through the paint at appropriate areas to simulate age. My mantra for aging paint is "less is best." Overdoing it is easy.

It's obvious that we've pulled our Shaker Cupboard back to an earlier day in its history. But the big question is: Did the detective work pay dividends? The feet are of a Shaker design and accurately scaled for this size cupboard. The moulding is in balance with the new base and the overall design is proportionally pleasing. Job done. There's no way you could walk past this cupboard without giving it a look-see.

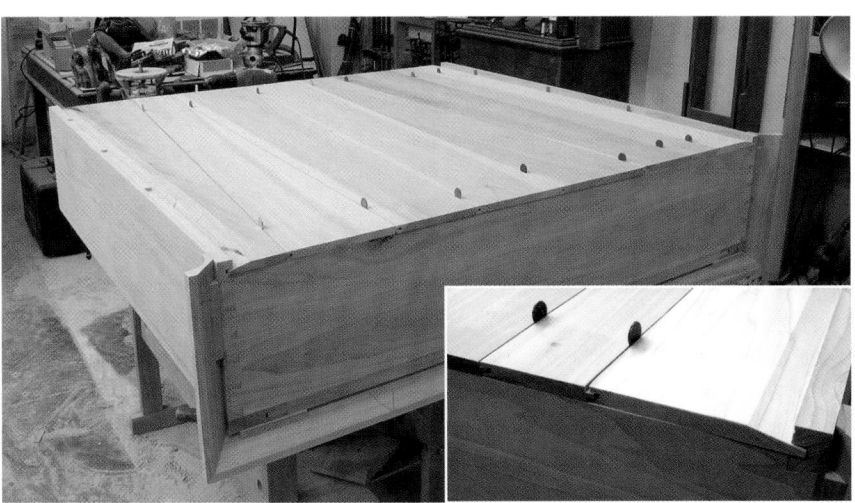

SOMETHING DIFFERENT. The treatment of the backboards on the Shaker cupboard is unusual. The thin boards have tongue-and-groove joinery and the end boards are beveled into dados in the case sides. To be true to the original, not one of the top section's backboards is rectangular.

A CORRECT TIME AND LOCATION. It's best to attach the top after dye and shellac, but just before adding the paint to the cupboard.

Shaker Storage Cabinet

BY TROY SEXTON

The Shakers always had a knack for packing a lot of storage into a small space and making it look good. The three-sided built-in in the Center family residence at Pleasant Hill, Ky., is a prime example. You've probably seen a photo of it. It's the impressive cherry unit that's in an attic with a skylight that illuminates all 45 drawers.

It is in that spirit that I designed this two-door cabinet for a client in Ohio. The family needed to store an enormous number of board games and toys in a small space. The doors had to hide everything.

How to Pack Lots of Stuff Into Small Spaces

Organizing clutter is an interesting problem that you also might face as you design storage in your home or case pieces. Here's what I did: Behind the left door I put a series of five ¾"-thick adjustable solid-wood shelves. These would handle the heavier games and books. Behind the right door is a series of ¼"-thick tempered Masonite shelves. These 10 shelves slide in and out of ¼" x ¼" dados.

The Masonite won't hold a lot of weight, but it's just right for storing lightweight objects. Think home office, and you'll know what I mean. Masonite (sometimes called "hardboard") shelves are perfect for storing letterhead, envelopes, CDs and any other paper goods in an office. The other challenge in this piece was getting the shelves, doors and face frame positioned so they didn't interfere with one another. As you'll see

in the drawings, it took a few pieces of "blocking" to get everything to work in this cabinet.

Face Frame First

This seems backwards, I know, but begin construction by building the face frame. The size of the case and doors are determined by your face frame, so it's clearly the place to begin.

When ripping out the material for the face frame stiles, cut them each about ¹⁄₁₆" wider than the dimension called for in the cutting list. This will make your face frame hang over the edge of the case sides. Once the face frame is attached, you can trim it flush for a perfect fit.

I use mortise-and-tenon joinery to build both the face frames and doors. The tenons are ⅜" thick and 1" long, and I usually cut a ⅜" to ½" shoulder on the edges. Be sure to cut your mortises 1¹⁄₁₆" deep so your tenons don't bottom out. When everything fits, put glue in the mortises, clamp the frame and allow the glue to cure.

Doors are Second

Next, build the doors. It's much easier to fit the doors into your face frame before it's attached to the case. Build the doors much like you did your face frame by using mortise-and-tenon joints. The only difference is that you need to cut a ⅜" x ⅜" groove in the rails and stiles to hold the door panels.

I cut my grooves along the entire length of the stiles; as a result, I cut my tenons with a "haunch" to fill in that extra space on the ends of the stiles. The panels

are flat on the front, and beveled on the backside so they fit in the grooves in the rails and stiles. I cut that bevel by setting my table saw blade to 7° and slicing off a little of the backside of each door until the panels fit snug and without rattling.

Sand the panels up to your final grit (120 will be fine for a painted piece) and assemble the doors. Sand the assembled doors and face frame and then peg the tenons if you like. I used square pegs that I pounded into round holes.

Shaker Storage Cabinet

NO.	LETTER	ITEM	DIMENSIONS (INCHES) T	W	L	DIMENSIONS (MILLIMETERS) T	W	L	MATERIAL	COMMENTS
FACE FRAME										
2	A	Stiles	¾	2½	51¼	19	64	1301	Poplar	
1	B	Top rail*	¾	2	45	19	51	1143	Poplar	
1	C	Bottom rail*	¾	5½	45	19	140	1143	Poplar	
DOORS										
4	D	Stiles	¾	2½	43¾	19	64	1111	Poplar	
6	E	Rails*	¾	2½	18½	19	64	470	Poplar	
4	F	Panels	⅝	17	18⅝	16	432	473	Poplar	
CARCASE										
1	G	Top	¾	19	50	19	483	1270	Maple	
2	H	Sides	¾	17¼	51¼	19	438	1301	Poplar	
1	I	Bottom	¾	16¾	47	19	425	1194	Poplar	
2	J	Dividers	¾	16¼	45½	19	412	1156	Poplar	
1	K	Nailing strip	¾	1½	46½	19	38	1181	Poplar	
1	L	Blocking 1	¾	2¼	45½	19	57	1156	Poplar	
1	M	Blocking 2	½	1¾	45½	13	45	1156	Poplar	
5	N	Adj. shelves	¾	16¼	22⅝	19	412	575	Poplar	
10	O	Masonite shelves	¼	16¼	20¼	6	412	514	Masonite	
1	P	Back	½	47	51¼	13	1194	1301	Ply	

*= 1" tenon on both ends

I'm not perfect, and neither are you. If your face frame is exactly the width of your case, it's going to be difficult to fasten it square. Make life easier by ripping your stiles ¹/₁₆" oversize in width. After you nail and glue the face frame to the case, use a flush-trimming bit in your router to trim the face frame flush with the side of the cabinet's case.

Supplies

Woodworker's Supply
800-645-9292

Amerock non-mortising hinges, #891-749, $2.95 each

Horton Brasses
800-754-9127

Maple knobs, #WK-3, 1½" diameter, call for pricing

You can see the haunch on the tenons on the rail closest to the camera. When it comes to fitting your panels, remember to work tight in summer and loose in winter. Panels of this size will shrink and contract noticeably.

Finally, the Case

The case goes together quickly thanks to my nail gun. Begin construction by cutting a ¾"-wide by ¼"-deep dado in the side pieces for the bottom of the cabinet. I like to use a dado stack in my table saw for this operation. Now cut a ½" x ½" rabbet on the back edges of the sides to hold the plywood back in place. Sand the inside of the case and get ready for the first bit of assembly.

Put the case together on its back. First put glue in the dados in the sides and fit the bottom in there. Nail the bottom in place from the outside of the case. I use a finish nailer for this task.

Now put the nailing strip in place at the top of the case. The diagrams show you where this needs to be, but essentially it's flush with both the rabbets in the sides and top of the case. Nail it home. Glue and nail the face frame to the case using brads. Trim the face frame flush to the case.

All the Insides

There's nothing complicated about the insides once you have a plan. Begin by cutting the ¼" x ¼" dados in the dividers. These are spaced 2" apart, and there

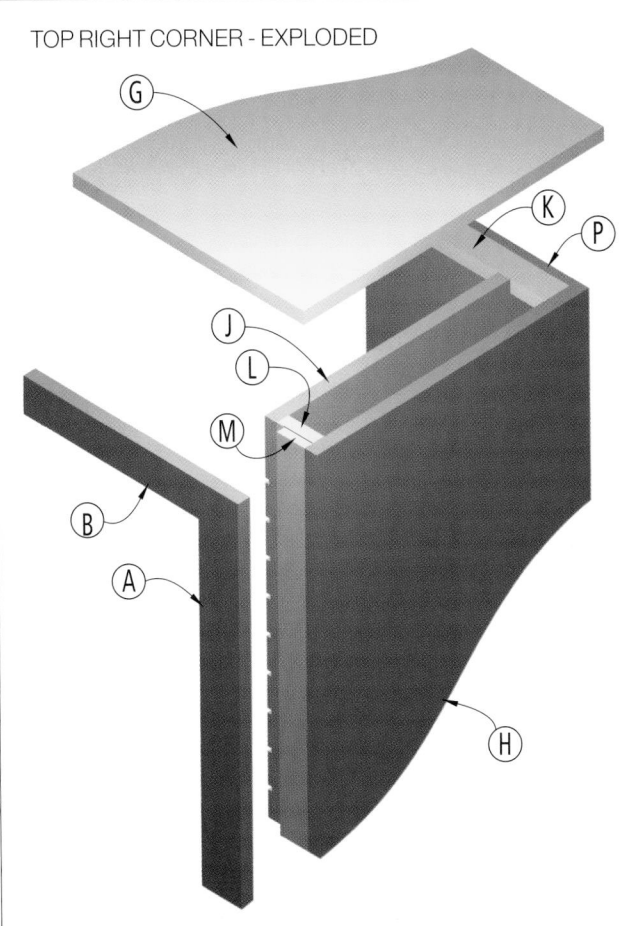

TOP RIGHT CORNER - EXPLODED

G
K
P
J
L
M
B
A
H

ELEVATION

48"
2 1/2"
16 1/2"
2 1/2"
2 1/2"
G
2"
2 1/2"
18 1/8"
2 1/2"
18 1/8"
2 1/2"
3"
51 1/4"
43 3/4"
B
A
F
E
D
C
3"
1"

PLAN - TOP REMOVED

47"
17 1/4"
19"
P
K
I
16 1/4"
1/2"
L
M
Outline of top

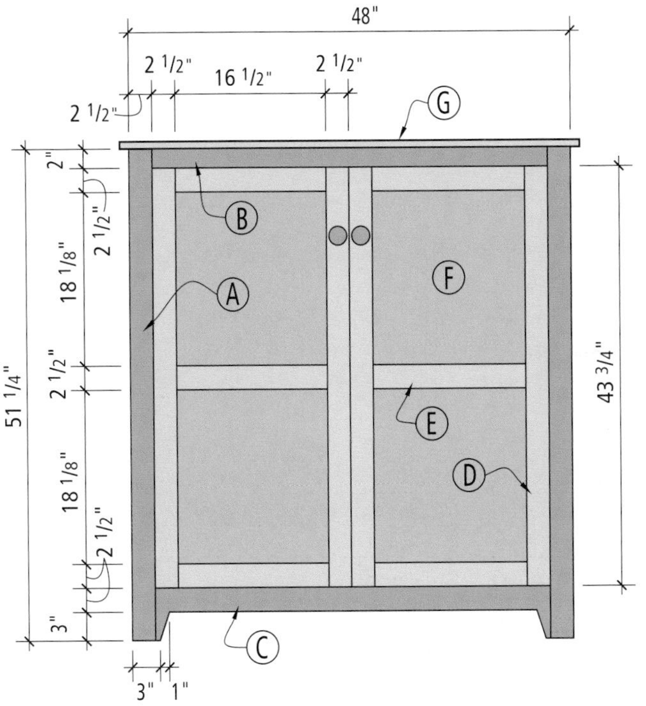

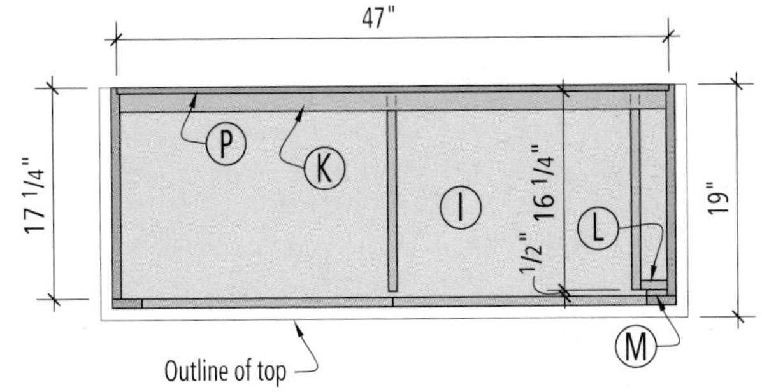

ELEVATION - FACE FRAME & DOORS REMOVED

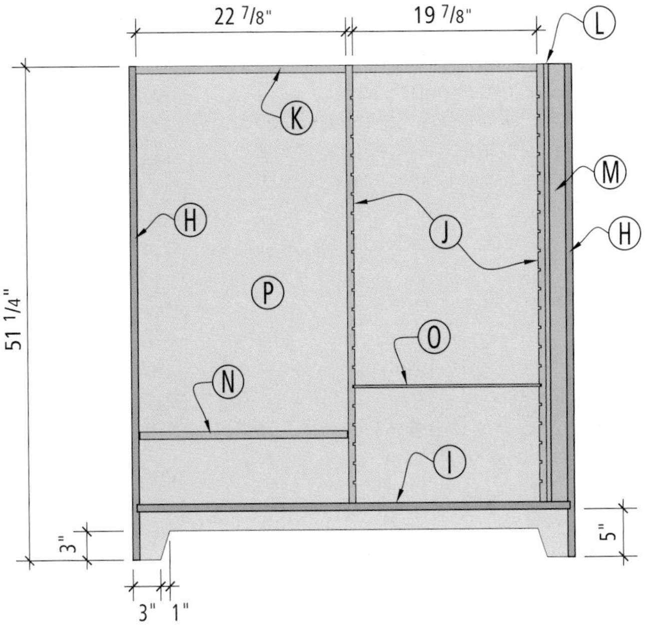

22 7/8"
19 7/8"
L
K
M
H
J
H
P
51 1/4"
O
N
I
3"
5"
3"
1"

are 21 of them. I used a dado stack in my table saw and simply moved the fence 1¾" after each pass.

Now it's time to add the dividers to the case. Turn the case on its head. Cut a notch in each divider so it will fit around the nailing strip. Get the divider right where it needs to be and nail it in place through the bottom and the nailing strip. Now nail the two blocking pieces shown on the diagram in place. The blocking does a couple things. First, it allows the Masonite shelves to be slid in and out without having to swing the doors wide open. Second, the thinner piece of blocking fills in the gap between the divider and face frame and leaves room for the hinges.

Now drill the holes in the left side of the case and the center divider for the adjustable solid-wood shelves. I'm partial to 5 mm holes spaced 1⅜" on center.

Mark the base cutouts on the sides, front and plywood back of the case using the diagrams as a guide. Use a jigsaw to

You could use a router and a straight bit to make this cut as long as you had a reliable way of guiding the router (such as an edge guide). I find a table saw is much faster for this operation.

make these cuts and clean up your work with sandpaper.

Cut your top to size. I used a piece of bird's-eye maple. You have a couple options for attaching the top. You could use pocket holes, figure-8 fasteners or wooden cleats. No matter which way you go, prepare the case for the top but don't attach it. I like to glue the top to the front edge of the case after finishing.

Finishing

On the knobs, top and all the inside pieces (except the Masonite), I wiped on a light honey-colored stain. Then I painted the case a dark red and added a topcoat of lacquer to protect the paint. Hang the doors, nail in the back and add the knobs.

I have no idea how the Shakers would feel about seeing one of their cabinets filled with "Parcheesi," "Connect Four" and "Uncle Wiggly" games. But I'm sure at least they would approve of the efficient use of space.

Once you nail the dividers in place through the bottom piece, turn the case over on its feet and nail through the nailing strip into the dividers.

In addition to cutting this detail on the sides and front, I also cut it on the bottom of the plywood back, which gives it a finished look when the cabinet is viewed from down low or from a distance.

Lingerie Chest

BY GLEN D. HUEY

If you have woodworking tools and a talent to build, there is a certain time each year that you are called upon to use both. Suddenly, Aunt Susan needs a cookbook holder or Grandma needs new picture frames as the holidays come into sight on the calendar. As a result, the plans you made to build your significant other that special gift get put on hold.

So this year I decided to get an early start and build this traditional-style dresser for my wife.

Joinery in the Sides

The case begins with the dovetails that connect the sides to the bottom. These dovetails will be hidden by moulding when the project is complete, so have some fun here. You could cut these joints by hand.

Lay out the pins in the sides and the matching tails in the bottom. This arrangement will prevent the case from ever loosening up across its width. After the pins are cut, transfer the layout to the bottom piece to create the tails.

Now lay out the location of the drawer dividers on the case sides. Begin from the bottom of the case. The joinery between the drawer dividers and the sides is a sliding dovetail (except with the bottom divider, which is butt-jointed against the case sides). I like to cut the dovetail socket into the case sides using a router with a ¾", 14° dovetail bit and a ¾" outside-diameter bushing. The bushing rides along a straightedge fence that you clamp directly on the layout lines, while the bit cuts the bottom of the slot in line with that fence.

The drawer dividers for the drawers located behind the doors are set into dados that are routed into the case sides. Use a straightedge fence in combination with a $\frac{1}{2}$" straight bit with a $\frac{1}{2}$" top-mount bearing set to cut $\frac{3}{16}$" deep. Run these dados to a point $1\frac{1}{4}$" from the front edge. Square the ends with your chisel.

The front top rail is attached to the case sides with a half-dovetail joint. Lay out the $\frac{1}{2}$"-long socket, make a cut with your dovetail saw that defines the socket and clean out the waste. Then cut the rail to shape and check the fit.

The dovetail joint that connects the back top rail to the case sides is arranged a bit differently. I chose to use a single wide pin on the end of the rail with two small half tail areas in the case side. Shape the rail then use that as a template for the sides.

To complete the work to the case sides you will need to create the $\frac{7}{16}$"-deep x $\frac{3}{4}$"-wide rabbet along the back edge of the side pieces for the back boards.

Dividers and Rails

The dovetailed drawer dividers are cut to fit the sockets in your sides using the same bit used to create those sockets. At your router table, set the bit to the appropriate height and then set the fence to leave the desired dovetail thickness. Make the cuts from both faces to ensure that the tail is centered on the divider. If you can push the pieces together tightly by hand you have the correct fit.

The dovetailed dividers also need $\frac{1}{4}$"-wide x 1"-long x $\frac{1}{2}$"-deep mortises to accept a tenon on the drawer runners. For all the rails except the bottom one, the mortise begins at the shoulder of the sliding dovetail. The mortise for the bottom rail is cut completely to the end of the rail.

Cut and fit the front top rail to the half-dovetail socket that you made earlier. Glue the dovetails at the case bottom and slide the joint together. Add glue to the two dovetail sockets at the top of the case and position the rails to their respective mates. A few clamps will hold the case. Check the measurements from corner to corner to make sure that it is square.

Speed up the dovetailing process by setting the angle on your jigsaw to match the layout lines and define the pins at the bottom of the case. You'll only be able to cut one side without changing the angle to complete the cuts.

This is one of my favorite methods for cutting dados for drawer runners (or dividers in this case). Use a double thickness of plywood to make a straightedge fence. The bit's bearing will ride against the fence creating a straight dado.

For the dovetail dividers mill an extra piece of scrap for setup. A snug fit will get tighter when you add glue. Note the backup block behind the work. This keeps the divider stable as it is cut.

Begin the installation of the drawer dividers with the bottom divider. Make sure it fits snugly, add a thin bead of glue to the bottom of this divider and attach it to the case through the bottom with $1\frac{1}{4}$" wood screws.

The dovetailed dividers are installed into the case after adding a small amount of glue into each socket as well as on the leading edge of the sliding dovetail.

After the first cut for the sliding dovetail slots, and with the router off, slide the bit to the back of the cut and draw a line where the base sits. This will be the stopping point of each cut in this operation.

This dovetail on the back top rail accepts a great deal of tension if the case is ever lifted using the top.

The "step" method involves plunging one cut, skipping the second $\frac{1}{4}$", and making the next plunge allowing equal pressure on all sides of the chisel. Work the entire length of the mortise then remove the remaining waste.

Once those dividers are in place it is time to install the $\frac{1}{2}$"-thick dividers for the drawers behind the doors. Be sure to mill the drawer runners for the interior drawers before you install the dividers. To install all these pieces you simply slide the divider into position. Then add the drawer runners directly behind the dividers to hold them tightly to the front. There is no mortise-and-tenon joint used

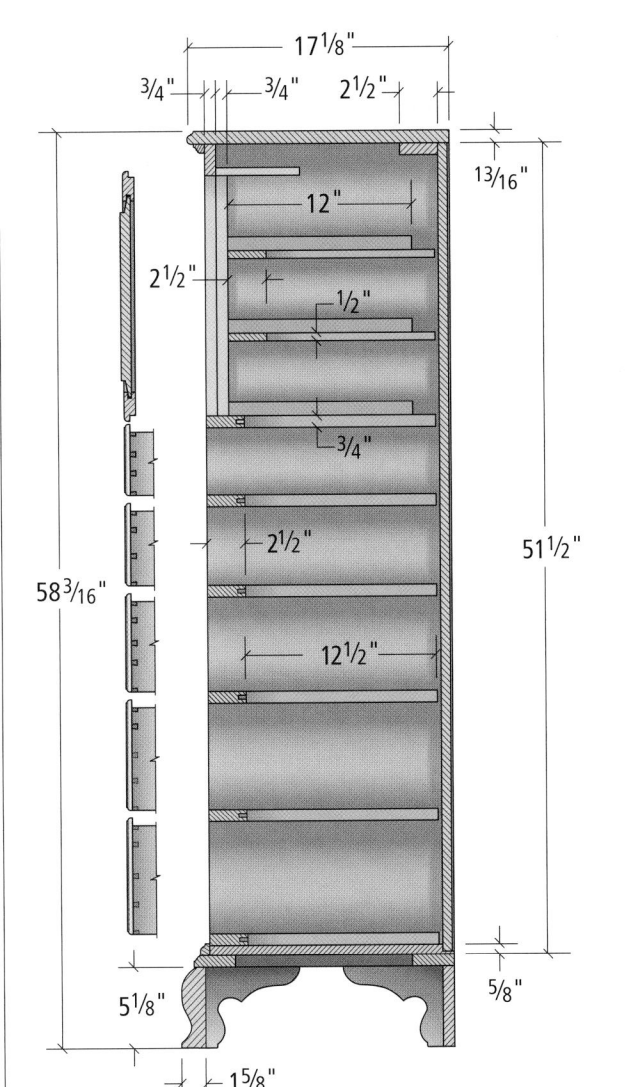

PROFILE SECTION

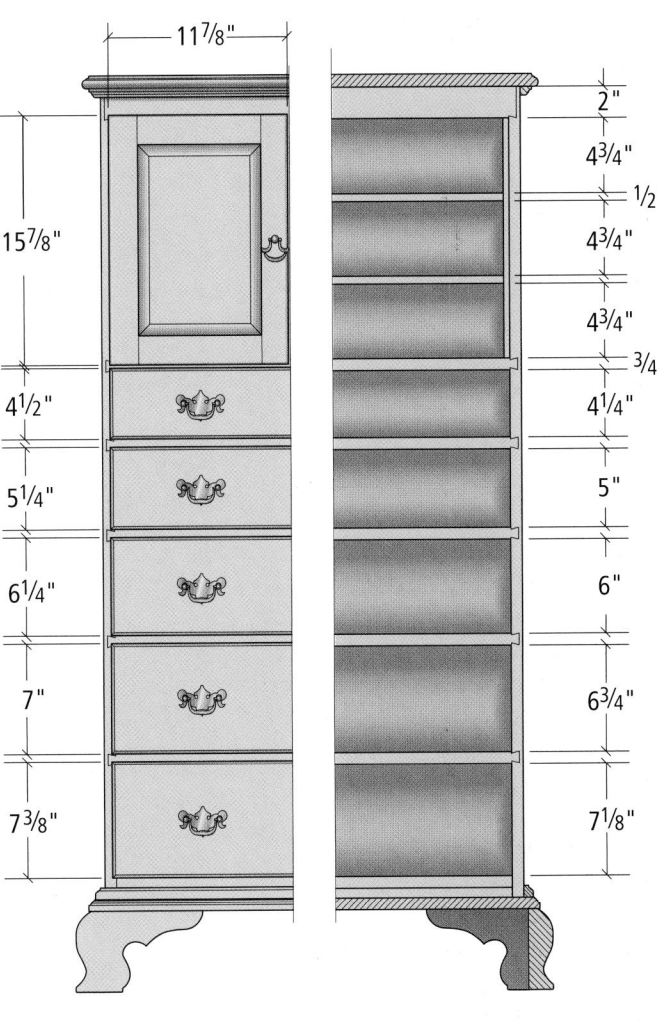

ELEVATION   ELEVATION SECTION

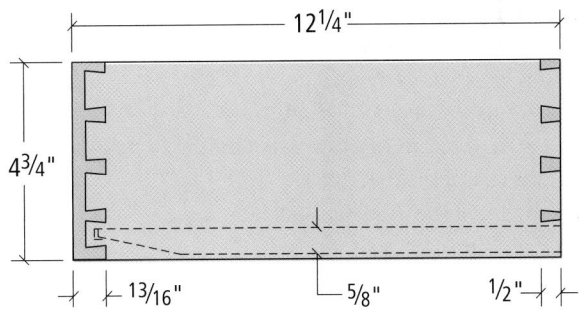

INTERIOR DRAWER DETAIL

with these dividers. Add a bead of glue to the edge of the runner that meets the case sides and install it into position. A brad at the front and rear will secure the runner to the case side. Above the topmost drawer, install the drawer kicks by gluing and nailing them to the side pieces.

Because you need clearance to properly operate the interior drawers while avoiding the hinges of the doors, you need to build out the interior case sides. To do this you need to add the interior side spacers. These spacers have a moulded edge and fit tightly from top to bottom. Hold them tight to the front edge of the installed dividers. Attach them with a small bead of glue and brads. To finish the interior area you need to cut and fit the interior drawer guides.

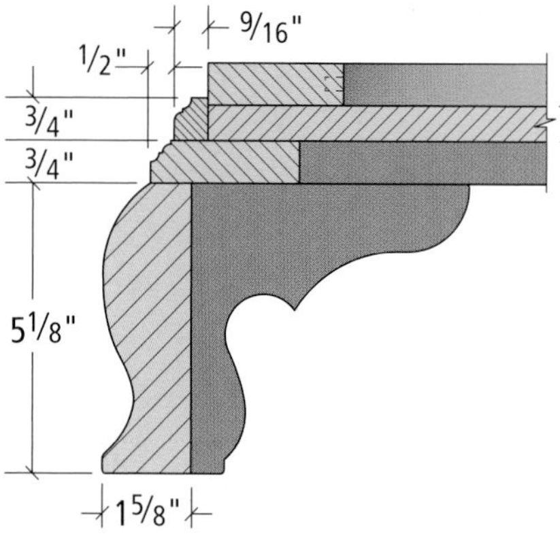

BOTTOM MOULDING DETAIL

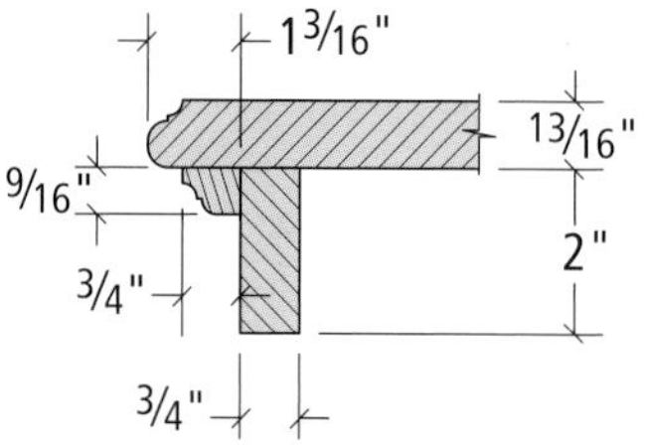

TOP MOULDING DETAIL

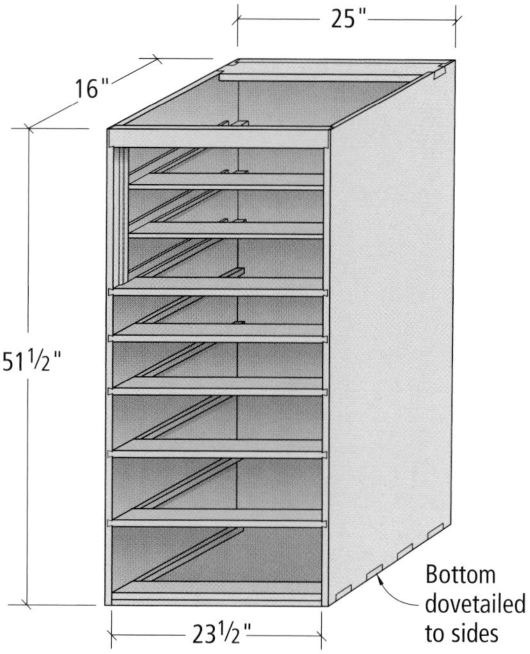

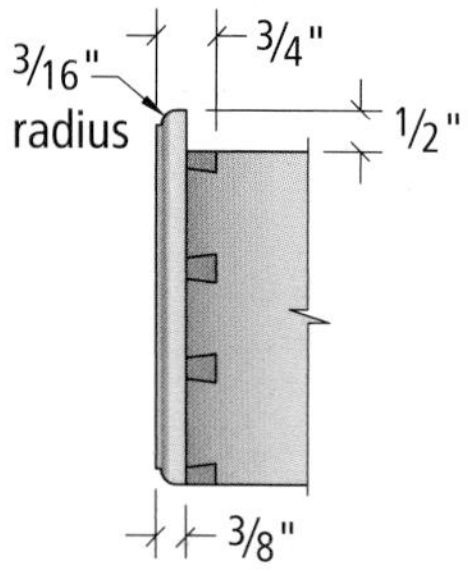

MOULDED DRAWER DETAIL

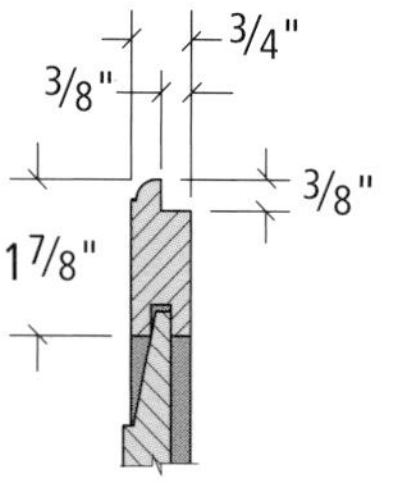

DOOR DETAIL

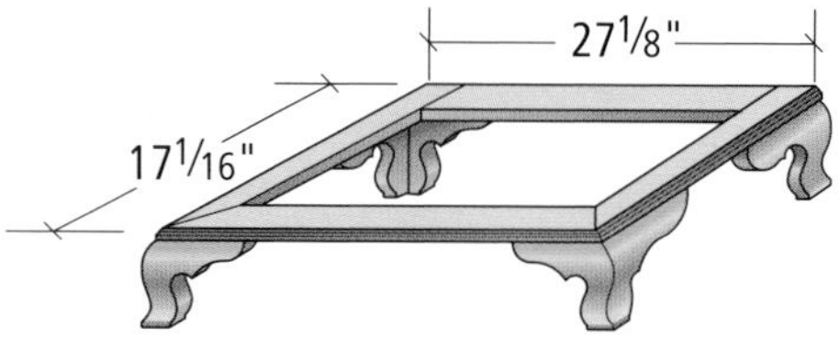

Bottom dovetailed to sides

EXPLODED VIEW

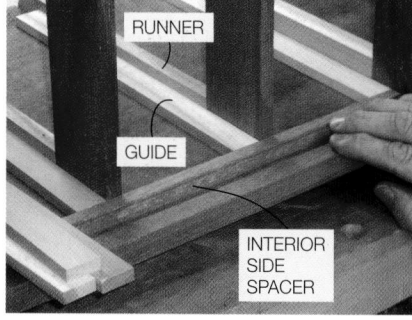

The drawer guides are glued and nailed at the front with a nail only at the back.

Make a ¼" tenon on one end of a wide piece of secondary wood. Once the tongue is fit to the mortise in the dividers, rip the board into the 1" strips that will be the drawer runners.

Clamping the base frame in this manner is the most effective method. You will need to work all four clamps in unison to simultaneously close the joint and square the frame.

Lingerie Chest

	NO.	ITEM	DIMENSIONS (INCHES)			DIMENSIONS (MILLIMETERS)			MATERIAL	COMMENTS
			T	W	L	T	W	L		
❏	2	Case sides	3/4	16	51½	19	406	1308	P	
❏	1	Case bottom	5/8	16	25	16	406	635	S	
❏	1	Back top rail	3/4	2½	25	19	64	635	S	
❏	1	Front top rail	3/4	2	24½	19	51	623	P	
❏	5	Dovetail drawer dividers	3/4	2½	24½	19	64	623	P	
❏	1	Bottom divider	3/4	2½	23½	19	64	597	P	
❏	12	Drawer runners	3/4	1	13	19	25	330	S	½" tenon, one end
❏	2	Interior drawer dividers	1/2	2½	23⅞	13	64	606	P	
❏	4	Interior drawer runners	1/2	1	11	13	25	279	S	
❏	2	Top drawer kicks	1/2	1	5½	13	25	140	P	Glued, nailed to case sides
❏	2	Interior side spacer	3/8	3/4	15⅝	10	19	397	P	Glued to case sides
❏	6	Interior drawer guides	3/8	5/8	12	10	16	305	S	
❏	1	Base frame front	3/4	2¾	27⅛	19	70	689	P	Miter both ends
❏	2	Base frame sides	3/4	2¾	17 1/16	19	70	434	P	Miter one end
❏	1	Base frame back	3/4	2¾	24⅛	19	70	613	S	1¼" tenon, both ends
❏	2	Feet blanks	1⅝	5⅛	26	41	130	660	P	For front & sides
❏	2	Rear feet blanks	3/4	5⅛	8	19	130	203	S	For rear of case
❏	1	Case top	13/16	17⅛	27½	24	435	709	P	Attached with buttons
❏	2	Front moulding	9/16	3/4	28½	14	19	724	P	
❏	4	Side moulding	9/16	3/4	18½	14	19	470	P	
❏	3	Door stiles	3/4	1⅞	15⅞	19	49	383	P	
❏	1	Door stile	3/4	2¼	15⅞	19	57	383	P	Wider for lip
❏	4	Door rails	3/4	1⅞	10⅛	19	49	257	P	1" tenon, both ends
❏	2	Raised panels	5/8	8¾	12¾	16	222	324	P	5/16" tongue, all sides
❏	3	Interior drawers	4¾	22¾	12¼	121	578	311	P & S	Overall drawer dimensions
❏	1	Moulded drawer #4	4½	24⅛	14⅜	115	613	366	P & S	Overall drawer dimensions
❏	1	Moulded drawer #5	5¼	24⅛	14⅜	133	613	366	P & S	Overall drawer dimensions
❏	1	Moulded drawer #6	6¼	24⅛	14⅜	158	613	366	P & S	Overall drawer dimensions
❏	1	Moulded drawer #7	7	24⅛	14⅜	178	613	366	P & S	Overall drawer dimensions
❏	1	Moulded drawer #8	7⅜	24⅛	14⅜	188	613	366	P & S	Overall drawer dimensions
❏	6	Interior drawer stops	5/8	3/4	3	16	19	76	S	
❏	28	Foot blocks stacked	3/4	1⅛	1⅛	19	29	29	S	Makes 4 pieces
❏	2	Foot blocks	3/4	3/4	14	19	19	356	S	Makes 4 pieces
❏		Back boards	5/8	24⅜	51½	16	620	1308	S	Many pieces
❏	5	Wooden clips	3/4	7/8	2¼	19	22	57	S	
❏	1	Door catch	5/8	5/8	2¾	16	16	70	P	

P= primary wood; S=secondary wood

Now install the drawer runners behind the dovetailed dividers. Cut a tenon on the runners that fit the mortises in the dividers. For aesthetic reasons I opt to clip the non-mortised end with a 45° cut. Add glue to the mortise and tenon as well as the first few inches on the runner and slide the joint together. The runner is nailed to the case sides at the rear.

Wooden clips attach the top to the case. The slots for the clips should be ¼" wide and are placed from ½" to ¾" down from the top edge of the sides. I use my biscuit joiner to make the slots.

Make the Base Frame

Mill the stock for the base frame pieces to size and cut both ends of the front piece at a 45° angle. While the miter gauge is set for 45° you can cut one end of each of the base frame sides.

The other end of the side pieces receives a mortise that is ¼" wide x 2¼" long x 1¼" deep. The angled cuts are to be joined with a #20 biscuit. Then cut matching tenons on both ends of the base frame's back.

To assemble the base frame, add clamps to square the frame as shown in the photo above and set it aside for the glue to dry.

Once the glue in the frame is dry, level the mitered corners and the mortised areas then mould the edges on the two sides and the front with a router.

Ogee Bracket Feet

Shape the ogee feet using a cove-cutting technique on your table saw. Trace the ogee foot profile on both ends of your stock. Set the table saw's blade height to the top edge of the cove of the foot while laying the stock face down on the saw's

Supplies

Horton Brasses
800-754-9127 or
horton-brasses.com

2 pr. • door hinges
#HDH-4, semi-bright

1 • door cupboard turn
#H-40, semi-bright

1 • door pull
#H-40, semi-bright

10 • drawer pulls
#H-17, 2½" bore, semi-bright

6 • int. drawer knobs
#H-42, ¾" semi-bright

• nails
#N-7, clout or shingle

surface. Set an auxiliary fence so that the blade starts in at the cove of the foot and exits at the opposite end of the cove, then clamp the fence in place. Lower the blade, then gradually cut the cove in small steps until the shape is complete.

Then, at the table saw with your fence aligned with the blade and the blade tilted to an appropriate angle, remove as much of the waste as possible by running the stock through the blade with the top edge against the tabletop.

Next, use the pattern below to lay out the foot profile. Trace the scrolled profile onto the stock and mark the center point of the area to be drilled to create the spur.

Remove the area that will create the spur using a 1⅜" Forstner bit and then cut each foot to shape using the band saw.

Set one of each profile of the feet aside to use as the rear foot on the case side. The remaining feet will be paired to make the front foot assemblies. Cut a 45°

miter on each of these feet. The first two will be cut with the miter gauge and auxiliary fence set in the standard position. Place a stop block to keep the blank from moving away from the blade as it is cut, and with the top edge of the foot against the fence make a cut to form the angle.

The second two pieces will be cut with the miter gauge set up reversed in the same slot of the table saw. Adjust your stop block and make the cuts while you are keeping the top edge of the foot tight to the fence with a push stick. Now you have a matched set for the front foot assembly.

Before changing the blade angle, set the fence to make a ¼"-wide x ⅜"-deep groove for a plywood spline in each foot.

Now assemble the front feet for the chest. Add glue, insert the spline and use duct tape or clear packing tape to immobilize the feet as the glue sets.

The two remaining moulded feet pieces are for the rear feet assemblies. They are dovetailed to the rear foot blanks, which are flat and made from a secondary species, such as poplar.

Before attaching the foot assemblies to the base frame, sand the edge profile and finish shaping the face of the feet. Attach the feet to the frame using glue blocks. Place the blocks in the corner of the foot vertically, as well as along the return of each foot. For the vertical blocks I stack squares of stock so the grain is alternating.

Now attach the completed base to the case with #8 x 1¼" screws along the front edge and nails at the back. The screws hold the relationship of the two constant with movement forced to the rear, which the nails will allow.

Create the transition moulding on your router table and attach it to the case covering the joint of the two assemblies. Use glue along the front piece and about 4" back along the side pieces, then finish the installation with brads.

I selected a classic ogee bit for the top edge and a ¼" roundover to soften the bottom edge of the top. Sand the top to #180 grit and attach it to the case. Use nails into the rear top case rail and screws through the wooden clips, which are rabbeted, leaving a ¼" tongue that slips into the slots cut in the case sides and front rail. Add the moulding below the top.

Building the Doors

For the lipped doors, I chose the right stile of the left-hand (or fixed) door to be the wide stile. This is the stile into which the opposite door will lip. Each stile receives mortises that are ¼" x 1½" x 1" in depth. They begin at ½" in from the end of the stile. Then cut matching tenons on the rails, being sure to leave material for a ⅜" haunch that will fit into the door's groove.

Cut a ¼" groove for the panel in the center of each rail and stile. That groove needs to be ⅜" deep. To raise the panel, tilt the table saw's blade to 12° and set the fence at exactly ³⁄₁₆" away from the blade from where it tips below the table surface. This will create the appropriate fit of the panel into the groove of the door frame parts. To create a classic raised panel you need to set the saw blade so that the outer edge of the blade is flush with the outside surface of the panel.

The setup for the second cut can be the most difficult (if you need more pictures and direction, visit woodwork-

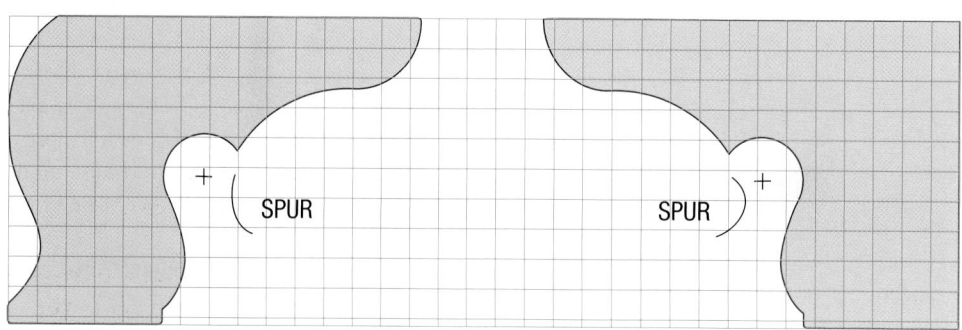

1 square = ½"

FRONT LEG PROFILE

BACK LEG PROFILE

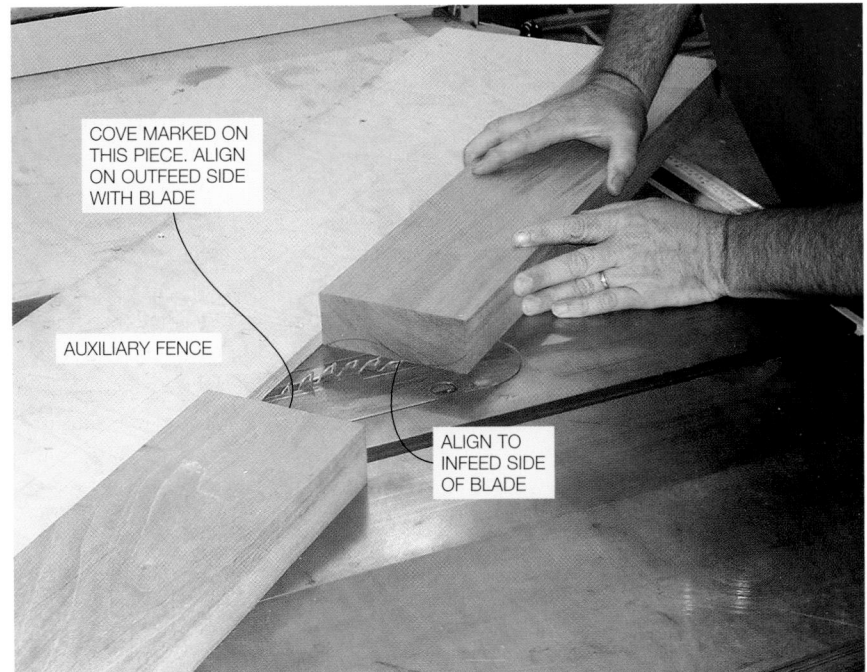

COVE MARKED ON THIS PIECE. ALIGN ON OUTFEED SIDE WITH BLADE

AUXILIARY FENCE

ALIGN TO INFEED SIDE OF BLADE

Set an auxiliary fence onto the saw with one piece of stock on each side of the blade and angle the fence until the point of the blade matches both end points of the cove of the foot just as it passes above and below the table top.

It may take a couple of passes to accomplish removing the waste from the top edge of the feet. Be sure not to cut the profile lines.

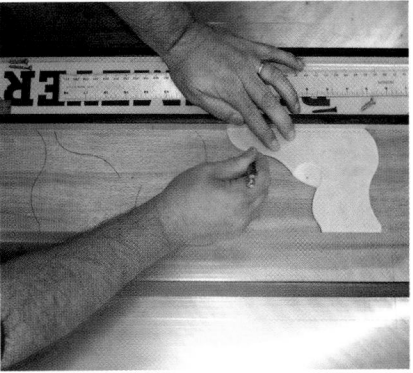

Mark the location for the center point of the drill area that will form the spur of the foot with a small drill bit. You will need three profiles facing in both directions.

Carefully hold the stock both down to the table and tight to the fence as you complete the cut. It is important to use a push stick to complete this cut!

Transfer the layout of the dovetails to the secondary blanks. Do not change or straighten the lines. If you adjust the lines you will not have a tight fit of the dovetails joint when complete.

HAUNCH

Here are the completed rails and stiles. You can see how the haunched tenon fills the groove area of the stiles.

Adjust the height of your cut first, then set the ovolo cutter to leave a ³⁄₈" flat area on the wide stile of your fixed door.

ersedge.com). You will need to raise the blade to just the height of the previously cut area and set the fence so that you are just nipping the 12° cut. This creates the square arris between the panel's flat field and the raised edges. Once set you can make the cuts on all four locations on each panel. Then glue up the doors.

Rout the profile on the perimeter of both doors. Then set up a rabbeting bit and create a ³⁄₈" rabbet on the top and bottom edge of both doors and the middle stile of the operable door. On the two outer or hinge edges of the doors create an ¹⁄₈" rabbet.

Next you need to create a matching edge profile and lip against which the second door will close. An ovolo bit will handle this task. Run this door with the raised panel flat on the table.

Drawers Come Next

Begin the drawers by measuring the openings. For the five lower drawers, add an additional ⁵⁄₈" to the length of the opening and a ¹⁄₄" to the height to arrive

SUPPORT BLOCK

HINGE MORTISE

I find it most helpful to add a block to the back of the door to stabilize the router as it is used to cut the area for the hinge.

at the needed sizes for the drawer fronts. Next use a $^3/_{16}$" beading bit to profile the drawer edge. The interior drawer fronts are cut to fit the openings, less an $^1/_8$" from side to side and a $^1/_{16}$" from top to bottom with no edge profile.

Create the lip on the drawer fronts by cutting a $^3/_8$" x $^1/_2$" rabbet on all but the bottom edge of the lower drawers. Then use the finished drawer fronts to get the measurements for the balance of the drawer parts. The width of the drawer backs is $^3/_4$" less than the width of the drawer sides to make room for the bottom to slide in.

Everyone makes drawers differently, depending on their preferences. Here's how I make mine: I use through dovetails to join the sides to the back. The dovetails at the front are half-blind. The bottom fits into a groove in the sides and drawer front.

The drawer bottom is made the same way as the raised panel for the doors. The difference is that this time you allow the blade to extend completely through the panel – not stop as the blade is flush to the panel. Once complete, sand the bottom and slide it into the drawer box then just inside the back, draw a small line. That line will be the height of the cut for the addition of a nail that will hold the bottom to the drawer back.

Slide the drawers into the case. On the exterior drawers you don't need stops, but the interior drawers need stop blocks attached to the case sides.

Hardware and Finish

To install the hinges, first position the hinge at the door. You need to cut the

lip of the door only to the width of the hinge – not the pin tips – with a saw and remove the material until it is flush with the door edge. I use a router to clean most of the waste from the hinge area then finish with a chisel. The short leaf of the hinge should be flush with the door edge after it is installed.

To mark the hinge locations into the case, position the doors and transfer them onto the case. You have access to the hinges with the drawers removed from the interior through the back of the piece. Next, scribe the hinge profile to the case with a sharp knife. Complete the work with your chisel. The balance of the hardware is installed after the piece has had the finish applied.

The fixed door is held in place with a small catch. To use the catch it will be spun to a vertical position to catch the top rail of the case. Attach the catch in place with a #8 x 1" wood screw.

To finish this piece I elected to use Moser's water-based aniline dye in dark antique Sheraton. It works well with the mahogany. After staining I knocked down any raised grain with #400-grit paper and applied a coat of clear shellac with my HVLP system.

Because I wanted a smooth finish and mahogany has an open grain, I added a coat of oil-based filler to the areas that would show on the final project. Apply the filler, allow it to flash off or turn white and wipe away the excess by wiping across the grain.

That was followed by two more coats of shellac to seal in the filler and after sanding it once, I applied one coat of dull rubbed effect Sherwin-Williams lacquer.

Complete the piece by adding the back boards, which are shiplapped and run horizontal to the case. They are attached with reproduction nails. No finish is applied to either the back boards or the secondary drawer parts.

My holiday is safe because I have my gift finished. But, even if you cannot get your cabinet built in time, I bet a picture folded in an small envelope will work wonders. Remember that good things come in small packages.

Distributed in Canada by Fraser Direct
100 Armstrong Avenue
Georgetown, Ontario L7G 5S4
Canada

Distributed in the U.K. and Europe by
F&W Media International, LTD
Brunel House, Ford Close
Newton Abbot
TQ12 4PU, UK
Tel: (+44) 1626 323200
Fax: (+44) 1626 323319
E-mail: enquiries@fwmedia.com

Distributed in Australia by Capricorn Link
P.O. Box 704
Windsor, NSW 2756
Australia

Visit our website at www.popularwoodworking.com or our consumer website at www.shopwoodwork-ing.com for more woodworking information projects.

Other fine Popular Woodworking Books are available from your local bookstore or direct from the publisher.

16   15   14   13   5   4   3   2

Acquisitions editor: David Thiel
Designer: Brian Roeth
Production coordinator: Mark Griffin

About the Authors

MEGAN FITZPATRICK

Megan is the managing editor of *Popular Woodworking Magazine*. She prefers using hand tools because they rarely make loud noises.

KARA GEBHART

Kara is the former managing editor of *Popular Woodworking Magazine*, and now a freelance author, editor and full-time mom.

GLEN HUEY

Glen recently has been a contibuting editor and senior editor of *Popular Woodworking Magazine*. He is the author of a number of books on building furniture, and teaches and hosts DVDs about furniture building.

ROBERT W. LANG

Bob is executive editor with *Popular Woodworking Magazine* and has been a professional woodworker since the early 1970s. He is the author of several *Shop Drawings* books about furniture and interiors of the Arts & Crafts Movement of the early 1900s.

CHRISTOPHER SCHWARZ

Chris is the former editor of *Popular Woodworking Magazine* and now serves as a contributing editor, covering the world of hand woodworking, as well as teaching and creating videos.

TROY SEXTON

Troy has been a contributing editor for *Popular Woodworking Magazine* for many years, and a professional woodworker for even longer.

STEVE SHANESY

Steve has worn many hats at *Popular Woodworking Magazine,* over the years, including editor and publisher. He has now returned to the ranks as senior editor.

JIM STACK

Jim was editor of *Popular Woodworking Books* for a number of years and now works as a freelance author, editor and illustrator.

JIM STUARD

Jim was associate editor of *Popular Woodworking Magazine* for a number of years and has now gone over the gentile world of fly fishing.

DAVID THIEL

David is a former senior editor of *Popular Woodworking Magazine* and is now executive editor of *Popular Woodworking Books*.

Metric Conversion Chart

TO CONVERT	TO	MULTIPLY BY
Inches	Centimeters	2.54
Centimeters	Inches	0.4
Feet	Centimeters	30.5
Centimeters	Feet	0.03
Yards	Meters	0.9
Meters	Yards	1.1

Read This Important Safety Notice

To prevent accidents, keep safety in mind while you work. Use the safety guards installed on power equipment; they are for your protection.

When working on power equipment, keep fingers away from saw blades, wear safety goggles to prevent injuries from flying wood chips and sawdust, wear hearing protection and consider installing a dust vacuum to reduce the amount of airborne sawdust in your woodshop.

Don't wear loose clothing, such as neckties or shirts with loose sleeves, or jewelry, such as rings, necklaces or bracelets, when working on power equipment. Tie back long hair to prevent it from getting caught in your equipment.

People who are sensitive to certain chemicals should check the chemical content of any product before using it.

Due to the variability of local conditions, construction materials, skill levels, etc., neither the author nor Popular Woodworking Books assumes any responsibility for any accidents, injuries, damages or other losses incurred resulting from the material presented in this book.

The authors and editors who compiled this book have tried to make the contents as accurate and correct as possible. Plans, illustrations, photographs and text have been carefully checked. All instructions plans and projects should be carefully read, studied and understood before beginning construction.

Prices listed for supplies and equipment were current at the time of publication and are subject to change.

Ideas. Instruction. Inspiration.

These and other great *Popular Woodworking* products are available at your local bookstore, woodworking store or online supplier.

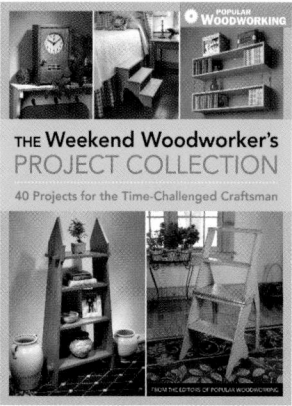

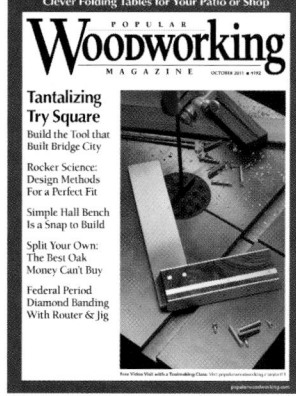

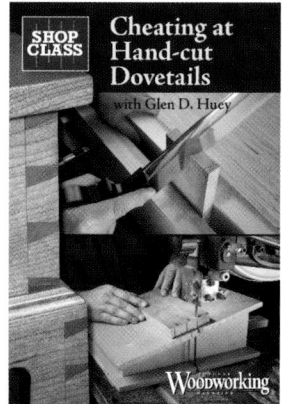

WOOD FINISHING 101
By Bob Flexner
Wood finishing doesn't have to be complicated or confusing. Wood Finishing 101 boils it down to simple step-by-step instructions and pictures on how to finish common woods using widely-available finishing materials. Bob Flexner has been writing about and teaching wood finishing for over 20 years.

paperback • 128 pages

WEEKEND WOODWORKER'S PROJECT COLLECTION
This book has 40 projects from which to choose and, depending on the level of your woodworking skills, any of them can be completed in one or two weekends. Projects include: a game box, jewelry box, several styles of bookcases and shelves, mirrors, picture frames and more.

paperback • 256 pages

POPULAR WOODWORKING MAGAZINE
Whether learning a new hobby or perfecting your craft, *Popular Woodworking Magazine* has expert information to teach the skill, not just the project. Find the latest issue on newsstands, or you can order online at popularwoodworking.com.

SHOPCLASS VIDEOS
From drafting, to dovetails and even how to carve a ball-and-claw foot, our Shop Class Videos let you see the lesson as if you were standing right there.

Available at shopwoodworking.com
DVD & Instant download

POPULAR WOODWORKING'S VIP PROGRAM

Get the Most Out of Woodworking!

Join the Woodworker's Bookshop VIP program today for the tools you need to advance your woodworking abilities. Your one-year paid renewal membership includes:

• *Popular Woodworking Magazine* (1 year/7 issue U.S. subscription — A $21.97 Value)

• *Popular Woodworking Magazine CD* — Get all issues of *Popular Woodworking Magazine* from 2006 to today on one CD (A $64.95 Value!)

• The Best of Shops & Workbenches CD — 62 articles on workbenches, shop furniture, shop organization and the essential jigs and fixtures published in *Popular Woodworking* and *Woodworking Magazine* ($15.00 Value!)

• 20% Members-Only Savings on 6-Month Subscription for Shop Class OnDemand

• 10% Members-Only Savings at Shopwoodworking.com

• 10% Members-Only Savings on FULL PRICE Registration for Woodworking In America Conference (Does Not Work with Early Bird Price)

• and more....

Visit **popularwoodworking.com** to see more woodworking information by the experts, learn about our digital subscription and sign up to receive our weekly newsletter at popularwoodworking.com/newsletters/

FOLLOW
POPULAR
WOODWORKING

6-8-15